CULTURE AND CONTEXT IN SUDAN

SUNY series in Middle Eastern Studies
Shahrough Akhavi, Editor

CULTURE AND CONTEXT IN SUDAN

The Process of Market Incorporation in Dar Masalit

Dennis Tully

STATE UNIVERSITY OF NEW YORK PRESS

For my parents

Published by
State University of New York Press, Albany

Printed in the United States of America

For information, address State University of New York Press, State University Plaza, Albany, N.Y., 12246

Library of Congress Cataloging-in-Publication Data

Tully, Dennis

Culture and context in Sudan.

(SUNY series in Middle Eastern studies
Includes index.
1. Dar Masalit (Sudan)—Economic conditions.
2. Agriculture—Sudan—Dar Masalit. 3. Economic anthropology—Sudan—Dar Masalit. I. Title.
II. Series.
HC835.Z7D377 1987 338.1'09627 86-23180
ISBN 0-88706-502-3
ISBN 0-88706-504-X (pbk.)

10 9 8 7 6 5 4 3 2 1

Contents

List of Tables

List of Figures

Introduction

Transliteration

The transliteration of Arabic into English letters is always unsatisfying, and the systems that are most exact are also the most cumbersome for reader, writer and typist. As a compromise, I have endeavored to follow the first occurrence of each Arabic word with an italicized exact transliteration, in the singular spoken form unless

Arabic letter	*Exact transliteration*	*Simple transliteration*
أ	^{I}	omit
ح	H	h
خ	x	h
ش	ʃ	sh
ص	S	s
ض	D	d
ع	^{c}	omit
غ	G	gh
ق (Modern Standard)	q	does not occur
ق (colloquial)	g	g

otherwise indicated, in which each Arabic consonant is represented by one character. The system is a modification of Trimingham's system for Sudanese Colloquial Arabic (1946). Subsequently, I either use the common spelling or a simpler transliteration, which should allow the reader who is unfamiliar with Arabic to remember the words and approximate the correct pronunciation; *s* is used to pluralize as in English. My intention with letters used in English, such as b, d, f, etc. will be clear, but the following may require explanation:

Gemination or *taʃdi:d* is indicated by a doubled letter. As for vowels, *a, u* and *i* are used for fatha, damma and kasra; in the exact transliteration they are followed by a colon if lengthened. The letter *e* is sounded like the *a* in "cake," *o* as in "north," and *o:* as in "foam."

Archival Citations

Archival material is entirely from the Sudan government's Central Records Office, Khartoum. I have followed the practice of Kapteijns (1985) in referencing this material by file numbers (e.g. Darfur 3/15/22); where a file is long and the location of the information is not clear from my text, I have added the name of the particular document.

Identification of Flora

Because the same Arabic or English name may be applied to different species in other regions, I have attempted to provide the scientific binomial identification for plants mentioned. I have relied on translations in the following sources: Barbour 1950; FAO 1968; Ibrahim 1978; Roth-Laly 1969–1972; Tothill 1948; Tubiana and Tubiana 1977. My identifications are not based on any personal knowledge of biology.

Currency

The standard unit of currency is the Sudanese Pound (LS) which is composed of 100 piastres (PT). In the colonial period, the Egyptian pound (LE) was in use. At the start of my research period, the exchange value of a Sudanese pound was $2.50, and at the end it was $1.25. During most of 1979 when price data were collected the value was $2.00.

Place Names

"Dar Masalit" means home of the Masalit, and is sometimes simply referred to as "the Dar." "Dar Fur" is the name of the land under the

Fur during the Fur Sultanate. After its conquest a province called "Darfur" was created, and later it was divided into "Northern Darfur" and "Southern Darfur."

Acknowledgements

Without the assistance of a great many people, this research would not have been possible. I would like to express my deepest gratitude to my friends and neighbors in Masterei, who welcomed me into their lives and patiently assisted me for friendship's sake, even when they thought my questions absurd, prying or both. I would like to thank Sultan Abd al-Rahman Bahr al-Din, Fursha Mohammed Arbab, Dr. Abdalla Ahmed Abdalla, and the schoolteachers of Masterei, especially Tijani Bashir, who extended their hospitality and solved many practical problems at crucial stages of the research. Officials of the Sudan Socialist Union, Dar Masalit Rural Council, and the Government of Sudan Economic and Social Research Council, Central Records Office, Meteorological Office, Office of Statistics, Plant Protection Office, Department of Health, and Veterinary Services all contributed their time to educate me and help me collect needed information. I am also grateful to the Institute of African and Asian Studies of the University of Khartoum, with which I was an associate while carrying out this research.

I am particularly grateful to Edgar V. Winans for stimulation and challenge from the earliest stages of planning until the present, including extensive comments on drafts of this manuscript. Dorene R. Tully has helped me understand many central issues, and painstakingly criticized drafts of these chapters. Lidwien Kapteijns has provided valuable discussion, both during and after field research, and has commented on draft chapters; her work in Dar Masalit sets a high standard to follow. John R. Atkins has challenged my imagination and given me insight into many levels of data analysis. Eugene Hunn supplied me with helpful comments on earlier drafts.

Research has been funded by a grant from the Social Science Research Council and the American Council of Learned Societies, and by the University of Washington Department of Anthropology. The analysis and writing have also been supported by these institutions, as well as a Lockwood Foundation Fellowship, a W. W. Stout Graduate Fellowship, and National Resource Fellowships. I am grateful to these institutions for their confidence and assistance.

1. *World Systems and Local Processes*

Social scientists have been stimulated to reconsider the theory and method of their disciplines by the underdevelopment, dependency and world systems literature of the last twenty years. Anthropology has long had a broad perspective in terms of comparative or cross-cultural approaches, and over forty years ago anthropologists such as Godfrey Wilson (1941–42) and M. Gluckman (1941) consciously placed their research on African cultures in the context of international economic and political relations. Economic anthropologists have made many contributions to our understanding of the effects of market participation on formerly autonomous societies or regions. However, an integration of anthropological insights concerning local change with more recent approaches to understanding global processes has only begun to be accomplished. There is an obvious complementarity of interests and experience here which can be developed.

An exclusive focus on local culture may not explain those features that are responses to external economic and political forces; on the other hand, study of world-scale processes does not explain the tremendous diversity of local responses and initiatives that have been observed (Cooper 1981; Comaroff 1984). Macro-level approaches rarely analyze units smaller than the nation, which leaves a serious gap between the study of local cultures and their global context. It is necessary to try to do both, in concrete case studies, to test the relevance of anthropological models in explaining change, and to see if world market incorporation is a relevant concept at the local level. Such a marriage has much to offer both to a world systems perspective that is top-heavy with theorizing and to an economic anthropology that needs to clarify its theoretical goals.

World systems theory is most commonly associated with Immanuel Wallerstein (1974a, 1974b, 1978, 1979), who built upon Andre Gunder Frank's theory of Latin American underdevelopment (1967, 1969, 1972). Frank argues that underdevelopment is not a primordial condition equivalent to the lack of development; rather, the underdevelopment of part of the world is a necessary counterpart to the development of the other part. "Traditional" ways of life are merely appearances; the reality is that rural areas of the Third World are fully incorporated into the capitalist world economy as "satellites" of the industrialized "metropole." Satellites do not direct their own development, but are dependent on and dominated by the metropole. The links from the metropole to the farthest hinterlands are made through a series of intermediate centers which act both as metropoles to the hinterland and as satellites of the next higher level; thus, industrial centers of underdeveloped countries are dependent on the western metropole, while dominating their own rural areas. Like Frank, Wallerstein emphasizes the global and connected nature of world development, conceiving it in terms of a world division of labor between center and periphery. He gives greater emphasis to the role of states as competitors in the world economy. The policies or strategies of states may affect the position of their capitalist classes, as well as the general population, in the world division of labor.

Both Frank and Wallerstein have been criticized from a number of theoretical perspectives for their limited treatment of local processes of underdevelopment or market integration (Bradby 1975; Peoples 1978, Goodman and Redclift 1981). Their location of the dynamic of capitalist development in the "metropole" or "center" treats the Third World as a passive victim, and ignores ways in which particular societies influence their own incorporation into the world market through resistance, selective response to incentives or pressures, or maintenance of precapitalist forms (Nash 1981 reviews this point; compare Smith 1978). As Alejandro Portes and John Walton point out, "the result of analyses and debates dealing exclusively with the world level is the perpetuation of the gap between research and theory inherited from modernization times" (1981:13).

Furthermore, because of their insistence on a single capitalist mode of production covering the entire world, Frank and Wallerstein are unwilling to consider that societies or regions can be partially involved in world capitalism. For example, in formulating his well-known argument about plantations in Brazil, Frank (1967) argues that they only appear feudal if considered in terms of local economic relations. They are obviously capitalist enterprises in terms of their place in the world economy, because their existence is founded on production for the world market. While this is a valuable insight, in making it he feels obliged to reject models of penetration or transition to capitalism or any concept of partial integration (Frank 1967:227–237). Perhaps in the Latin American cases studied by Frank, where market participation has a history of several hundred years, he can argue that the observed structures are fully a part of the world market (Barnett 1975:183). However, the insistence that all the world is now one capitalist system suggests a uniformity that does not exist.

Similarly, in spite of an obvious awareness of process and diversity in his discussion of European history, Wallerstein's formulation leads to an arbitrary division between members and non-members of the current world system. To do this he must distinguish "between *essential* exchanges and what might be called 'luxury' exchanges." Even though he recognizes that this distinction rests upon the social perceptions of a given culture, and furthermore that these are subject to change, "this distinction is crucial if we are not to fall into the trap of identifying *every* exchange activity as evidence of the existence of a system" (Wallerstein 1974b:397–398; compare 1978:230). I agree that this distinction is crucial to his "either-or" formulation, but I also believe that it is impossible to apply it objectively. Wallerstein's position suggests an immediacy to market incorporation which does not elucidate how it occurs; just as one touch from King Midas turned his daughter to gold, one touch of the market turns a formerly autonomous society into a part of the international division of labor. It is not clear why a process which was very complex and slow in Europe should be so simple and immediate in the Third World today—if true this point demands explanation.

An appreciation of the global reach of the market does not require this neglect of both the process by which it occurs and the diverse local conditions which it encounters. Samir Amin (1972, 1976), Claude Meillassoux (1972) and others have discussed ways in which societies may be transformed by market incorporation and yet maintain or be reinforced in certain aspects of the preexisting socioeconomic structure. Much work in this vein has been carried out in terms of the "articulation of modes of production," whose main formulation can be attributed to Pierre-Philippe Rey (1973).[1] As David Goodman and Michael Redclift (1981) point out, not only is there an ongoing debate between proponents of articulation and those of world systems theory; but there is also considerable diversity among the advocates of the articulation of modes of production approach, both in the development of theory and in its application to concrete cases. It is not the intention here to attempt to resolve these issues. However, there are a number of valuable aspects to the articulation approach which seem to be quite compatible with and complementary to the world systems model if one looks beyond terminological disputes. These derive from the greater emphasis on local process and diversity which it includes (Bernstein 1977:69).[2]

The articulation model accepts the ultimate integration of all parts of the world into a capitalist market, but takes the process by which this occurs as an object of study. Rey (1973) has attempted to derive a theory of the transition of precapitalist Third World societies to capitalism from Marx's analysis of the transition from feudalism to capitalism in Europe, as described in *Capital*. In his model, any particular society goes through a process of transition, for which he suggests three general stages. At first, contact with the market is limited to a simple exchange of goods produced within the precapitalist mode of production, thus reinforcing the existing mode. At this level, market contact could be stable; however, colonization or force is used to impose a deeper participation in the market. Capitalism comes to dominate the local economy and transforms productive relations; production for the local market is destroyed, agriculture is converted to commodity production, and a limited labor force is created. Colonization is not needed after a point, because once the capitalist mode dominates, the process has a dynamic which continues under independence (that is, neocolonialism). Precapitalist forms are partially maintained and subsistence agriculture continues to play a part in supporting the labor force for a substantial time. Eventually Rey foresees this leading to a full capitalist agriculture and the destruction of peasant agriculture; however, this last stage has not yet been reached in the Third World (nor, as Goodman and Redclift (1981) note, has it been reached in Europe to date).

There is an obvious similarity of this model to Paul Bohannan and George Dalton's classification of societies according to the role of "the market place and the market principle" in them (1962:1). This is a result of the fact that Rey's model of stages has been developed in criticism of that typology. George Dupre and Pierre-Phillippe Rey (1973) have accused Bohannan and Dalton, as well as Karl Polanyi, of viewing the market as a contagious mentality; that is, having implied that market incorporation spontaneously grows out of "peripheral" contact because of the spread of an "economic man's" state of mind. The criticism is not entirely just. In the very work Dupre and Rey criticize, Bohannan and Dalton state that "foreign administrators have had to do more than establish market places to create a market-dominated economy—in many instances, production for the market has been made mandatory, by separate and special legal means with heavy sanctions" (1962:22).

What is of secondary interest to Bohannan and Dalton is primary to Dupre and Rey; they argue that force is needed to make capitalism dominant, and thereafter capable of spontaneous growth in the current neocolonial period. Then, although capitalism takes root, some elements of precapitalist modes are maintained within transitional or hybrid structures. Thus, local diversity is of importance because it leads to a diversity of transitional forms. Several authors also point out that variations in the nature of capitalist forces at different times and places affect the articulation that is established, and certainly this is true; the nature of a particular company or colony's needs or abilities, as well as politically determined strategies for the colony or empire as a whole have important effects on the way a particular region is pressed to enter the market (Bradby 1975; Scott 1976; Cliffe 1977; D. R. Tully 1985).[3] These authors join with Rey in stressing the study of local structures and the history of their interaction with the particular market forces facing them.

The focus of the modes of production approach at the local level tends to be upon the transformation of structures of inequality and exploitation. This is reasonable because articulation is often accomplished through changes in the roles of local elites. If those with a degree of control over production in a precapitalist system are integrated into the world market, they will tend to use their position in the local economy to expand market production and therefore their own consumption possibilities (Samoff and Samoff 1976). Market ties may allow precolonial elites to develop new forms or degrees of control as well. For example, Dupre and Rey (1973) discuss the process of articulating the world market with West African lineage societies through the elders, who exerted some control over production and substantial control over reproduction. Stephen M. Soiffer and Gary N. Howe (1982) consider the role of patron-client relations and their transformations in a Brazilian case, and Lionel Cliffe and Richard Moorsom (1979) discuss the process by which market forces and national policies allowed the cattle-owning Tswana nobility to increase its control of the rest of the population as well as environmental resources. Indeed, this is an issue with some history in anthropology, as witness the studies of S. F. Nadel (1947), James B. Watson (1952), and many others.

However, precapitalist power structures are not the only important elements affecting the articulation process. Anthropological studies of social change, while often cast in a functionalist or adaptationist framework, also show the importance of preexisting patterns of family and gender relations, community organization, settlement, consumption, law, ritual practices, and local values in determining the course of market integration.[4] The holistic analysis of culture, which takes these factors into account, can bring a more complete understanding of the process of articulation to studies of the global economy. For instance, it may illuminate processes by which commodity production and market participation intensify in many cases, once they have begun, without violence, external pressure or purposive action by local elites.

Rey has been criticized by both Barbara Bradby and Aidan Foster-Carter for his position that violence is needed to break down precapitalist social structures. While violence has certainly played a role in a large number of cases, it is simply not true that it is always employed; also, Dupre and Rey's argument that precapitalist modes never give way to capitalism without colonialism is overstated. It is more useful to look to the motivation for conquest or violence at particular moments in particular places. Nevertheless Rey has a point about the stability of peasant production and the resistance shown to participation in the market in many cases. Indeed, Goran Hyden (1980) argues that capitalism is *not yet* dominant in rural Africa and that more force will be required to overcome the propensity of peasants to withdraw from the market. From a farmer's point of view, a combination of subsistence and market production may be preferred in order to maintain a degree of autonomy at the household level (Arizpe 1982; Tully 1981b). On the other hand, Joan Smith, Immanuel Wallerstein and Hans-Dieter Evers (1984) see nothing contradictory about incomplete incorporation into the market, but rather consider it a normal feature of modern capitalism that increases the possibilities for exploitation and accumulation.

In any event, whether before conquest or within Rey's second stage, both the processes by which participation increases and the mechanisms of market incorporation that operate in transitional structures remain to be elucidated. Some mechanisms are fairly clear. For example, after colonial occupation, taxation or other administrative obligations may force commodity production or wage labor (for example, Arrighi 1973). These obligations can be imposed within precapitalist social structures, as the Sudan attempted to do in collecting taxes through the former channels of tribute. At a more subtle level, Barbara Bradby (1975:150–151) discusses economic pressures such as the destruction of local industries by competition with imported consumer items. Many writers have described the distorting effect of labor migration induced by government policies, which removes an important part of the labor force while obliging the remaining population to intensify production (Amin 1972; Lipton 1982). Gervase Clarence-Smith and Richard Moorsom discuss how the induction of a local arms race required local populations to increase production in order to maintain their independence. Below I consider ecological processes that may compel market participation.

Such mechanisms of incorporation can interact with cultural factors in ways that sometimes exceed the anticipations of colonial administrators. Bohannan, for example, has demonstrated how the production of cash crops among the Tiv was accelerated by the connection of general-purpose money to bridewealth (1959); similarly labor migration has been stimulated in many cases by competition for marriage partners (e.g. Watson 1958; Sudanow 1979; Murray 1981). In an autonomous economy such inflation is impossible. Migration or commodity production may also interact with community labor exchanges or the division of labor by sex in ways that increase dependence and transform social relations (Erasmus 1965; Guyer 1980). Watson has suggested that local competition of "big men" accelerated adoption of a sweet potato and pig economy in New Guinea (Watson 1977; compare Boyd 1985). His 'Jones effect' (as in keeping up with the Joneses) may play an important role in the spread of capitalism as well. The elucidation of these sorts of mechanisms of change, which incorporate cultural variation in the analysis, is needed to add depth to what is in Rey's formulation primarily a typological model of the steps of market incorporation. In so doing one simultaneously eliminates the suggestion, inherent in Rey's model, that the development of a market economy proceeds by free choice if there is no violence.

Another aspect of local variation which needs to be incorporated into studies of market integration is the human place in the ecosystem. This has been of particular concern to anthropologists, and K. P. Mosely and Immanuel Wallerstein (1978) recognize the contribution of ecological anthropology to the understanding of precapitalist social structures; however, ecological studies have often been locally oriented or static or both. Benjamin S. Orlove calls for an ecological approach that goes beyond "neofunctionalism" to examine the global context (1980:252). Peggy F. Barlett points to a trend "toward joining the approaches of economic anthropology and cultural ecology in the study of production processes in peasant communities" (1980:545), including government policies, marketing conditions and price structures in the environmental context of human action (1980:551–552). Many local studies of market incorporation do not consider ecological factors, but interesting results have been reported in several cases. These illustrate ecological issues affecting the spread of the market that may have general application.

First, market integration may produce unequal and destructive exploitation of communal resources. Garret Hardin's "tragedy of the commons" model (1977) points out the possibility for overuse of shared environmental resources, but his model assumes that an outlet for these resources or their products exists. In the context of articulation with a market which demands commodities from previously autonomous societies, it is the effect of the introduction of such an outlet that is at issue. In many cases the ability to control the production and marketing of environmental assets is not equally distributed even though rights to these assets are; thus, the marketing of these resources may foster an intensification of local relations of inequality. For example, Hardin's *gedenkenexperiment* is played out in Botswana, where although pasture is a community asset, cattle are and have been unequally distributed.

When cattle became a source of high income, the owners of large herds were able to exploit the communal resource (Cliffe and Moorsom 1979; compare Grossman 1983 for a related New Guinea case, and DeWalt 1982 on Honduras). Mining of agricultural land, often communal fallow, through agricultural techniques oriented to short term profits is another common occurrence in the Third World with the same effect; community resources are appropriated and the profits accrue to those who are wealthy enough to buy the equipment needed to carry out the appropriation first (Duffield 1978).

As in Hardin's model, everyone loses in the destruction of shared resources. However, some experience net gains in the process by accumulating the income from the sale of these resources. Thus, the tragedy is greater than Hardin's model indicates. Overuse of communal resources is likely to be unequal, patterned by preexisting socioeconomic relations, and to perpetuate or strengthen those relations in new form.

A second, related ecological consideration is that production for the market may produce a more intensive use of farmland or range by small producers. This may lead to erosion or reductions in soil fertility, and thus further intensification to maintain a minimal level of income or to meet obligations (DeJanvry and Garramon 1977:211–12; Wasserstrom 1978; Murray 1981; Frankenberger 1983; Collins 1984). Eventually an area may become unlivable.

Third, environmental changes have different effects in a society that is engaged in market production than in one that is autonomous. Rural populations may turn to migration or wage labor to cope with land scarcity or crop failures, thus maintaining a high population density in rural areas (Arizpe 1982; Bohannan and Dalton 1962:21–22; Collier 1975). In the case to be described in this book, drought, population growth, and loss of forest resources all contributed to increases in commodity production and labor migration.[5]

Fourth, market production by part of the population may destabilize the ecological adaptation of an entire region. In the Sahel, cash cropping and extension of farmlands in the higher-moisture areas left many herders with no alternative to becoming wage laborers when drought struck (Franke and Chasin 1980). Finally, an aspect of human ecology which will not be studied in this work, but requires mention, is disease, which decreased the viability of many independent small-scale societies (Richards 1983; Turshen 1984; Feierman 1985).

Such aspects of the environmental and demographic context of market integration must be taken into account to understand fully the forces impinging on the farmer. By integrating these factors into a study of market incorporation, one can demonstrate the inadequacy of explanations of Third World poverty solely as a result of ecological factors such as drought or overpopulation. The interaction of ecological factors and world market forces is crucial.

In spite of the greater appreciation that the articulation approach has for local processes, a difficulty remains concerning the concept of exploitation. To a certain extent the articulation of modes approach has been supported by those who reject the Frank-Wallerstein concept of exploitation through unequal exchange, rather than in the process of production (compare Emmanuel 1972 for development of the concept of unequal exchange). Rey defines exploitation as occurring "when that part of the produce of the producer's labour which is taken from him serves to reinforce the producer's position of dependence" (1975:62). This is a qualitative definition which can actually be applied to relations of exchange as well as production, *but only where the original producer participates in the exchange.* For example, small farmers can be exploited in this sense through sales to merchants, further increasing the wealth and power of the merchants. The definition is thus in harmony with orthodox Marxist analysis in which exploitation only occurs in production.[6]

However, if a rural capitalist class, which exploits the original producers also engages in exchange with urban capitalist classes, then relative prices would determine the flow of surplus value; no matter how poorly the rural capitalists fare, this is not considered exploitation.[7] Fully developed, the rejection of the concept of exploitation in exchange reduces all relations beyond the immediate production stage to hegemonic conflicts among exploiters. This is an awkward analytical approach to the current multilevel world economy. It renders secondary the power gradient from the metropole to the periphery which determines relative prices, and therefore obscures the question of where surplus value can be accumulated for reinvestment. Furthermore, the focus on local relations of exploitation ignores common interests between rural exploiters and rural exploited. Indeed Michael Lipton (1977) argues that it is rural-urban conflicts of interest in the Third World that form the most important "class" division today.[8]

If class analysis is employed to understand possible bases of political action, such practical considerations are important. They are better represented in Frank's model of stepwise accumulation, which recognizes that the flow of surplus value to the metropole involves a series of unequal, exploitative relations. Orthodox Marxists may legitimately argue that this is a redefinition of the concept of exploitation (Pilling 1973), but the charge of circulationism (and neglect of production) is misplaced. As Dupre and Rey (1973) argued, exchange and production are intimately related; it is through exchange that capitalism dominates productive relations within formerly autonomous societies. William Hansen and Brigitte Schulz also suggest analysis of the symbiotic relationship between internal structures of exploitation and external accumulation through trade (1981:19–24). However, as Henry Bernstein points out, important questions remain: "One set of issues concerns how the conditions of production are determined by the circuit of capital, and the question of effective possession of the means of production and effective control of the production process'' (1977:69). Production must still be the focus of study to discover how it is controlled, how capital is accumulated and employed, and how the options available to men and women with varying amounts of assets are altered at different stages; in short to comprehend the mechanism of market incorporation. These aspects of production take place in a context largely determined by exchange relations located many levels away from the farm.

There are also difficulties in this analysis of exploitation that derive from its usage of a labor theory of value, which has been receiving severe criticism from within Marxism in recent years (Lippi 1980; Steedman 1978). It is perhaps this which prevents the articulation school from going beyond qualitative overviews of relations of exploitation. Indeed, complex issues are raised in attempting to quantify surplus value in a society where producers are not separated from the means of production, and in attempting to apply the labor theory where a good deal of labor is domestic, prestige oriented, or directed at the circulation rather than the production of goods (DeVroey 1982). Such considerations apply in a very large proportion of rural populations; indeed, the transport of commodities is a major activity, and often a source of high incomes, in almost all cases where production for the market is important. There has been little effort to conceptualize such 'nonproductive' labor in rural societies.

Thus, even if a labor theory of value were unquestioned, it is not clear how to apply it to Third World peasantries in transition from a precapitalist to capitalist modes of production, and the theoretical problems of working out the adaptation are immense. Were this done, the interface between the newly adapted value theory and a price theory would still need to be developed in order to calculate international and inter-regional flows, which Frank and Emmanuel have shown to be important elements of the underdevelopment process. The articulation approach has not presented an adequate substitute for the study of exchange and price relations to date, but neither is the approach inconsistent with such analysis in practice. In the following study of Dar Masalit, it will be clear that even at the local level, capital accumulation is carried out through relations of exchange much more often than through relations of production, due to the present form of market incorporation. While the focus of this study is on production, it is in large part exchange relations and prices in the context of market integration that determine what is and will be produced.

Finally, neither articulation nor world systems approaches have yet integrated the level of the individual as an active participant in social change. As Lawrence Grossman points out, a focus on structures rather than human agency can lead to teleological explanations of change (1983:60). In the study which follows, I have therefore attempted to represent the options that are available to individuals at different stages in the process of market incorporation. On the other hand, decision making approaches can suggest a level of voluntarism which mystifies the process of the extension of the market (Amin 1974b:87–93). This can have implications in terms of the current evaluation of underdevelopment; for example, Keith Hart states that ". . . in West Africa's case, 150 years of peasant rationality have left the region in a backward economic condition and with a precarious political future. It is no use claiming that colonialism produced this mess. Even if it did, the successor states are now nominally sovereign, and it is their responsibility to devise an escape route" (1982:119). While admittedly the issue of moral responsibility does not weigh heavily in international relations, it plays some role. Such blame-fixing arguments as this are commonly heard as part of the ideology of the wealthier nations, and are employed to justify self-serving policies; as such should not be used uncritically.

So how to discuss individual decisions without supporting the illusion of voluntarism? Marx provides a key in what has probably become his most quoted statement in recent years: "Men make their own history, but they do not make it just as they please; they do not make it under circumstances chosen by themselves, but under circumstances directly found, given and transmitted from the past" (1972:437). This expresses the division between the individual's choice on the one hand, and the limitations on his or her options on the other. This division has been (fairly amicably) recognized in recent anthropological studies of decision making, which include both cognitively oriented studies (Gladwin and Butler 1984) and other "actor-oriented" models which focus on the decision context and adaptive behavior of individuals, but not on what goes through their minds (Chibnik 1980; Orlove 1980; Barlett 1980; 1982).

It is the latter approach that is followed in this work. I am not dealing with the psychological modeling of decisions, but rather with understanding the transformation of the structure of choices available to individuals in the process of incorporation. This is necessary to show that market integration does not proceed by free, fully informed choice of most persons, but rather by altering the strategies available to individuals for survival. Decisions by a minority of the population may have undesirable effects on all; this is commonly the case when nonrepresentative authority figures use their positions for their own ends (Samoff and Samoff 1976). However it is not only politicians who can change the strategies available to others. For example, Barlett (1982) presents a case where a new option of extensive beef production by the large landowners forces the land-poor into intensive tobacco production. They choose this, yes, but they have no other viable options within the system.

The description of options available to individuals who are living the process of market incorporation is intended to bring home the deep reach of market forces into everyday life. It is clear that the options are limited for most and little would be gained by psychological modeling; the poorest farmers have no choice but to fully utilize all of their resources to survive. However, my analysis does not fully explain the different choices of individuals with several viable options. Why does one person with savings spend it, another use it to finance a stable occupation, while another invests in trade to multiply the savings? I cannot say whether this question is best studied through psychology or some other approach.

In the following study of rural life in Dar Masalit, Sudan, I have attempted to integrate anthropological approaches to culture with an understanding of global market expansion in order to analyze a particular structure of underdevelopment. In chapter 2, the social organization of the Masalit before, during and after colonial occupation is discussed in terms of the political history of the region. Chapter 3 presents an analysis of environmental and demographic processes taking place in these periods, and relates them to colonial policies and market forces. In chapter 4, a detailed economic analysis of productive activities is presented in terms of their former and current place in Masalit society and in the world market. In chapter 5, I analyze changes in the control of productive assets and change in the relative value of assets as a result of these political, ecological and economic changes. From this basis, I consider the effect on structures of inequality within the village. The emergence of a class structure is not yet clear, but there are nascent classes with obvious conflicts of interest that will play a part in future political processes.

2. *Masalit History, Society and Culture*

The Masalit of Northern Darfur, Sudan, inhabit one of the most remote areas of the Northern Sudan, on the western border over 1000 km from Khartoum (figure 2.1). Dar Masalit, "home of the Masalit," is separated from the rest of Sudan by the Jebel Marra range, and even its rivers drain into Lake Chad rather than the Nile. Geneina, its capital, is connected by road to El Fasher and Nyala, but the trip takes at least two days and is impossible for several months each year. Air connections and mail are frequently interrupted for months at a time.

It was this isolation that first attracted me to Dar Masalit, since I was interested in studying labor exchange in a relatively autonomous society whose economy was oriented to production for local use. It seemed that such a remote area would have been most likely to have avoided market integration. However, I soon discovered that the isolation of Dar Masalit was more apparent than real.

While retaining a local orientation and a degree of autonomy in many respects, the Masalit have also become firmly embedded in the context of social, political, cultural and economic processes at the national and international level. These processes involve forces and policies that are felt throughout the Sudan, for example, increasing market orientation, penetration of national political structures, economic pressures on family structure, and movement towards a stricter interpretation of Islam. However, such general trends may not necessarily lead to a homogenization or 'Sudanization' of the nation. Local populations like the Masalit absorb, adapt, incorporate, or reject these forces in terms of their existing values and social organizations,

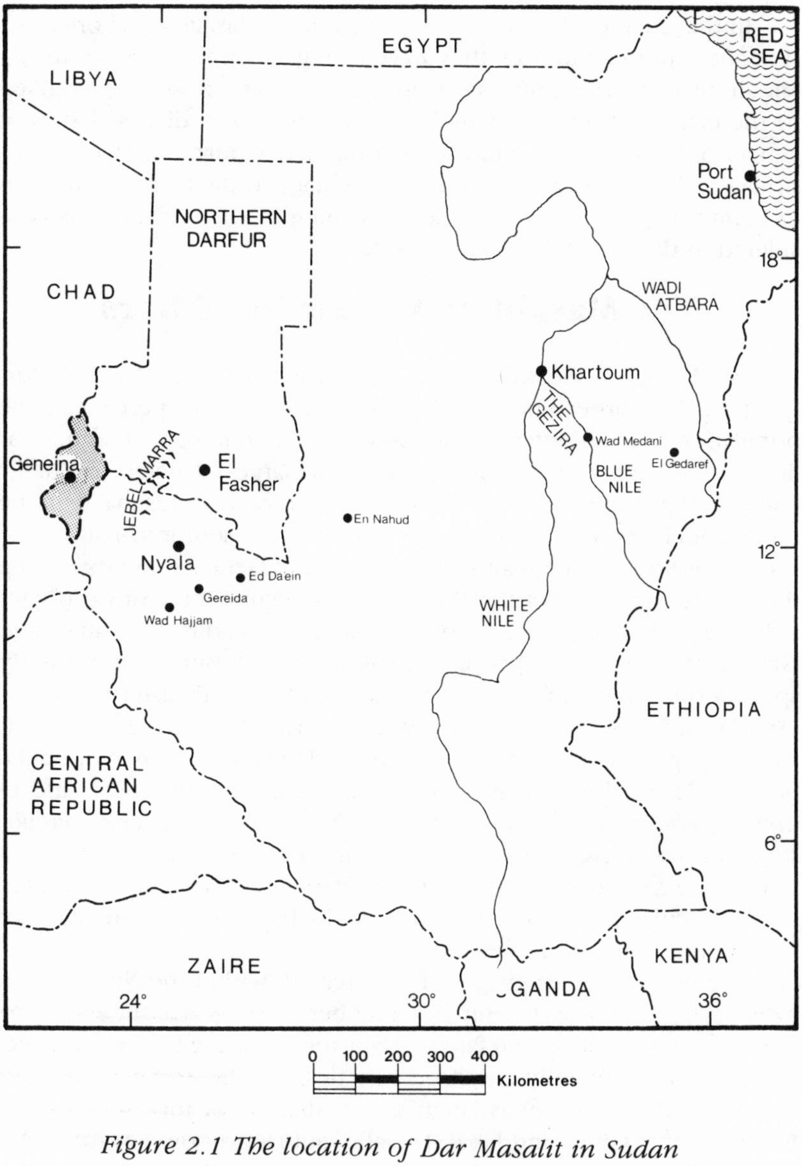

Figure 2.1 The location of Dar Masalit in Sudan
Source: Republic of Sudan, Survey Office Map of Sudan and maps ND–34, ND–34G, H, K, L, O, P. NC–35.

and the result is a product of this contact between the local and the global.

In this chapter, I describe some aspects of Masalit social organization and culture, and how they have changed in the course of recent Masalit history. The emphasis is on issues that are most closely linked to the economic analysis which follows, but I also discuss issues of general anthropological interest for comparative purposes. The discussion of political history is limited at this stage to the formal structures of administration; the process and meaning of these changes is considered in detail in subsequent chapters.

The Masalit and Their Neighbors

Dar Masalit is the westernmost subprovince of Northern Darfur, lying on the border with Chad (figure 2.2). Over 72 percent of the population are sedentary rural people of a number of ethnic or linguistic groups, of which the Masalit is the largest. Geneina residents make up 9 percent of the population, while rural nomads make up the remaining 19 percent.[1] The Masalit occupy the southern half of the Dar, including the goz plains east and west of Geneina, but excluding the southernmost tip of the Dar, which is occupied by Sinyar (figure 2.2). North of Geneina are found, successively, Erenga, Jabal, and Gimr territories.[2] The peoples mentioned each speak or formerly spoke a *rota:na* or non-Arabic language. In the northeastern Dar, five 'Arab' groups also have small territories. These Arabs are Terjim, Hottiyya, Otriyya, Mahadi, and Darok. Other significant sedentary populations of Maba, Tama, Zaghawa, Daju, and others may be found in homesteads, villages, or clusters of villages within Dar Masalit, sometimes with rights to small areas within a larger territory. In addition, Geneina and some towns have districts traditionally associated with particular ethnic groups, some of which, such as Bornu, may not have a substantial rural presence.

The non-Arabic languages of the area fall within the Nilo-Saharan category specified by Joseph H. Greenberg (1966). Masalit and Maba are languages of the Maban family; Daju and Tama are Eastern Sudanic, and so also presumably are those varieties classified by A. V. Tucker and M. A. Bryan (1956) as languages or dialects of the Tama group: Erenga, Awra, Gimr, and Jabal (Jabaal). Paul Doornbos (1984b) places Sinyar in the Central Sudanic family.

The use of Arabic by the non-Arabic ethnic groups is considerable, but varies in ways similar to those reported by Bjorn Jernudd (1968) for the Fur. In the city of Geneina, Arabic is quite common; many Masalit and other people use Arabic in the home, even with children.

Figure 2.2 Ethnic and linguistic groups of Dar Masalit and vicinity

However, in the Masalit villages, Arabic is never a first language. Many children and elderly people do not speak Arabic at all in the villages, and few women of any age know more than some greetings and polite phrases, numerals, and market words. Young and middle-aged men do tend to have a fairly good speaking ability; this is because almost all have spent substantial time in eastern Sudan, working. Some Arabic may be learned locally, in Qur'an schools, or through contacts with Arabic speakers, but at the village level the contribution of local learning is small. Because village women rarely migrate, few learn Arabic. However, the use of Arabic by both men and women is spreading, most noticeably in the towns intermediate in size between the villages and Geneina. In such towns, market activities bring different ethnic groups together, and both men and women participate; Arabic is the *lingua franca.* Also, substantial numbers of town children attend school and learn Arabic in that way. Furthermore, in the villages of the northernmost part of the Dar, Arabic is much more commonly spoken than among the rural Masalit, and has apparently replaced the Gimr language completely (Doornbos and Kapteijns 1984).

As an ethnic identifier in Dar Masalit, the word 'Arab' is applied to people whose language is now and by reputation always has been Arabic. It is strongly associated with nomadism or a tradition of nomadism. Twenty-four Arab omdas (heads of tribes or segments) are inscribed on the tax roles; they include the following Arab groups, in addition to those listed above: Awlad Zait, Bani Halba, Shatta, Junub, Jululi, Rashidi, Xuzam, Mahari, Hamidi/Rashidi, Nowayba, Awlad Eid, Shigerat, Eregat, Salami, and Misriyya (some groups have two omdas). The five omdas with territories are all primarily *baqqa:ra* (cattle herders), while the remainder are about half baggara and half *jamma:la* (camel herders). It should be noted that the terms "baggara" and "jammala" have no ethnic connotation, but are used solely to describe the predominant herding activity of the group. Also, one should note that this list of tribes is not a direct representation of the Arab population of Dar Masalit, which varies seasonally and yearly, as well as in response to international and provincial policies and politics. Because this research concentrated on the Masalit, it is not possible to provide full information on the Arab populations (but see Reyna 1984).

A review of the peoples of Dar Masalit should not neglect the eastern and northern Sudanese, from Northern Province, Khartoum, El Obeid, El Fasher, and other towns, who make up much of the urban population of the Dar. In Geneina and in some of the towns of the Dar, merchants, teachers, officials, businessmen, and others in positions requiring education, capital or both, tend to come from the Nile Valley. Some are very short-term residents, but others are following family predecessors and settling in Geneina, forming a fairly stable community.

None of the ethnic or linguistic groups above, except perhaps the Jabal, also called Mileri or Mun, are restricted to Dar Masalit. In addition to the Masalit in Dar Masalit, numbering approximately one hundred fifty thousand at the time of the 1955–56 census (see chapter 3), there is a large Masalit population just across the border in Chad, in an area lost to the French at the beginning of the twentieth century; these numbered fifty-one thousand in 1954 (Lebeuf 1959:78). To the west in the Wadi Batha area, near Abesher, live another fifteen thousand Masalit, also called Masalat (Lebeuf 1959:78). In Southern Darfur, thirteen thousand people are listed under "Masalit" omdas in the 1955–56 census. These three populations of Masalit are the result of precolonial population movements that are characteristic of the Sahelian region. In addition, new population centers of Masalit and other western Sudanese have grown up in the rural eastern Sudan, as well as in Khartoum and many smaller cities of Sudan. These are composed of emigrants responding to the investment policies of the colonial and postcolonial Sudan, which neglected the west while developing the Nile Valley. There is no information available on the number of these people, but migration is now so closely linked to the existence of the Masalit that it would be absurd to consider their home to be restricted to Dar Masalit (see chapter 4).

The people of the Dar are almost entirely Muslims. The nature of Islam in Dar Masalit is characteristic of the cultural position of the region in the Sudan; that is, Dar Masalit maintains a "little tradition" within a "great tradition" (Redfield 1960). While the Dar has many practices that are only locally valid, it considers itself part of the larger world of Islam, and as such is both elevated and reduced. Elevated, because most Muslims feel that they are much better off to have the one true faith; reduced, because the rural people can never hope to attain the level of sophistication in their religion that they would like. The same holds true for the cultural world in general. As the Masalit come to be a part of the Sudanese world, and as temporary migrants come to be exposed to urban life and values, these farmers find themselves losing their independence and ethnic pride, and gaining a position as exploited country bumpkins, only marginally citizens in a large cultural entity. This cultural level of awareness is coordinated with the shifts in the political and economic positions of the Dar that have occurred under Turkish and British colonialism, and which continue today.

Nevertheless, the little tradition of the Masalit continues to be vital and valuable to the people. They are proud of their history, and their reputation as fighters and survivors who are fiercely independent in nature. Masalit values and institutions continue to dominate rural life, and most people consider it an honorable life with many satisfactions, including a greater degree of autonomy and self-sufficiency compared to the eastern Sudan. Even as the Masalit come to participate in the world market and international politics, they work to preserve this autonomy. It remains to be seen whether the trends toward reduced independence and greater external orientation will continue, or whether this local autonomy will be safeguarded into the future.

Political History and Organization

Dar Masalit was a frontier area between greater powers for hundreds of years. The empires of Dar Fur and Wadai to the east and west respectively demanded tribute from, did battle with, and ruled over varying portions of the Masalit region in different eras. In the late nineteenth and early twentieth century, it became a point of contact and contention between French and British imperialist efforts, and the final demarcation of Dar Masalit was established in treaties negotiated in Europe. The political organization was conditioned by these forces and went through many changes.

It continues to do so; therefore, one must discuss the political structure in terms of these processes, not as a static system. The precolonial and early colonial political history of this area, especially for the period 1870–1930, have been thoroughly studied by Lidwien Kapteijns (1983; 1985), and the following brief summary owes a great deal to her work. I also draw on other published works, my own interpretations of the colonial archives, and interviews with Masalit elders, particularly for the colonial period. Certain related historical topics are discussed in greater detail in later chapters.

The period before 1874 is called the "Ancien Regime" by Kapteijns. The status of the Masalit region in the seventeenth and eighteenth centuries is not entirely clear; it was a period of expansion and contest between Wadai and Dar Fur, and this area probably was conquered or overrun from both sides several times. The nineteenth century brought a degree of stability, with the westernmost Masalit under Wadai jurisdiction, the eastern population under the Fur, and those in the center occupying a 'no-man's land' or buffer zone. The situation changed in 1874 with the occupation of Dar Fur by Turkish forces, which freed the Masalit from Fur overlordship.

Even those Masalit under Fur administration did not form a unit before the conquest; they were divided among three different Fur districts. With the conquest of the Fur, the outlying parts of their empire were in a position to negotiate with the new regime. Hajjam Hasab Allah, who was a high Masalit official under the Fur, took advantage of this situation to forcibly unify the Masalit, including previously unadministered peoples to the west. He was successful but unpopular, and he was deposed in 1883, just as the Mahdiyya was reaching Dar Fur.

The Mahdiyya was a period of independence for the Sudan, achieved under the leadership of Muhammed Ahmed, who proclaimed himself the Mahdi in 1881. Mahdism was a millenarian movement, calling for the reform and revitalization of Islam in preparation for the day of judgment. The religious message of the Mahdi was a rallying ideology for resentment against Turkish rule, and led to the Mahdist conquest of Khartoum in 1885 and Mahdist administration until the Anglo-Egyptian reconquest of Sudan in 1898. In the west, the Mahdiyya began earlier, with the surrender of the governor of Dar Fur in 1883; at that time the Mahdiyya became another large-scale force with which local politics had to contend.

After the Mahdi proclaimed himself, a number of Masalit visited him, including Ismail Abd al-Nabi, a religious teacher. They brought back the Mahdi's message of reforms, including the prohibition of alcohol, reduction of bridewealth, and the forbidding of certain pre-Islamic ceremonies, as well as instruction in praise songs and religious texts. Ismail developed a following, and took power after the deposition of Hajjam; he laid the basis of a Masalit Sultanate and founded the dynasty that continues to this day. He was also accepted by the Mahdists as a loyal agent. However, after a few years and the Mahdi's death, Ismail became disenchanted with the Mahdist regime; his loyalty suspect, he was called to Omdurman where he died. His son broke with the Mahdists, and the sultanate entered a period of independence and expansion; however, this was not without cost. There was continual warfare with Mahdist, Fur, French, and other armies, and, as a result, the Masalit lost the western part of the area they inhabited to the French in 1912; nevertheless, the independence of the sultanate was largely preserved until British occupation in 1922. At that time, Dar Masalit was incorporated into the Anglo-Egyptian Sudan with the sultanate maintained as a Native Administration, which continued to be the official basis of government until the May Revolution in 1969. Since then, the government has been gradually replaced Native Administration institutions with branches of the national political structure.

From the Ancien Regime to the present, the structure of administration and political organization has undergone considerable changes. Under the Ancien Regime, the basic unit of organization was the territory of a patrilineal clan (*xaʃm al-bayt*). Each clan or clan segment was associated with one or more territories (*balad, da:r* or *Haku:ra*), in which they had primary control of the land, but clan members were not restricted to their territories, and individuals or groups from one clan often lived in the territory of another. We do not know if there were titled rulers in the areas outside Fur administration, but where the Fur exercised authority each territory's leading clan or clan segment had a representative called a "*malik*," "*dimlij*," or "*dimlik*." According to Kapteijns, the malik allotted land to newcomers, settled disputes, managed a public granary, represented the clan, or more likely residents of the clan territory, to the Fur overlords, waged war on other clans, collected taxes,and received ivory, runaway slaves and other precious export goods found in his territory. He was obliged to forward part or all of the latter to his superiors, but in practice sold much to itinerant traders. He was also entitled to a percentage of taxes. According to Kapteijns, under the maliks were village sheikhs (*ʃayx*), who collected taxes for the maliks and directed affairs to them; however, since most villages at that time were small and impermanent, it was unlikely that the sheikh was an important official at this time, and probably many people were under the direct jurisdiction of their malik.[3]

Above the malik level was the fursha level (*furʃa* or *firʃa*), also a Fur title. However, this level did not exist in all of Dar Masalit under the Fur.[4] Masalit clans in two of the three Fur districts were grouped under two furshas who acted as maliks for their own clans, and also represented other clan territories to the Fur. In one of these districts, two large maliks were later able to establish separate furshaships, making a total of four furshas in the Ancien Regime. In the south, a number of maliks continued to represent their people directly to the Fur. This hierarchy of sheikhs, maliks and furshas was transformed into something rather different as a Native Administration, although the titles persisted.

The local political elite, according to Kapteijns, carried out the same productive activities as the commoners (*masa:ki:n*, poor people) who composed the bulk of the population: farming, herding, hunting and gathering. However, the furshas and larger maliks, by virtue of their control over export goods and their privileged position in terms of sumptuary laws, enjoyed imports such as foreign clothing, rifles, tea and coffee, as well as "more horses, wives, slaves, and hangers-on than the average commoner" (1985:43).

The extent and exact nature of slavery under the Ancien Regime was not fully understood although Kapteijns has considerable qualitative information. According to Kapteijns, the defining characteristic of slaves was that they did not belong; indeed, one older informant she quoted considered non-Masalit immigrants generally as slaves (1985:48)! While most slaves appear to have been freely bought and sold, others might better be considered to have been clients, captives or temporarily servile. Slaves were captured in raids, but also took refuge from war, famine or drought; if they could return to their homes they would again be free. For example, after the Turks conquered the Fur, many men and women of the Fur political elite came to Dar Masalit where they were given 'refuge' as slaves, though they were of elite families. In the wars fought in the period of Masalit independence, many war captives were also enslaved. On the other hand, when the Masalit took refuge with their neighbors in times of trouble, they were 'enslaved' as well.

Thus, it would appear that slavery was in part a way of incorporating members of other ethnic groups, comparable to the Nuer-Dinka interaction reported by E. E. Evans-Pritchard (1940:221–7; compare Newcomer 1972; Glickman 1972; Southall 1976). Some Masalit clans or sections are said to be descended from other ethnic groups, although they are now considered Masalit, just as Dinka could come to be considered Nuer after a time (compare Tornay 1981 for another case of ethnic assimilation).

However, as in the Dinka case, there was also an export trade in slaves, which Karen Sacks (1979) suggests increased the number of Dinka refugees and dependents, and provided Nuer aristocratic clans with new opportunities to increase their power. It is not yet clear to what extent regional slaving activity interacted in the Masalit case with the raiding and export trade, which was so important to Dar Fur and Wadai in the nineteenth century.

Kapteijns states that the slave trade from the south was a more important source of slaves for Masalit use than regional slaving (1985:53–54), but this may have been a result of the export trade. In any event, it is possible that changes in the nature of slavery due to development of an export trade in slaves are at the source of the theoretical debate that Kapteijns reviews (1985:4–16) concerning the nature of African slavery.

Slaves relieved their owners of labor while essentially supporting and reproducing themselves; female slaves as wives or concubines also expanded their owner's family. Due to their greater access to export goods, as well as their greater responsibility to receive refugees and maintain "hangers-on," the maliks and furshas were the main owners of slaves in the Ancien Regime.

With the emergence of the Masalit sultanate, especially under Abakr after 1888, the term "political elite" acquired a new meaning for the Masalit. Abakr, son of Ismail Abd al-Nabi, expanded the power of the sultanate, created estates, and established a privileged class of landed aristocrats and powerful bureaucrats. As the Masalit entered directly into the trans-Saharan trade, which had formerly been largely restricted to the Fur and Wadai aristocracies, new flows of guns, clothing and special foods were absorbed by a Masalit aristocracy, primarily of the sultan's clan. Abakr made sure that import goods were status symbols restricted to the political elite by sumptuary laws. The new aristocracy made efforts to settle the expanding numbers of war captives and refugees on their estates in order to make the most use of their lands; in the short run, at least, power was directly related to the number of subjects under one's control, partly in their capacity to produce revenues, and also as constituents.

The expansion of the top of the local administrative hierarchy reduced the power and autonomy of the maliks and furshas. They lost judicial and other authority, as they were placed under direct observation by agents of the sultan. They also lost some taxes and other sources of income, including export goods found in their territories, which had formerly allowed them independent access to import goods. They became dependent on the favor of the sultan for their position as well as their income. Some maliks managed to join the new elite, while most sank in position and prestige. The effect of the sultanate on commoners was more far-reaching; more taxes and labor demands were levied than ever before, with less chance of escape. As for slaves, they came to be concentrated in the hands of the new sultanic elite, and much less in the hands of the maliks. Thus, under Abakr the political structure of the Masalit was drastically transformed, from a clan based organization with local elites, who interfaced with distant Fur overlords, to a centralized system with a large local bureaucracy living from slave estates, and the exploitation of the free farming population. The clan elites declined in power even as they represented the sultanate in despoiling the countryside. Later sultans were milder, but their relatives became even more exploitative and independent in their extractions from rural areas, and at least two popular uprisings occurred between 1911 and 1913. It was this sultanate, with twenty years of 'traditional' authority behind it, which was adopted as the basis of a Native Administration under the policy of indirect rule by the Anglo-Egyptian Sudan.

The Sudan conquered Dar Fur in 1916, after coexisting with it as an independent state since 1898. The British did not proceed to occupy Dar Masalit until 1922, although they established a border post at Kereinik in 1918. Sultan Andoka had actually submitted in 1912 to the French, and was paying tribute and receiving support for his regime from them, but border negotiations in Europe placed the Masalit—except for territory ceded to the French in 1912—in the Sudan. Reginald Davies, who had worked in the Sudanese administration since 1911, became the first resident in 1922; he was a strong proponent of Lord Lugard's theory of indirect rule (1965). In 1935, the governor of Darfur wrote of this event "Dar Masalit was taken over 13 years ago . . . as a going concern, with a complete and effective judicial system, and a full (if somewhat primitive) organization for all branches of its administration" (Darfur 1/34/174).

The irony of this comment becomes clear as we examine the record of British occupation. As elsewhere in the Sudan, indirect rule was applied in a utilitarian way only, with no concern for maintaining a precolonial system of authority for its own sake; after all, the British went on to create the appearances of traditional rule elsewhere in Sudan even where there were no pretenders with which to work. In this spirit Davies set about restructuring the sultanate into an effective arm of British administration.

Davies was of the opinion that the new administration should be firmly centralized around the sultan, a sentiment that Andoka agreed with wholeheartedly. Although his power to carry out foreign policy was curtailed, and his judicial decisions were subject to overrule, he received the full support of the British for his position, at the expense of the rest of the sultanic bureaucracy that was overrunning the Dar. Although it took years, the estates were brought under the sultan's control, which included the collection of taxes and administration of justice. The British also supported the Masalit sultan's power over other ethnic groups; Sir Harold MacMichael in 1918 stated that the Jabal and Erenga were "grumbling" and would break away if not for British support (Intel 1/19/98). Most importantly, the sultan was placed on the Sudanese payroll and was provided with a large regular salary. As Davies put it to the Governor in 1924: "His personal revenue should be so much greater and more secure than it has ever been before, that we achieve the political end of making the idea of a return to pre-occupation conditions thoroughly repugnant to him'' (Darfur 3/3/24). His rivals in the bureaucracy became his dependents, and he was able to build a palace, buy a car, make the pilgrimage to Mecca, support many retainers, and generally live a very comfortable life of secure wealth and power.[5]

The reduction of the power of the sultan's relatives left a void especially when it came to tax collection, a central concern of the colonial administration. It was Sultan Andoka, perhaps experiencing trouble with his relatives and the landed aristocracy, who suggested collection of taxes through furshas and maliks (Intel 2/51/429). Thus, in the first decades of colonial rule, the clan leaders, both maliks and furshas, were brought into the Native Administration in a hierarchical structure. Apparently a good deal of fluidity had developed, and many maliks had somehow become furshas; there were over thirty in 1936. Perhaps they were created by the sultans during their period of independence. The power of granting land—thus, establishing a fursha's or a malik's office—was a prerogative of the Fur sultan in the Ancien Regime, but Hajjam Hasab Allah arrogated this right (Kapteijns 1985:70) and Masalit sultans later did likewise. The resident took part in this process after occupation: ''He therefore persuaded the sultan to bring all *maliks* who were still independent under *firshas*, and to reduce the number of *firsha*ships by dismissing 'the more useless firshas' and amalgamating their districts'' (Kapteijns 1985:220; compare Darfur 3/3/21, 1921 Annual Report, where it appears that it is the sultan who is enlisting the resident's support in this policy).

Reduction of the number of furshas took place over about fifteen years; in 1938 there were twenty-six furshas, of whom seventeen were Masalit (Darfur 1/34/175, 1938 Annual Report). The number increased slightly afterwards, but the basic structure of administration was now established. The level under the sultan became something larger than a malikship had been under the Ancien Regime, but smaller than a furshaship,and this was apparently a convenient size for the administrative purposes of the government. The fursha became an official comparable to the *omda*, the basic local official of other Sudanese Native Administrations. Arabs in Dar Masalit were also brought under officials first called sheikhs and later omdas who were directly responsible to the sultan (Darfur 1/34/175, 1938 Annual Report). The recognized furshas were given small salaries and tokens of office, and were secured in their authority by the support of the sultan and the British, although they were easily replaced or dispensed with if they were not useful to the administration. Apparently they were aware of this: "It would appear that they [the furshas] are at last beginning to regard themselves more as servants of the administration subject to obligations and less as feudal chiefs possessed of rights," wrote the resident in 1932 (Darfur 1/34/175, 1932 Annual Report).

This change in the nature of the fursha's office of course affected maliks as well; they became a somewhat redundant official. Most furshas only had a few maliks under them, which made their office an impractical level at which to delegate authority or to pass on information. It was in this context that the village sheikhs became an important part of the administrative hierarchy; being several times more numerous than maliks, they could be significantly more effective as local agents of the fursha. The first mention of sheikhs as village heads and tax collectors that I found is in the 1934 Annual Report, although it is not entirely clear that the sheikhs mentioned are not those of Arabs (Darfur 1/34/175). Villages also were growing; in 1924 the resident estimated village size at only 6–50 houses, but as will be shown in the next chapter, immigrants were recruited to join villages and share the tax burden. With the expansion of the population due to immigration of Masalit and others from Chad (see chapter 3) and the decreasing importance of the clan territory as a concept, the maliks faded into insignificance, such that many villagers today do not know who their maliks are or where their clan boundaries lie. The fursha and sheikh became the standard officials of the Native Administration, mirroring 'chiefs' and 'headmen' elsewhere in Britain's African colonies (compare Gartrell 1983).

Thus, the political structure of Dar Masalit went through several transformations in its known history. At some point Fur titles were imposed on an unknown organization; a sultanate based on the Fur model then came to exist above them; and these were both drastically reconstituted under colonial rule. The Native Administration structure was maintained at independence in 1956. After the May Revolution in 1969, it became official policy to abolish Native Administrations; however, the sultanate of Dar Masalit was one of a few that were temporarily retained on the grounds that it was not yet practical to replace them. In 1978 and 1979, I found that a hybrid structure continues to exist.

Furshas are still the basic units of administration. There are twenty Masalit furshas plus the Masalit omda of Geneina, as well as eight non-Masalit furshas, the Gimr sultan, and twenty-four Arab omdas. The Masalit furshas govern 1,463 sheikhs, with fifteen to one hundred eighty-six under each fursha. However, rather than taxing and administering on behalf of the sultan, the furshas are grouped under three rural councils that are part of the national political structure; these are joined with the council of Geneina into a "majlis al-montaga" or district council. (The sultan, incidentally, was the elected president of that council in 1978.)

This organization is also temporary, and the government is working through its several agencies to penetrate Masalit society at least with its major institutions—the Sudan Socialist Union and the majlis or council structure of legislative assemblies. The boundaries of malik territories are being ignored in the establishment of new rural councils, but fursha boundaries are being respected. The Department of Cooperatives has also expanded greatly in recent years. Both rural councils and cooperatives require local participation, in that a large number of people have to request the establishment of a council, and buy shares in the case of a cooperative. In both cases, interest is being generated through subsidized sugar, because both councils and cooperatives are entitled to certain allocations.

The government also revamped the judicial system in 1978 and 1979, and organized courts that were not based on fursha boundaries. Thus, the old order is being supplanted in its most important administrative and judicial functions. Powerful people of the old order continue to be influential and well-placed, for example, the sultan is the highest district court judge, and took part in appointing the new lower court judges, which include a large number of furshas as well as clansmen of the sultan, who had been judges before the May Revolution. The sultan and some of the furshas are also influential by virtue of wealth. Nevertheless, in the long run, the government will probably be successful in reducing the offices of sultan and fursha to empty titles, and then fully incorporating Dar Masalit into the national political structure.

One should not leave the discussion of Masalit political structure without mentioning one problematic figure called the wornung. He was the leader of the young men of the village, training them in warfare, leading hunts, raids, and communal labors. According to Kapteijns, he was active in setting the barter equivalents for local commodities. My informants mentioned that he determined the opening of the seasons for the major gathered goods as well. Kapteijns notes that the wornungs acted as police or seconds-in-command for the maliks, but, in view of their essential functions, it seems likely that they existed before Fur administration, and were then incorporated into that structure. Nowadays, wornungs still exist, but not in every village, and with no official status; however, they can still raise a work party from time to time (compare Haaland 1978).

Thus, the political organization of Dar Masalit has gone through a series of transformations, but in general it has consisted of an extractive hierarchy superimposed upon local relations of community and family. Under the Fur, political power was rather decentralized, and the maliks and furshas had a measure of independence. Part of the tribute extracted stayed with them in rural areas for redistribution. During independence this structure was destroyed, only to be reconstituted under a highly centralized Native Administration after independence. Thus, an articulation of administrative structures was established between the colonial center and a local hierarchy. As will be shown in subsequent chapters, the political changes at this stage did not radically transform the local economy, which continued to be oriented to subsistence production and the reproduction of the community. It was not until colonial rule was near its end that economic flows between Dar Masalit and the Nile Valley became significant. Only at that stage did market incorporation take place at the level of village and family. Local forms of social organization partly determined the process of incorporation and were themselves transformed by it.

Local Social Organization

For the majority of the population, the intricacies of Dar-level political organization are not a constant factor in their lives, but the policies of these organizations are. These policies are locally expressed through the actions of sheikhs, councils and courts; these coexist with some elements of local social organization and replace others. The clan or clan segment probably has been of major importance in social life, affecting settlement, marriage, warfare, compensation for murder, as well as lesser suits, and other activities. Nowadays, the clan is a minor theme, and the village is the basic unit of organization. The majority of the population live in rural villages of 100–500 people; between these villages also exist smaller camps, many of them seasonal but some permanent, in which one or several families may live. Perhaps five to ten percent of the Masalit outside Geneina live in the towns that have grown up during and since the colonial era. These are market centers, furshas' headquarters, and sites of schools, dispensaries and police posts; they have populations of approximately one to five thousand people. Even they are frequently organized as a set of contiguous villages rather than as units.

Most villages have a sheikh; some larger villages have two, while a few villages have no sheikh and the people are listed with sheikhs of neighboring villages. Each sheikh is chosen by popular approval, commonly from among the close relatives of the previous sheikh. Primarily, they are the village intermediaries with the fursha, police, courts, councils and other institutions of government. They are responsible to the government for overseeing the tax listing and collection, as well as communicating orders and bringing cases into the court.

In 1979 sheikhs were paid LS 6.00 per month, which is neither a lot nor insignificant, plus 10 percent of taxes that possibly amounted to an additional LS 10 per year. Formerly sheikhs were able to conduct hearings in the village on cases of many types, and collect fines, but the centralizing policy of the government is also at work here. Several cases in 1978–79 were brought into court against the sheikhs' will; some sheikhs were even fined for not reporting small theft and assault cases to the police.

Sheikhs, as well, are responsible to their villagers; they should use their influence to be sure that the tax listings of livestock numbers are kept low, accompany villages to court and act as their guarantors if necessary, and help newcomers find fields or places for their houses. The position is, however, not well respected, and many villagers refuse to act as sheikhs or to cooperate with them. Sheikhs are frequently in difficulties either with the government or their people or both. Nevertheless, it seems that people can always be found who are attracted to the activities of this office and the opportunities they present.

Most villagers conduct their daily affairs as much as possible without reference to sheikhs, police or courts; the primary idioms of social organization are kinship and neighborliness. In socializing, sharing ideas or information, and cooperation, as well as dispute settlements people look to their close kin and close neighbors, who are often the same people. Villages usually have one or several large kinship groups of cognatically (primarily patrilineally) related men and women, and their spouses. Members of these large kinship groups may interact almost exclusively with the descendants of a common grandparent and their spouses in everyday life. On the other hand, those without a large number of local close kin may activate more remote relationships. Aside from some particular observances towards the immediate family of one's spouse, kinship is a general idiom of cooperation and friendliness that may be extended as far as one likes. Thus, people act as kin to those relatives who are also local and with whom they get along, not unlike the Tunisian villagers described by Barbara Larson (1983).

Those without local kin rely on the strength of ties of neighborhood, which are often neglected in descriptions of African societies (but see Abrahams 1965; Lewis 1974). Frequently kin live near each other, but one is expected to be friendly and cooperate with one's immediate neighbors in any case. Neighbors as well as kin are called in to intercede in family disputes, and close neighbors may be counted on to come to work parties. The men of a neighborhood often eat together as a group, or in each others' compounds at different times; women frequently go to the well together, help each other with child care, work together to feed people at wakes or ceremonies, and cooperate in many other ways. To a certain extent, this neighborly idiom is extended to the whole village; certainly this is true in small villages and most especially in the camps, where common meals are the norm and fences are rare.

In the larger villages there are usually several neighborhoods, each one concretely expressed by a masik (*masi:k*), which is usually a clearing protected by trees and sun-shelters where men eat, pray, socialize and work together. Women of the neighborhood often work and pass time together in each other's compounds. In the masik, wakes are observed, disputes are heard, and boys are given religious instruction. One feki usually has responsibility for each masik. (The village in which I lived, with less than five hundred residents at its seasonal maximum, had six active masiks—this excludes the camps.) Nevertheless the entire village and people of camps surrounding the village should pray together on major religious holidays under the *ima:m* of the village, who is one of the fekis chosen by the villagers for this purpose.

The social spheres of men and women are somewhat separated; there is in fact a woman called a "sheikha" who sometimes represents female interests in village affairs.[6] However, the division of the sexes is far less in this area than in other parts of the Muslim world, and women are by no means secluded. They farm and own animals, cooperate with male friends and relatives, go to the market where they buy and sell from strangers including men, and celebrate together with men at parties and ceremonies. There is an element of separation that prevents close relations between the sexes except in terms of kinship and marriage, but there is room for a good deal of friendly interaction and mutual support.

Age and generation are not the basis of any formal grouping institutions, such as sets or grades, although circumcision is an important rite of passage in the life of boys. However, as everywhere people of similar age find themselves in similar situations that are the basis of friendship and interaction. Children and adolescents form friendships that may lead to migrating together, living as neighbors, or marrying each others' siblings. Older men, especially those of a religious inclination, usually enjoy each others' company best.

One young man, who built a house near mine on the edge of the village, complained about the age of village men, as most young men had either emigrated or were in the camps for the rainy season. He was busy trying to persuade young men to build near us in order to form a youthful neighborhood, and he was already discussing the location for the masik.

However, age is a minor theme in Masalit social life, and in general adults interact freely regardless of age. There is a degree of respect for one's elders, but in village councils and general interaction young adults are also heard and respected. Children and adolescents mingle with adults but are expected to be respectful and obedient; however they are often encouraged to converse and take part in adult activities as well.

Cross-cutting all of these idioms of social organization is another factor that is of considerable importance, or rather two closely related factors: attitudes about alcohol and religion. Although virtually all Masalit are Muslims, there is a range of piety and strictness of observance. Drinking is a salient distinguishing feature between groups. Millet beer has important social functions and symbolic significance; it is forbidden by Islam, but the prohibition on alcohol was not effectively preached in Dar Masalit until the late nineteenth century. Currently, in the villages I studied, close to half of all adults abstain from alcohol, while half continue to drink. In general, abstention from alcohol is a sign of greater interest in religion, although there are religious men of the old school who continue to drink, and a few non-drinkers who abstain for other reasons. Mutual tolerance usually rules, but the distinction between the pious and the drinkers is an important factor in daily social interaction, marriage and residence choices, and other activities. The pious pray together, take instruction together, and share many values; in at least one village the non-drinkers withdrew to form a separate neighborhood.

All of these factors—kinship, neighborhood, gender, age, drinking, and religious orientation—as well as practicing the same handicraft, owning adjacent fields, and many other circumstances—may predispose people to have a relationship, and also provide the idiom and structure for that relationship. From the individual's point of view, these idioms are the basis for a personal network, with some relationships having greater obligatory content than others regardless of intervening factors. However, friendship and personal choice permeate all relationships expressed by these idioms, such that within a family some brothers are more brotherly than others, and some neighbors more neighborly. There are few ascriptive corporate groups that structure Masalit society in important ways. Even the family is, for many purposes, better considered as a collection of individuals rather than as a simple unit.

Family and Household

Villages are composed of families, which are best defined as ever-married women with their co-resident children and/or spouse. In the two villages where I collected data on family structure, the most common type of family is made up of a monogamously married couple with children; however, the majority of families do not conform to this description (table 2.1). There are nearly as many women in polygynous marriages, and there are large numbers of widowed, divorced women and women whose husbands are absent at any given time. Many of these women have children. For resident men, monogamy is most common; only about one third of them have two or more wives. However, from the viewpoint of women and their children, only 36 percent of families have a full-time resident husband and father. In part this reflects the effects of emigration, temporary and permanent, which has been predominantly by males; as a result among resident villagers over the age of twenty there are 1.6 females to every male. A few single men exist at any one time, but it is rare for a man to stay single for long.

It is common in economic studies to assume that families such as these are "household firms," which implies that production and consumption are primarily joint activities, characterized by pooling of resources and decision making at the family level. While for certain purposes Masalit families can be considered as households, this obscures a good deal of the intra-household economic behavior. The Masalit economy, like many others if examined closely, is characterized by individuation and personal independence in consumption and especially in production (compare Turner and Turner 1955; Guyer

Table 2.1 ***Marital Status of all Ever-married Women in two Rural Villages***

	NUMBER OF WOMEN[a]	PERCENTAGE
Monogamous, Husband Present	66	36
Monogamous, Husband Absent	17	9
Polygynous	62	33
Widowed or Divorced	39	21

a N = 184

1981; Reynolds 1982; Jones 1983). Fields and livestock are individually owned, as are harvests. A husband and wife may help each other, or even make a joint field, and children help parents. However the norm is for individuals to take responsibility for their own cultivation and to do most of the work. Older children frequently have fields and animals of their own, and use the proceeds to buy clothing or other needs.

A husband and wife operate a joint household for most consumption activities and in raising children. However, they do not establish a joint estate by marrying. Many economic responsibilities are separate, and each must meet these out of his or her own harvest. The husband must provide clothing for the family, build and maintain dwelling and work places, and provide the more expensive foods, such as meat and sugar for family consumption. As a result the husband is most involved in the cash sphere, growing more cash crops and making the larger sales and purchases. Also, the better paid positions in the manufacture and distribution of consumer goods (trade, tailoring, etc.) are almost exclusively male. A wife's contribution to the household is mostly in direct labor. She is responsible for cooking, gathering firewood, fetching water, and care of small children. She often barters small quantities from her crop stores for vegetables and spices needed on a small scale for the family food. Both men and women may also make independent purchases of clothing or other items; women can get money by sale of their crops or animals, by gathering forest products, or by making oil, butter, prepared foods, or millet beer.

Independence of husbands and wives in crop production, to the extent of keeping separate granaries, is commonly reported among speakers of Nilo-Saharan languages (Barth 1967b; Oboler 1982; Doornbos 1984b; Haaland 1984). Among the Masalit, I was told that in the past the man's harvest would be sealed and would not be opened until the woman's was finished.[7] Thus, any grain surplus in a given year would be accumulated by the husband. However, although grain harvests are still kept separate, millet does not have the position that it formerly had; since men put more time into cash crops, millet is of less importance, and, even before the wife's millet is finished, the man may have used much of his own in feeding a camel or horse, making a work party or ceremonial feast, or in sales for cash needs. Nevertheless, the present system perpetuates the older pattern, in that for married couples the surplus—now in cash crops—is still largely controlled by men.

Thus, it would be an over-simplification to assume that the household is the most important decision making unit. The error would be compounded if one considered polygynists and their wives as a single unit. On the contrary, polygyny decreases the level of control that husbands and wives can exert over each other's economic activities. A polygynous man's resources are spread over two or more distinct families, each composed of individuals with needs and wishes of their own. For this reason, in the chapters that follow, polygynous men have been considered to be members of each of their families in inverse proportion to their number of wives, and their resources have been weighted accordingly.[8]

Having stated that there is a good deal of independence and economic individuation, I do not wish to imply that the family is unimportant. In fact it is the most important group to which anybody belongs. The agreement to form a household and share in raising children is a serious one and establishes substantial rights and duties. Certainly for the most part it is in the interests of husbands and wives to plan their activities together and help each other to be successful, for there is room within the institution for a good deal of cooperation as well as competition. I have emphasized the individual aspects to point out that this cooperation is that of partners, each of which is doing their best to meet their personal goals within their set of personal constraints. The constraints on men and women and their obligations to their families differ, and this must be kept in mind in order to understand the processes of socioeconomic change that are discussed in the following chapters.

Thirty-three of the one hundred eighty-nine families (including one hundred eighty-four women-based units and five single men) in the two villages censused lived at the time of the village census in joint compounds; that is, the dwellings of two or more families were surrounded by a common fence. Because of the importance of extended families as economic units elsewhere in Africa, I made efforts to determine the extent of pooling and familial cooperation within the compound. Except for a few cases where an elderly person was infirm and unable to farm and cook, families in joint compounds operated separate households; greater levels of cooperation occurred, but these were in the idiom of neighborliness. While the men of a joint compound, in those few cases where there were two men, ate together, it was repeatedly stressed to me that each woman cooked separately every night. Grain stores, fields and livestock were kept separate. Although many of the joint compounds involved parents and children, it must be clear that there was no extended household under control of a parent, such as the *gandu* unit in Nigeria (Hill 1972; Goddard 1973). Families lived together by convenience and mutual choice. Usually these arrangements emerged early in the developmental cycle of the family.

Men and women are usually married by their early twenties. The groom, usually with the assistance of his parents, pays a bridewealth of approximately three cows, ten goats, and variable amounts of cash; this is primarily distributed to the bride and her mother, and then more distant relatives. The groom must build a house in the bride's mother's compound, and live there with his wife for at least a year, working in the fields of her mother. Bride-service is sometimes replaced by an additional cash payment, especially in the towns. In the first year the groom is to a great extent a dependent of his wife's mother, the *aju:s*, "old woman", eating from her grain stores, but in the second year he cultivates his own field and becomes more independent. The couple usually stays until at least one child is born. They may also stay permanently, if it is convenient, or they may move nearby in the neighborhood; if the husband is from a different village, they may move there, possibly into his father's compound. Alternatively they may move to a different village entirely.

The main factors affecting the residence decision are the availability of fields and compatibility with kin and neighbors. Many men have told me how happy they are to build their own place, but there are also good reasons to continue a joint arrangement. If a man intends to migrate, a young wife might best be left with her parents and siblings rather than alone. If a parent is ill or needs a lot of help, one child may stay along with his or her spouse. Or, simply, if a compound is big, fields are nearby, and things are going smoothly, why bother to build another house? One might as well put up a small symbolic fence and continue to live as neighbors with one's parents or in-laws. However, uniting an extended family into a household firm is not among the reasons for residing in a joint compound.

Summary

I have outlined those aspects of Masalit social organization which are most important to an understanding of the socioeconomic processes which are taking place, and I have tried to give the reader a general idea of who the Masalit are as a people with a history and a culture. I have briefly described the history of the political incorporation of Dar Masalit, which set the stage for its economic incorporation, and also established new patterns of privilege defined by linkage with British power. I have also described the forms of social organization at the village and family levels, which have been undermined by political and economic incorporation, but have also played important roles in determining the nature of market integration and its effects on the community. These themes are taken up in more detail in subsequent chapters, but first the discussion of the context of incorporation must be extended to the environmental and ecological situation of the Masalit as well as the changes it has undergone.

3. *Dar Masalit In Context: Environment, Ecology and Demography*

Understanding human actions requires a knowledge of their context. While this book is primarily concerned with social and economic aspects of Dar Masalit life, they cannot be understood in isolation. The environment and major environmental trends, which concern an area far larger than Dar Masalit, are active forces with which farmers and herders must cope. Similarly, with the political and economic incorporation of Dar Masalit into the Sudanese nation, administrative decisions made on a larger scale have local effects to which farmers must adapt. The ecological effects of the farmer-government-environment interaction change the context of future human action.

Environmental constraints vary within Dar Masalit, especially in terms of rainfall, which results in different regional patterns of adaptation. Rainfall also varies over time; Dar Masalit has been affected by recent reductions in Sahelian precipitation. Because rainfall is so essential to life in Dar Masalit and is a major determinant of ecological possibilities and variation, a large part of this chapter will be focused on rainfall patterns and trends, and the interaction of these trends with the current position of the Masalit in the market economy.

A people is also a population, as understood by demographers—a collection of human beings that exhibits an objective structure and characteristics, irrespective of cultural details or personal situations. Demographic trends also are both the results of human action and the context of future decisions. Immigration and emigration are particularly salient in the recent history of Dar Masalit, and have had major effects on its ecological condition. The evidence for these patterns from colonial records and census materials is discussed.

Finally, just as Dar Masalit must be situated in a larger context, the site of the most intensive fieldwork must also be situated within Dar Masalit. Thus, after discussing the larger-scale processes and regional characteristics of Dar Masalit, the field site that occupies us in future chapters is briefly described.

The Physical Environment: Rainfall and Groundwater

Dar Masalit is long—320 km from north to south, and approximately 100 km west to east—and because of this shows considerable variation on some environmental parameters that determine much of the cultural and ecological variation. Rainfall is primary. As elsewhere in Sudan, there is more rain and a longer rainy season in the south than in the north, because the intertropical convergence (ITC) between the desert high-pressure zone and the southern moist zone moves north over the summer months, then slowly returns (Barbour 1961). This results in a general pattern of richer, denser vegetation in locations further south, yielding increasingly to sparse, short-season vegetation towards the north. Although it lasts from April to October in the south, the rainy season (*xari:f*) is at its height in July and August; it is followed by a cool season (*ʃita*) in which abundant groundwater persists, yielding in December or January to the heat of the dry season (*Sayf*).

Rainfall is the primary determinant of agricultural possibilities, as well as of grazing. But the groundwater and drainage system determines the availability of much of that water. The wadis or riverbeds concentrate water, and thus, usually the thickest and most stable vegetation in a given area is found along the wadis, as are the reliable wells. Wadi vegetation provides fodder for goats and camels both before and after the rains when the plains are bare of vegetation. Cultivation of wadi fields also proceeds using only groundwater. Thus, throughout Dar Masalit the pattern of wadis is a major determinant of settlement patterns, permitting or restricting various economic uses of the regions of the Dar. Where wadis drain large areas, their flows (including subterranean water) are more secure and permit more stable settlement patterns.

The entire northern Dar drains into the Wadi Kaja system (figure 3.1), which flows with considerable volume and consistency through

Geneina during the rainy season. Kaja then proceeds south, mostly along the western border of Dar Masalit, draining the western section of the southern Dar as well as areas in Chad. Meanwhile, the Wadi Barei drains the eastern Dar until it joins the Wadi Azum, which reaches Dar Masalit from Jebel Marra at Murnei. Azum then follows the eastern border of the Dar and drains the southeast. The Azum and Kaja systems, which form the eastern edge of the Lake Chad basin, meet at the southern tip of Dar Masalit and flow west.

It is impossible to overstate the importance of rainfall and resulting groundwater in Dar Masalit. The level of rainfall determines the feasibility of growing millet, sorghum, or groundnuts; the amount of drinking water for people and animals; quality and quantity of grazing; and the state of the forest areas, which are the source of building materials, wild foods and game. In any given year, the distribution of the rains is also of great importance for agriculture, and this may vary substantially over short distances. A rainless ten days when crops are young may spoil a season, even though total rainfall is sufficient. Such drought periods are less likely to occur when total annual rainfall is high than when it is low. Also, timing is less crucial with respect to the recharging of groundwater reserves. Thus, in direct ways the total amount of rainfall and groundwater affects the quality of life and the suitability of an area within Dar Masalit for habitation, and this in turn affects the distribution and adaptation of people within the Dar. Changes in total rainfall over time are also occurring, affecting the habitability of the entire Dar.

Since the regional variations of adaptation in the Dar are partly a result of the long term rainfall levels and partly of the recent low levels, rainfall trends are considered before discussing the varying adaptations of the people.

Rainfall Trends

In Dar Masalit, mean annual rainfall in different stations ranges from 351 to 654 mm (table 3.1). Overall, the southern half of the Dar gets about 25 percent more rain than the north.

The records for Geneina demonstrate that rainfall was fairly stable for the years from 1928 to 1968, but in the decade 1969–78, mean annual rainfall at all stations in Dar Masalit fell markedly below earlier levels. Following the range from 439–702 mm in the previous decade, in 1969–78 rainfall ranged from 253–574 mm. In effect, any point in the Dar had average rainfall for that decade that was formerly

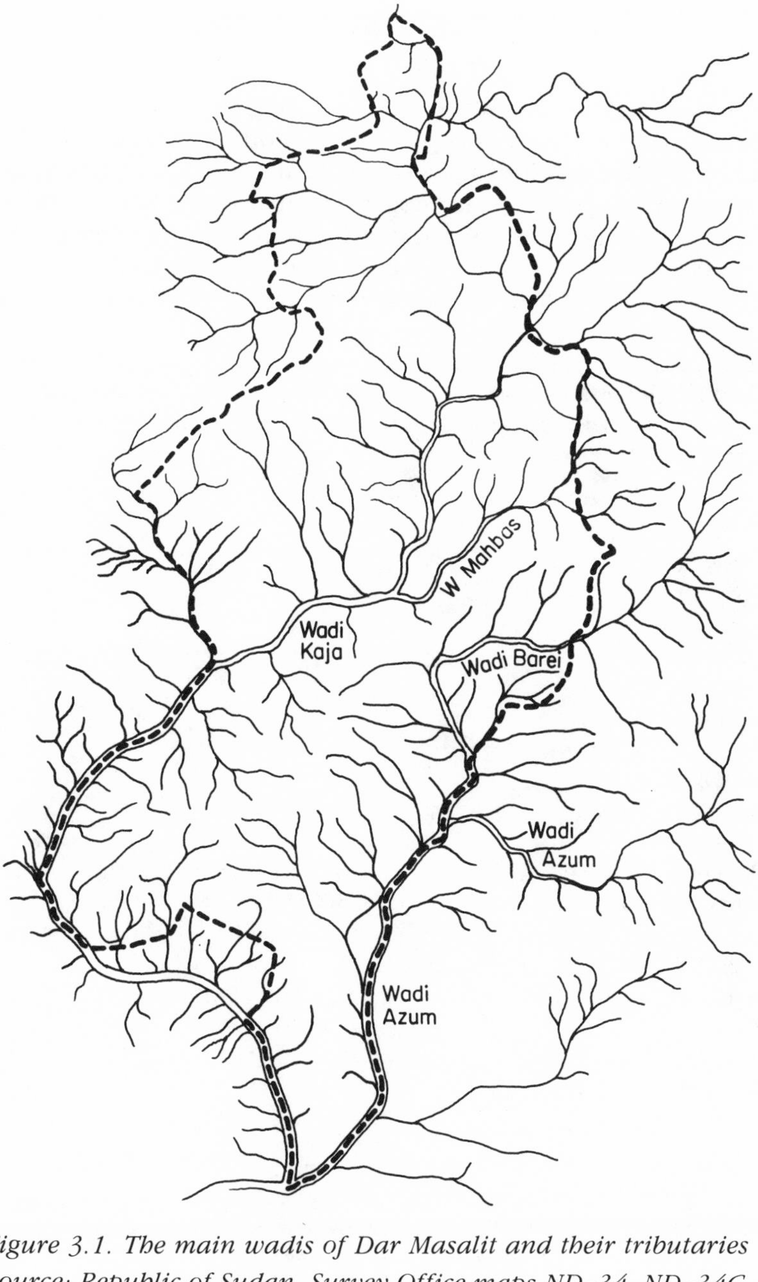

Figure 3.1. The main wadis of Dar Masalit and their tributaries
Source: Republic of Sudan, Survey Office maps ND–34, ND–34G, H, K, L, O, P; United States Air Force, Operational Navigation Chart K4 (1967); Landsat images 8111408223500, 8111408225500, and 8120408230500.

characteristic of an area 100 kilometers nearer the desert. The years 1972 and 1973 were especially dry in the northern and central Dar, and also in areas north of Dar Masalit, such as that inhabited by the Zaghawa. Many people emigrated from the northern territories in those years. While the rains in the rest of the 1970s were better than the worst drought years, they did not return to pre–1968 levels; then, they were followed by another brutal drought.

Table 3.1 ***Mean Annual Rainfall in mm by Decade at Dar Masalit Stations and Zalingei***

Station	1929–1938	1939–1948	1949–1958	1959–1968	1969–1978	Mean	SD
Northern Region							
Hajar							
Kulbus				439 (9)	253 (8)	351	175
Sileia			528 (8)	457 (9)	372 (3)	473	128
Abu Suruj				477 (7)	417 (7)	447	130
Sirba				570 (9)	394 (7)	491	161
Central Region							
Geneina	571	518	574	578	415	531	132
Kereinik			574 (8)	480 (9)	343 (8)	466	160
Masterei				627 (8)	546 (6)	592	152
Murne				526 (3)	402 (1)	495	55
Southern Region							
Arara				628 (8)	417 (9)	517	147
Beida				702 (8)	526 (3)	654	122
Habila			737 (6)	587	501 (6)	604	160
Forobor-anga				694 (6)	574 (7)	630	153
External							
Zalingei	606	688	682	668	535	632	128

Source: *Republic of Sudan, Meteorological Department records.* Where data are incomplete, the number of years recorded is shown in parentheses.

Most meteorological data available to me are for the years 1978 and before, but the African drought of the early 1980s is well known;

personal sources confirm that this has severely affected Dar Masalit (compare Dickey 1985). In this section, it will be argued that the drought of the 1980s should not have been such a surprise in the light of evidence available in the 1970s. Rainfall trends for Dar Masalit will be discussed first, and they will then be considered in the context of trends for the Sahel as a whole.

Rainfall data are available from twelve stations in Dar Masalit, and also from Zalingei, in Jebel Marra (figure 3.2). The Zalingei data are relevant because it is not far from the eastern border of the Dar, and particularly because Jebel Marra is the origin of the Wadi Azum, an important source of water to the people of Dar Masalit. For Zalingei and Geneina, data have been collected by meteorologists for fifty years. Other stations have data of varying time depth, mostly collected by medical staff at dispensaries and mailed to the Sudan Meteorological Department. These data are often incomplete, but sufficient in combination to indicate local patterns.

In table 3.1 are listed the twelve Dar Masalit stations in order of latitude, and Zalingei. Mean annual rainfall is tabulated for the 1969–78 decade and all preceding decades for which data are available. It is clear that for all stations there has been a substantial decline in the 1970s compared with the preceding decade. Figures from Geneina and Zalingei suggest that rainfall levels have been stable for forty years before this last decade, while three stations (Sileia, Kereinik, and Habila) show a declining trend since the 1950s.

Throughout the Sahel, a drought took place in a period generally agreed upon as 1968 to 1973. In Dar Masalit, the most distinct drought years were 1972 and 1973, in which eight of the ten stations with records showed the lowest rains of the decade (table 3.2.) The northern and central areas showed the greatest declines from normal rainfall. One must consider whether the decade means were low because of the drought years alone, and whether subsequent rainfall has been "normal." Also, there was a high rate of missing data, especially for the latter half of the decade. To examine whether rainfall returned to normal levels after the drought, while reducing the effect of missing data, the records were grouped into northern, central and southern regions, and Zalingei. For each year, in each region, the mean of all data points was taken. Thus, for those years with missing data from some stations, the data of nearby stations were given greater weight. After this step, only one value for regional rainfall remained lacking, northern region, 1976. Then, five-year means of these regional values and Zalingei were calculated, including the 1974–78 'post-drought' period. The results are given in table 3.3

Figure 3.2. Rainfall monitoring stations in Dar Masalit, and Zalingei station

Source: Republic of Sudan Survey Office maps ND–34 et al (See Figure 3.1); Republic of Sudan, Meteorological Department.

Table 3.2 ***Annual Rainfall in mm Recorded by Station, 1969–78***

Station	1969	1970	1971	1972	1973	1974	1975	1976	1977	1978
Hajar Kulbus	335	281	95	94	219	–	293	–	404	301
Sileia	364	–	480	273	–	–	–	–	–	–
Abu Suruj	400	456	330	252	292	–	488	–	–	698
Sirba	–	336	418	243	260	437	614	–	–	451
Northern Mean	366	358	331	216	257	437	465	–	404	483
Geneina	532	459	514	343	214	404	350	417	533	384
Kereinik	420	–	558	183	305	260	463	200	–	354
Masterei	–	789	744	418	331	506	–	–	–	488
Murne	402	–	–	–	–	–	–	–	–	–
Central Mean	451	624	605	315	283	390	407	309	533	409
Arara	503	460	429	371	336	581	–	295	501	278
Beida	535	–	559	–	–	–	–	–	–	484
Habila	619	489	269	437	–	–	–	–	795	397
Foroboranga	477	585	661	383	468	785	659	–	–	–
Southern Mean	534	511	480	397	402	683	659	295	648	386
Zalingei	597	554	767	610	412	468	546	498	410	491

Source: *Republic of Sudan, Meteorological Department records.* Regional means are calculated for each year from available data. A dash indicates incomplete data for that station in that year.

Table 3.3 ***Regional and Zalingei Five-year Means of Annual Rainfall (mm)***

Region	1949–1953	1954–1958	1959–1963	1964–1968	1969–1973	1974–1978
Northern	487	569	495	465	306	447
Central	552	578	585	537	456	410
Southern	780	716	679	602	465	534
Zalingei	653	710	698	638	588	483

Source: *Republic of Sudan, Meteorological Department records.*

It appears that although there has been a dramatic recovery in the northern region, which was hardest hit by drought, in the southern region, the second half of the decade was only slightly wetter than the first half, and in the central region and Zalingei, rainfall has actually been less. In all areas, the amount of rainfall has continued to be below pre–1969 levels.

Whether recent low rainfall is part of a long-term trend may be examined using simple linear regression. For the period 1949–78, rainfall totals are plotted by region in figure 3.3 with best-fitting lines shown. For the thirty year period, linear trends are downward, and the coefficients of correlation, intercepts, and slopes are all significant at the 0.01 level or better. This is in spite of the fact that there is considerable variation from year to year, which makes the downward trend difficult to perceive in the short term.

A model to be discussed below has suggested that rainfall levels in the Sahel have dropped steeply after a peak in the late 1950s. Also, the above discussion has been concerned with the question of a recovery after the drought period ended in 1973. For this reason, best-fit lines have also been plotted for the periods 1949–59, 1959–73, and 1973–78. In all regions, the 1950s are fairly level, followed by a drop in the 1959–73 period which is steeper than the thirty year trend. Finally, in the 1973–78 period, all four regions show an upturn. Due to the small number of points, many of the correlations are not statistically significant for these shorter periods. Only the 1959–73 periods for the northern and central region show correlation coefficients significant at the 0.05 level or better. Nevertheless, in combination these four graphs support the model of a downward trend over the 1960s culminating in the drought, followed by a partial recovery. These trends are discussed below in terms of global climatic theories.

Rainfall is inherently variable in the Sahel, and so the interpretation of incomplete data for a limited period must be cautious. However, the drastic effects of rainfall declines on people's lives, and the urgent need for decisions about appropriate action, counsels against patience. A tentative interpretation is that in the early 1970s, the northern region was affected by the same weather system that caused acute drought in the West African Sahel, and thus, it experienced a short-term reduction in rainfall. Dar Masalit as a whole, however, seems to be experiencing a long-term reduction which is less distinct but more persistent. This has already contributed to environmental deterioration, and these effects continue to accumulate. If rainfall levels continue at the levels of the 1970s, these trends will not be easily halted or reversed.

A long-term decline in rainfall has also been reported by Ismail Abdalla (1985) for a village in Kordofan, 700 kilometers east of Dar

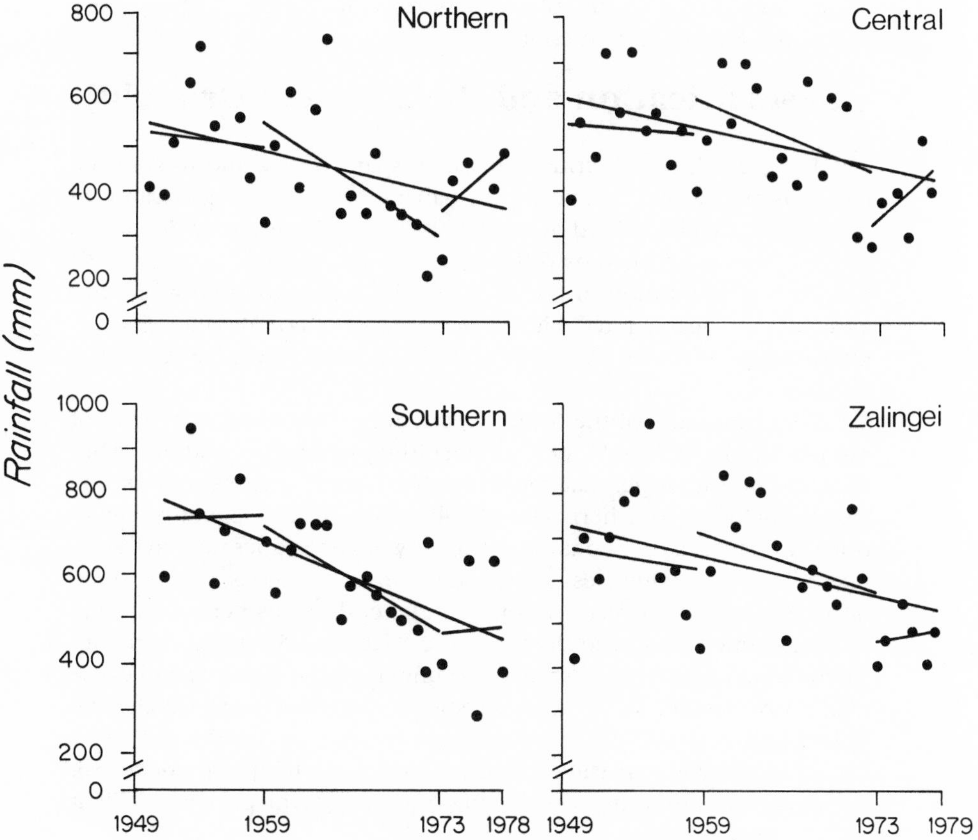

Figure 3.3. Regional rainfall trends. Linear trends for 1949–78 are downward and statistically significant for all regions. Trends for periods 1949–50, 1959–73, and 1973–78 are shown although most are not statistically significant.
Source: Republic of Sudan, Meteorological Department records, consulted March 1980.

Masalit. For Abesher, some 150 kilometers to the west, a declining trend has been reported by Kenneth Hare (1977) from 1957 until 1973. Thus, Dar Masalit appears to be part of a larger region which is experiencing rainfall reduction. Such trends have also been observed elsewhere in the Sahel, and theory has developed concerning the nature and causes of this phenomenon. A discussion of this theory places the Masalit case in context.

Desertification and the Sahelian Drought

The Sahel is a semi-arid zone which spans Africa, and west of the Nile it is transitional between the 'Sahara' and 'Sudan' geographical zones. It is usually defined by rainfall, but, as A. T. Grove (1978) points out, the figures adopted by different authors to define it vary. Grove's compromise definition of the Sahel, as the area getting between 200 and 600 mm mean annual rainfall, places most of Dar Masalit in it (begging the question of the time period for which average rainfall is taken!).

The drier parts of the Sahel experienced a markedly low level of rainfall in the 1968–73 period, resulting in famine and hardship throughout the zone. Rainfall was also less in areas south of the Sahel—including southern Dar Masalit—but the consequences were not as great, because rainfall variation in wet zones does not have such immediate consequences as it does in dryer areas. Over time, however, it was also very serious. By the end of this period, international attention had been drawn to the "Sahelian drought," and considerable efforts were being made to understand the nature and cause of the low rainfall levels. The questions addressed were usually the following:

1. Is rainfall decreasing? If so, is it a brief and temporary decrease, a medium-term downtrend, or a long-term process? Will it reverse?
2. If rainfall is decreasing, is the cause a nonhuman, global process? If so, what and how?
3. Is the cause human? Again, what is it, and how does it operate?

It is ironic that none of these questions are new in the literature on this area. Brynmor Jones, in 1938, reviewed several articles with varying points of view on all of these issues. The literature of the 1970s has provided some new insights and possible explanations, and the additional data of decades of observation, but has not come to agreement on the fundamentals.

Fluctuations in rainfall levels in the Sahel occur in several time frames. In the longest, over tens of thousands of years, major changes have taken place. Twenty thousand years ago the borders of the desert were hundreds of miles further south than they are now (Grove 1977;

Talbot 1980; UNCD 1977). The dunes of Dar Masalit, now fixed by vegetation, were bare and mobile. Over a succeeding period approximately six thousand to five thousand years ago, the current Sahel was considerably wetter than it is now (Nicholson 1980). These long–term changes were part of the global weather patterns affected by the earth-sun distance and other factors (Bryson 1974), and it is difficult to relate processes covering tens of thousands of years to those spanning a few decades. Yet it could be that long–term patterns are most noticeable in marginal areas such as the Sahel, and the reduction in Sahel rainfall is an indicator of global weather patterns of the future.

At the opposite extreme, opposing any conception of enduring trends in rainfall, it is pointed out by many authors (Hare 1977; Schone 1977; Warren and Maizels 1977) that short-term periods of drought are regular occurrences in arid zones. In the Sahel, previous droughts have occurred in 1911–13 and the early 1940s. A series of bad years occurs in the Sahel three or four times per century (UNCD 1977:6). Thus, the 1968–73 drought might be considered a normal event, to be endured with the expectation that it may be followed by better times. However, short-term fluctuations may occur in addition to long-term downward trends or upward trends, and no direct link between them has been demonstrated by these authors. In the circumstances, it appears that their counsel, that the problems will solve themselves, is unwisely optimistic.

Of more interest in the light of the data from Dar Masalit is the observation of trends spanning centuries, made possible by extended periods of data collection in semi-arid zones and efforts with new methods of investigation. Sharon E. Nicholson (1980) has assembled geological data, travelers' accounts, and chronicles from Sahelian states and has attempted a regional quantitative analysis of rainfall trends over hundreds of years. While historical records indicate that droughts recur in the Sahel, this does not mean that the normal levels of rainfall have stayed the same over the centuries. She finds that relatively wet conditions have existed in the Sahel during the sixteenth, seventeenth and early eighteenth centuries. They have been followed by an arid period comparable to the present, followed by a return to humid conditions in the late nineteenth century. Rainfall measurements confirm the latter.

Grove (1977) reported that rainfall was high in the Sahel in the last twenty-five years of the nineteenth century, followed by dry years in the early twentieth century. The period 1920–1960 was reported to be relatively wet in various parts of the Sahel, but at some time in the vicinity of 1957–64, a downtrend began (Berry 1975; Hare 1977). Hare observed downward trends over the 1957–73 period in West Africa and Chad, followed by an upturn in 1974; he found these to be comparable to patterns in semi-arid zones of Australia.

Derek Winstanley (1973), drawing on data from Africa, India and the Arabian peninsula, concludes that the summer monsoon in these places is part of a cyclical global system that also involves Mediterranean winter rains and westerlies in the British Isles. He finds that monsoon rains, including the Sahel, peaked in the late 1920s after a drier period, and have been in a gradual, steady decline since then. The 1950s showed an upward fluctuation from this trend, while the sixties showed a sharp downward trend. Writing in 1973, he said, "Monsoon rainfall is at a low point of an irregular fluctuation, superimposed on a longer term downward trend" (Winstanley:191). Basing his prediction on two hundred and seven hundred year cycles observed in the European part of the system, he has predicted recovery from acute drought, but a continuation of the gradual downtrend of monsoon rainfall for another fifty to three hundred years. The data from Dar Masalit fit this pattern well. As shown above, the 1949–58 period is relatively flat; the 1959–73 trend is strongly down, and there has been a certain amount of recovery since that time. If Winstanley is correct, the rainfall levels will not return to the levels of the 1929–58 period in the lifetime of current inhabitants.

A. T. Grove (1981) has criticized Winstanley's argument as an overly simple model based on too little data; certainly, such a model should undergo considerable scrutiny before being accepted scientifically. Nevertheless, we would have been more prepared for the famine of the 1980s had its predictions been taken as seriously by policy-makers as those of the optimists.

Peter J. Lamb, while not supporting Winstanley's model, was a lonely voice in 1982 arguing that rainfall levels continued to be very low at West-African Sahelian stations, and that this condition was not receiving adequate publicity. He pointed out: "The suggestion that the Subsaharan drought was not likely to disappear in the near future has so far not been disproved," and that there was as yet no support for the projection of gradual recovery from the drought (1982:47). Subsequent events, of course, proved him tragically correct.

Thus, the medium-term analyses, while not always in agreement, cause us to question the sanguine 'drought' point of view, which predicts a return to normal rains fairly quickly. An examination of the data gives no confidence that levels which were previously normal can again be attained, and, if an uptrend were to begin, there is every likelihood that it would be gradual. For the people of the affected area, it is not a matter of their enduring a short-term phenomenon, but rather of adapting to the environment as it presents itself now. In Dar Masalit, that means an environment that is drier and poorer in resources than that inhabited by the preceding generation.

The environmental changes that accompany reduced rainfall are commonly known as desertification; that is, an area suitable for human habitation is turned into desert. It is rare that the desert actually invades a wet area in the form of moving dunes, since dunes are fixed by vegetation where rainfall is sufficient (Jones 1938; Talbot 1980:43). Rather, desert conditons are created by lower rainfall, usually with human assistance, and the desert thus annexes adjoining areas. The relative importance of human and nonhuman forces in this process is the subject of considerable discussion, partly because what is human can presumably be controlled.

Nonhuman explanations of the drought consider that the changes are part of global weather patterns, which naturally change Sahel rainfall. The model of Winstanley, discussed above, does not propose an explanation of the global weather cycles, but certainly places them beyond human control. Others explain weather patterns in terms of changes in global pressure patterns, or the effect of sunspots (Schone 1977; Landsberg 1975). Another global theory traces the changes to volcanos and also to human agencies external to the Sahel; that is, the higher rate of particulates, pollutants and CO_2 produced by industry and the mechanization of farming (Bryson 1974). However, Bryson also gives personal estimates of increases in atmospheric particulates due to "slash and burn agriculture and . . . deflation of soil disturbed by agriculture and construction" in the subtropics, which approximately equal the above "human pollutant emissions," and are a result of "especially rapid growth in the subtropics" of population (1974:758).

Several other theorists agree with Bryson in blaming the reduction in rainfall on human overuse of the Sahel. N. H. MacLeod (1976) argues that increased dust comes from wind erosion of over-grazed or monocropped soils; this dust interferes with the mixing of wet and dry fronts at the intertropical convergence that ordinarily causes rain. J. G. Charney (1975) traces the effect to the increased albedo or reflectivity of lands brought under intensive herding or cultivation, which causes reduced rainfall. As Jeremy Swift (1977) points out, these theories are logical, but none of them has been proven. As yet, data and actual research directed at these issues are insufficient.

At a local level, many have described instances where human activities, before or in reaction to the drought, have led to degradation of the physical environment, although not necessarily to reduced rainfall. For example, M. Kassas (1970) and H. N. LeHouerou (1968) attribute desertification in the Sahel to mismanagement including overgrazing, overcultivation, and overcutting of forests, leading to "desert encroaching over steppe, steppe over savanna, and savanna over forest. . . . The initiation of these replacement changes results primarily from deliberate action of man" (Kassas 1970:124). One cannot avoid noticing in such writing an effort to blame drought, famine and desertification on the people who suffer most from them. Consider also J. L. Cloudsley-Thompson: "It is now generally accepted [he references two of his own articles] that the main causes of desertification are overgrazing and trampling of the soil by domestic animals, the felling of trees for fuel, and bad agricultural practices." While he allows that climatic change plays a role: "Man cannot escape responsibility for having created a very large part of the Sahara desert." (1978:416–418) This kind of explanation has a basic appeal since it is so simple, but it leaves us wondering why the inhabitants of the Sahel have suddenly started destroying their environment in the twentieth century. To understand this one must look to the larger context of their actions.

Use of the environment is part of a system including the market context. Rather than considering overexploitation as the *cause* of either desertification or low rainfall, it is better considered as a *response* to low rainfall and also to larger economic and political pressures, in ways that are developed below. A number of researchers have presented evidence to this effect.

Richard W. Franke and Barbara H. Chasin (1980) describe the destructive effects market integration and colonization have had on local ecosystems, leading to a loss of the ability of human populations to adapt to drought. Bob Shenton and Mike Watts (1979) point out that local relations of redistribution and reciprocity, which played an important role in coping with drought, have been destroyed by colonial taxation policies and commodity production. In the case of the Sudan, Samir J. Ghabbour (1972) discusses the problems of wells and other government services in concentrating populations where the environment cannot support them. Abdel Aziz Bayoumi (1983) also argues that service delivery has been politicized and conservation neglected, and states that: "In my opinion the Government, represented by the Ministries of Agriculture since Independence, is the main cause of desert encroachment in the Sudan." A/Hamid Bakhit also protests the lack of a conservation effort, pointing out that crop markets "tempted the local farmers to make the maximum use out of available land disregarding totally the deteriorating soil fertility." (1983:7) The effect of such policies can best be understood by considering precolonial adaptations to the environment, and the ways in which these policies disturbed them.

Typically, human populations of the Sahel adapted to rainfall patterns with flexibility in the precolonial period. Shifting cultivation was the usual form of farming, and herding was nomadic. Migration to areas that were receiving adequate rains was normal, and, in precolonial periods was an integral aspect of the regional social organization (Lovejoy and Baier 1976; Tully 1985). A flexible adaptation by herders and farmers, who exchanged both goods and population, increased regional stability and resilience in the face of drought (Baier 1976). Both herders and farmers expected drought years to occur, and so kept surplus grain or animals as a reserve for those years. In the high rainfall period of 1930–60, herds expanded, and populations of farmers grew locally in adaptation to the available rainfall. With the severe downturn in rainfall during the 1970s, areas under cultivation were increased to maintain production, and savings were consumed. The forest, always a reservoir of subsistence, was exploited by more intensive hunting and gathering, and herders pollarded trees to feed their animals. The population of the Sahel concentrated around the most secure water sources, and many people moved into towns searching for income. All of these adaptations to drought sustained the population for two or three years, as they had in the past, without permanently damaging the environment.

However, there were some differences with previous drought periods. For most populations it was no longer sufficient to produce their own subsistence; taxes and new consumption needs introduced during colonial occupation made higher levels of production and sale necessary. This meant that what savings people had were more quickly exhausted, while the pressure on the forest to produce income as well as subsistence was greater. Towns were larger than they had been in the precolonial period. As low rainfall levels continued, the reactions described above became destructive, and intensified the long-term damage to the environment. The concentration of populations around towns and water holes led to intense local degradation of environments, with the consumption of most trees, including food sources, as firewood and building materials. Pastures were degraded by overuse. Farmers also expanded into all arable land and increased the use of remaining forest to such an extent that game and wild fruits became scarce. The greater area cultivated and grazed and the reduced forest cover increased wind erosion; the lack of vegetative cover caused the rainfall, even though reduced, to run off in torrents, creating gullying, sheet erosion, and ever-lower water tables. Thus, the patterns of behavior that were adaptive for short periods of low rainfall were ineffective in the long term.

The only effective reaction to a long period of reduced rainfall is emigration by a part of the population. In the precolonial period, Sahelian peoples constantly resettled. In some cases, enduring relations between geographically separated peoples existed, while elsewhere populations moved and expanded into vacant lands or, by military means, into occupied ones. The large number of linguistic groups that are composed of populations separated by hundreds of miles indicates the frequency of population movements in the past. However, the option of migration was much less practicable in the recent drought period. National borders divided north and south in many areas, for example, Niger-Nigeria, which were formerly continuous and flexible of population. Pastoralists found the forest areas and grazing lands to the south to be cultivated. Farmers were unable to move where they were not welcome, and they found areas to receive them were scarce. Thus, the flexibility of the relationship of human populations to land has been much reduced by the intensification of agriculture in the colonial and postcolonial period.

Before the reduction in rainfall of the 1970s, farmers across the Sahel had already expanded their cultivation to produce a marketable surplus in order to pay taxes, buy market goods, or meet government production quotas (Franke and Chasin 1980). Also, urbanization at the level of small towns across the Sahel had begun, and a class of merchants and salaried government workers existed that purchased local products and were particularly high consumers of meat, building materials, and wood. Thus, the environment was already under pressure when the drought came. Strategies formerly employed only when needed for survival—that is, expansion of cultivated areas and consumption of forest resources—were being employed to meet new cash needs and supply new classes. Therefore, the flexibility of the ecosystem and the ability of the population to absorb the rainfall loss in the short-term were diminished, while the option of long-term adaptation through population movement was foreclosed by intensification elsewhere. Thus, many people became refugees or homeless wanderers, while others were forced to depend on temporary labor migration by some family members. Such migration by individuals did not reduce population pressure in the same way that resettlement of families in response to drought did in the past. Labor migration by sons and husbands was a short-term solution that maintained an expanding population in an area that could not support that population by local resources alone.

Although Dar Masalit did not experience six years of severe drought, it suffered many of the Sahelian problems. Fifteen years of gradually declining rainfall, culminating in the extremely low rains of 1972–73, had similar effects. As figure 3.3 showed, the decline did not present itself in a steady downward tendency; rather, it was erratic and therefore unobservable as a trend to many inhabitants. However, this downward trend had clearly observable effects on groundwater and forest resources. Formerly reliable wells in the northern and central areas dried up, forcing people to move. The ecological crisis added to the history of taxation, market participation and urbanization that not only obliged the people of Dar Masalit to exploit their soils and forests to the limit, but also made the accumulation of savings for bad years increasingly difficult for most of the population. By 1972 many people did not have the resources to survive one or two severe drought years; they left to seek farms or employment elsewhere.

The forest is suffering as well. Throughout the Dar, forests are being cut faster than they can grow back at current rainfall levels in order to supply a population that formerly enjoyed more rain than it now has. Further, in all areas informants report their flora much reduced from previous levels. Doornbos (1982:36) also describes reduced tree and game species in the southern tip of Dar Masalit. Thus, one of the major buffers for short-term drought has fallen victim to an enduring drop in rainfall levels.

Although there have been some good years since 1973, there have also been some terribly dry years. The regeneration of the forest and soils would take decades even under optimal conditions (UNCD 1977) and some loss will probably be permanent. With the pressures of market production, high elite consumption levels, and a high rural population density relative to current rainfall, it is likely that large areas of Dar Masalit will never 'recover' from the drought, in the sense of returning to previous levels of resource availability. Cash needs are increasing, towns are growing, and so forests are being cut in ever more rural areas, following the familiar Sahelian pattern. Instead of recovering, farmlands are being used more intensively with techniques that accelerate soil degradation (compare Abdalla 1983 for a similar case from Kordofan). Ultimately, the result is impoverishment of most of the people.

The main concern of this work is not with rainfall trends, but with the history and effects of the penetration of a rural area by global market forces. The process by which a peripheral area is incorporated is in many ways independent of the weather, except insofar as it speeds or slows the process, or makes certain activities possible or impossible. In Dar Masalit, weather patterns have forced many into labor migration in 1972 and 1973, marking another step in the increasing market participation of the people of the area.

However, this was not an inevitable effect of a caprice of nature; it must be understood as the 'choice' of people whose options were circumscribed and redefined by their position in the larger political and economic system. Labor migration was already a major economic activity in Dar Masalit, inevitable for many, well before 1972; the dry years were merely an additional pressure.

Similarly, the ongoing process of environmental degradation is easily deplored by urban experts as the wanton despoiling of their heritage by short-sighted Masalit, bent on profit at any cost to others; more realistically, the environmental heritage of the Dar is being sold piecemeal by those who have little else to sell and no choice but to sell something. Thus, while environmental changes need to be taken into account in the economic history of Dar Masalit, one must not lose sight of the larger picture, and mistake these changes for the basic causes of Masalit poverty and powerlessness.

Regional Variation in Dar Masalit

The climatic and social processes described above are proceeding with different effect in the several areas of Dar Masalit. To a large extent, this is related to climatic variation throughout Dar Masalit. Thus, before discussing data collected at a particular site in Dar Masalit, one must consider the overall situation of the Dar, and the typicality of the research site.[1] In the following, it should be noted that 'the North' and 'the South' do not define precisely the same areas as were convenient in the discussion of rainfall data; subsequent use of these terms will reflect commonality of human adaptations in these zones. They will be redefined below.

The landscape of Dar Masalit is diverse. Overall it is intermediate in geography, neither dramatic and massive like Jebel Marra to the east, nor flat and uninterrupted like much of Southern Darfur. While there are no hills that cannot be climbed in a few hours, there are many small hills and rocky outcrops. The land is full of contours and gradual slopes, and crossed by wadis and their tributaries. These wadis support diverse vegetation: acacias of many types, as well as large tamarinds, sycamores, and other trees. There are also rough areas, too hilly or rocky for agriculture, where forests are found; and in the south on the banks of the Wadi Azum, where the obliging *Acacia albida* sheds its leaves in the season of cultivation, forest and farmland are often one and the same.

In the height of the dry season, the countryside is bleak except for the wadis; most trees are bare, revealing the empty nests of storks; and the brown of earth, buildings, and dried vegetation is only broken by the occasional green of an usher bush (*uʃar, Calatropis procera*)—a succulent with a sap that irritates the skin, and causes the hair of animals to fall out should they brush against it. But with the first rains, the trees miraculously sprout leaves, attracting the camel-keeping nomads from the south. Then, suddenly the earth is covered with green pastures and young crops; the air is full of bird calls, and livestock get fat and frisky. The length of this season and the amount of rain that comes is an important variant not only from year to year, but also from north to south; it both complements and causes geographical differences, which result in contrasting settlement patterns and economies in different regions of Dar Masalit.

The Goz

The Goz is the central section of Dar Masalit, surrounding the capital city of Geneina, and extending eastward across the Dar. It is characterized by expanses of sandy or goz soil, so much that throughout Dar Masalit when people speak of "The Goz," they are referring to this area. It is the home of the northern clans of the Masalit, and the small clans of various ethnic groups that came to be jointly known as Erenga, as well as others (Kapteijns 1985:16).

It was the locus of most Masalit political activity during the last one hundred years, the home of the sultans, and the site of battles with enemies from east and west. Due to the relatively unhindering terrain, it was long crossed by pilgrims and caravans from the west, and was the area most effectively incorporated into the sultanate of Dar Fur.

Goz soils are favored throughout the Sudan for millet cultivation, and this is the main crop on the Goz. The area is also crossed by major wadis, including Kaja, Mahbas and Barei. In the alluvial soils of the wadis, sorghum and various vegetables supplement millet farming. The wadis are dry, but are the main locations of wells in the dry season, and so villages have formed along those watercourses where both water and fields are available. There are also varying amounts of pasture and forest resources, especially in the western and eastern Goz. Water, fields and forest are the essentials of the independent Masalit life, and in the Goz they have been combined in optimal proportions—in the past. However, recent trends have undermined this balance and have reduced the natural endowments of the area.

Throughout the Goz, a striking event of the nineteen seventies was the failure of some of the reliable wells and pools needed for dry season life. This forced people to concentrate in areas with water or to move seasonally to and from the remaining watering points. People with livestock were forced to go south during these dry years to better watered areas, and many of these people have not returned. In the 1970s the government undertook a drilling program in the Goz and successfully provided wells for a number of villages. However, the restoration of water cannot restore the pasture and forest resources which were also reduced by the low rains. Furshas interviewed throughout the Goz complained about the decline in the quantity and quality of grazing.

In addition, trees have been considerably reduced throughout the area. This is partly due to the low rains and the pollarding of trees by herders because of the scarcity of grazing. However, especially in the areas close to Geneina, the town demand for charcoal and building materials has been the major factor in denuding the landscape. Twenty years ago, forests with monkeys and game animals existed a few minutes away from Geneina, but the growth of the city has leveled the surrounding countryside.

Another economic problem on the Goz is the lack of rural opportunities for cash incomes. Groundnuts and sesame rarely yield well in this area, due to the low rainfall. A little gum arabic exists, but the Geneina gum market is not active and the prices are not encouraging. Near Geneina, those with alluvial land can grow vegetables to sell in town, or can get employment. But for most residents of the Goz, they can only grow surplus millet or cut down more trees to have something to sell on the market. In response to these pressures many rural residents of this area have moved to Geneina or to the eastern Sudan as laborers, or have resettled in vacant areas in Southern Darfur or the southern part of Dar Masalit. However, to some extent their numbers have been replaced by immigrants from Chad, fleeing the civil war. Thus, this area still exhibits some of the fluidity of population that has characterized the Sahelian zone for hundreds of years.

On the positive side, this region benefits from some government services. Perhaps due to the proximity of Geneina, or perhaps because the history of the area has left a tradition of active involvement in politics, the Goz has a relatively high number of small schools and dispensaries, and it has been the beneficiary of the well-drilling program mentioned above (figure 3.4). Proximity to the veterinary and medical services of Geneina, as well as the market, is valued by many residents. These services have led to a growth of some towns in the Goz where services are provided. However, in this area the services tend to be small branches that feed patients, students or cases into the larger Geneina facilities. In addition the various services are not highly concentrated in towns in this area, but tend to be spread among smaller centers. This is also true of markets; while some traders have set up shop in larger villages or towns, the proximity of Geneina and the paucity of exports from the area have limited the development of local trade. Thus, the towns of the Goz have remained small and overshadowed by Geneina.

The Far North

North of Abu Suruj and Sirba is the land of the Jabal or Mileri people, centered around Sileia, and north of them the Gimr, who have a separate sultan headquartered at Kulbus.

In the past, this area was much like the area just described—expanses of goz soil interspersed with wadis and forest zones. The trees were a little shorter, the millet season briefer and the wells deeper, but the area was quite livable. However, the decline in rainfall seriously afflicted this area. Whereas in the past one planted large areas to make up for low yields and high risks, many people no longer consider it worth trying. The population dropped in the seventies, except in the towns.

At Kulbus a little border trade profits some, and in Kulbus and Sileia government services exist that attract people. Grazing and forest resources are much reduced, and the number of animals has dropped. If the rains improve enough for millet cultivation, this area will still suffer the disadvantages of the Goz, but without the advantages of proximity to Geneina, and it is unlikely that many of the emigrants will return. Of the regions of Dar Masalit, this is the most clearly marginalized.[2]

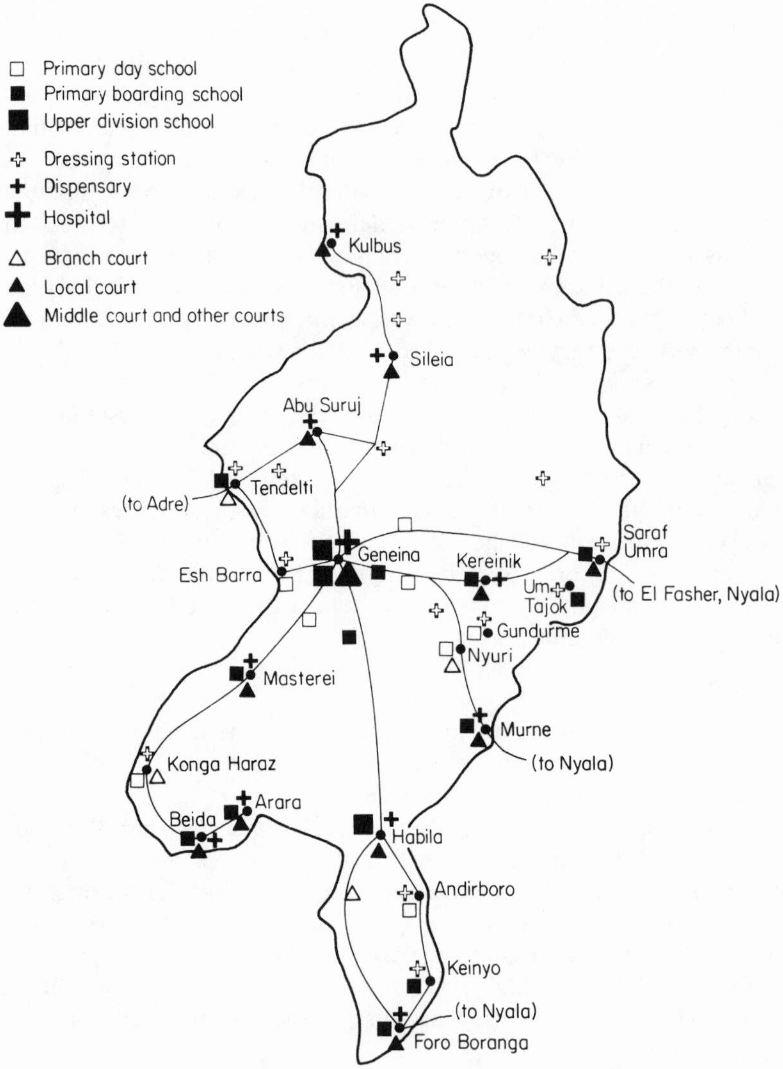

Figure 3.4. Medical, judicial and educational facilities in Dar Masalit

Source: Interviews with government personnel in Geneina, 1978–79; Republic of Sudan, Survey Office maps supplemented by my sketch maps.

The South

About ten miles south of Geneina, the expansive goz of the central area gradually ends, giving way to an area that is better watered, but rougher, with more hills and forest areas. Although in the past the population of the southern Dar had probably been a minority, this is currently the home of a majority of the Masalit. Senyar, Fur, and Daju people predominate in the southern tip of this region. There is goz soil in the south, but in limited areas. The broadest expanse of goz is around Masterei, with dozens of villages, but even it is surrounded by bush or forest on all sides. Further south goz plains are smaller, such that isolated villages may be found farming tiny goz fields deposited in the lee of the mountains twenty thousand years ago.

Cultivation of alluvial soils or clay plains predominates in these areas. Large forest areas exist, but these are marked by limited water, and so are mostly used only on a seasonal basis by Arabs and Masalit alike when rainy season pools or springs are available. Water is easily available in the tributaries of the large and reliable wadis, and thus the villages and the cultivated area are mostly distributed along them.

The relative abundance of both rain and groundwater has made the southern portion of Dar Masalit attractive to herders and farmers, especially in recent years. Large numbers of herders have brought their animals from the north, and Arabs have long used the Wadi Azum as a secure dry-season pasture. The southern area also presents opportunities for export crops. The goz soils of Masterei, Gokor and Gube are major groundnut producing zones, while the alluvial soils of Arara, Beida, and the Azum area are used to produce mangos, okra, coriander, onions, red pepper and other market crops. These are accumulated by merchants of the small towns, which act as "vanguards of exploitation" (Ahmed and Abdel Rahman 1979), and feeder points to Geneina, which in turn sends crops to Nyala, El Fasher, or Chad. Lorries travel daily to and from Habila, and twice a week in convoy down the western border to Beida and back, until the rains wash out the roads; then camels work through the rainy season, taking nuts and coriander to Geneina and returning with sugar and cloth.

These lorries also serve the border trade, which heavily involves (and profits) some of the growing towns. Beida and to some extent Arara, on the western border, support a good deal of trade with Chad, exporting and importing European, West African and Sudanese manufactured goods, sugar, livestock and crops. The direction for some goods, like sugar, depends on price and local supply; both eastern Chad and western Sudan are remote and subject to shortages.[3] Foro Boranga in the southern tip has a large livestock market, patronized by merchants who come directly from Nyala, site of the railhead to Khartoum, as well as from other parts of Dar Masalit.

Finally, government facilities service or employ substantial numbers of people in the south and government employees consume local products. Habila not only has a military base, but also has been upgraded to a district headquarters and center of administration for the area south of approximately 13 °N. A government plantation at Andirabiro, while not directly employing many Masalit, brings more civil servants to the area. Schools, dispensaries, veterinary services, courts and police posts add to the market functions of the southern towns, making them points of population growth. Unlike the situation in the Goz, these government agencies tend to be concentrated in a handful of towns which are also commercially active. This makes them increasingly important foci of activity for surrounding rural areas (figure 3.4).

However, as noted above, the southern region of Dar Masalit has also suffered from declining rainfall, and some sources of water are also drying up. Declines in grazing due to reduced rain and increased usage by Arabs are reported throughout this area. Forest resources, though relatively abundant, have been under intense pressure from herders, as well as from the increased numbers of villagers who need wood and bark rope for building, firewood, and crafts. But the pressure is most intense from the growing towns. Shopkeepers require very strong beams of wood for permanent structures, which requires felling the large trees that protect the forest, and there is great demand for wood for furniture and fences. The buildup of Habila draws heavily on local resources, and much lumber is sent to Geneina and even Nyala as well. Civil servants and soldiers—usually young men doing hardship duty in these outlying areas—send wood or furniture to families in the eastern Sudan, accumulating the necessities of marriage.[4] Game is much reduced and likely to be non-existent soon due to town demand and the export value of hides and dried game meat. Thus, the forest resources of the area, while abundant relative to population and needs in the past, are rapidly being depleted by the increased population, increased town consumption and increased export.

While urban centers can import wood and meat from ever greater distances, the typical villager, accustomed to gathering his or her needs from the forest, now has lost that possibility in many areas and will soon lose it in others. Thus, the woman who needs firewood or the man who needs materials to build a house must increasingly purchase these goods in the marketplace. This is but one example of the new relationship that has emerged between town and country, affecting the quality of rural life. In addition to the depletion of their environment and the increase in population, farmers must cope with new cash needs such as these. Their market participation adds to the formation of exploitative relationships between themselves and the commercial sector.

Demography

Environmental trends and ecological forces at work in Dar Masalit have been considered. In this vein, one may also now consider the people, or rather the population, of Dar Masalit in demographic terms. The area has an active history of immigration and emigration as well as population growth and expansion that certainly plays a role in the local ecology. Therefore, before addressing the very personal level of individual economic strategies and activities, I analyze the available archival, historical and census material for information that can help us to understand the situation of Dar Masalit.

It is difficult to evaluate the overall flow of population in the precolonial period; it appears to have been a very fluid situation. Much of the flow involved the enslavement of war captives, for which the wars of the first decades of the sultanate provided ample opportunities. For example, "in 1890 the Masalit acquired many slaves by nursing the victims of the cholera epidemic which was decimating the Mahdist army of occupation back to health. The Masalit Sultan ordered every Masalati to capture, confine and cure as many diseased Mahdist soldiers as he could. . . . When the epidemic died down . . . most captives were taken to Dirjeil [the sultan's headquarters] and settled there" (Kapteijns 1985:51). The Masalit themselves were enslaved by the thousands when they lost in war (Kapteijns 1985:64). The wars also provided ample opportunities for such local slaves to escape (Kapteijns 1985:168) although female slaves, who could be rapidly incorporated into the family of their master, would be less likely to escape (Kapteijns 1985:59–60). After colonial occupation, slaving was officially stopped, and many slaves fled Dar Masalit (Kapteijns 1985: 238); those who did not leave were presumably integrated into Masalit society.

This appears to have been a regional pattern. A study of the demographics of these flows, their ecological effects and feedback mechanisms that might have regulated these movements would be most valuable and interesting, but at present we do not know the net effect of regional slave trading.

In the early colonial period immigration appeared to be the most important source of population changes. Reports of immigration were recurrent in the colonial record of the 1920s and 1930s. For example, in 1923 the Civil Secretary in Khartoum wrote to the Governor of Darfur: "Redfern reports steady infiltration of Masalit from French territory. Immigrants absorbed in existing villages but numbers would be equivalent to about thirty villages" (Darfur 3/1/5). In 1924 the resident reported a party of two hundred Salamat Arabs coming from French territory, and in 1927 at least five large groups of non-Masalit were reported to have immigrated from Chad (Darfur 3/1/5). In 1928 the resident reported that "French subjects in very large numbers have poured across and settled down in the southern areas of Dar Masalit"; the sultan estimated them at one thousand households (Darfur 3/1/5). In 1931 the resident wrote to the Governor that "thousands of French subjects come annually" (Darfur 3/1/5), and in 1937 the resident Candole noted "there is still a steady immigration from French territory mainly of Daju and Senyar in the southern part of the district who are attracted by the easier conditions of life in Sudan territory. A similar movement of Arabs from Nyala district is encouraged by the Sultan's 'open-door' policy" (Darfur 1/34/175, 1937 report).

Resident's reports do not cover the 1940s and 1950s, but it was clear from my observations and interviews that Arabs, Masalit from Chad, and smaller populations of Daju, Tama, and Borgu continued to enter and settle in Dar Masalit during this period; for example, in the 1950s the fursha of Masterei allotted one of the broadest goz plains in the area to Arabs for rainy season cultivation (in the higher rainfall prevailing at that time it did not yield well, but now its loss is regretted by the Masalit villagers nearby). In the last two decades, continual civil war in Chad created new flows of refugees, both to the towns and to rural areas.

This immigration joined with natural increase to cause a quadrupling of the population in about thirty years. Resident Pollen estimated the population in 1923, exclusive of Dar Gimr, at 70–75,000 (Darfur 3/3/21); as will be seen below, the 1955–56 census count, excluding Dar Gimr, was over three hundred thousand.[5] This growth occurred in spite of the fact that there was substantial emigration to eastern Sudan over this time. It was also more population growth than can be attributed to natural increase. In the 1955–56 census, the crude population growth rate was measured to be 3.2 percent, and even if this high rate had obtained from 1923 to 1955 it would only account for 70 percent of the observed increase. Even this was too high for several reasons. First, the base number for the 3.2 percent rate was a population that was 55 percent female, due to levels of male emigration in 1955 that did not exist in 1923. Correcting on the assumption of equal numbers of each sex in the population, the growth rate would be only 2.9 percent. Second, venereal diseases were chronic in the 1920s and 30s and were repeatedly mentioned in colonial reports. As S. P. Reyna (1975, 1979) pointed out, in a nearby area of Chad this is a major cause of infertility in women. Finally, this area was beset with repeated epidemics of relapsing fever and cerebro-spinal meningitis throughout the period in question, which took an unknown toll on the population. Thus, natural increase was likely to have been limited, perhaps accounting for less than half of the population increase. The high level of immigration into Dar Masalit that took place at that time was probably a more important factor.

The explanation of this immigration was found in French and British colonial policies. While the British were not yet in effective control of Dar Masalit, the French were imposing a heavy tax burden on the population to the west, and they promoted other unpopular policies as well: "During the month there has been a large influx of natives of French Equatorial Africa into Dar Masalit and Zalingei districts. The immigrants are partly Arabs from Abesher and further west, and partly Masalit and Dage [Daju] from Adre and Goz Beida. According to native reports this migration is due to intensive tax collecting and other drastic measures on the part of the French authorities, and as the majority of the refugees have left their cultivations behind, some even abandoning their cattle, it may be assumed that the measure of their discontent, or their fear is considerable" (Sudan Government Monthly Record No. 409, 1928, in Balamoan 1976:110).

On the other hand, immigrants were well received in Dar Masalit, for a number of reasons. "Since villages, not individuals, were assessed, village heads welcomed newcomers who would of course share the tax burden" (Kapteijns 1985:238). Immigrants also added to the constituency and prestige of local sponsors who would find a field for them and help them get started. This was a typical political process in systems of shifting cultivation that involve continual dissolution and reformation of villages over the countryside. Immigrants were easily integrated into this pattern as long as land was abundant. In so far as immigrants came to seek refuge with local rulers, in the case of non-Masalit the distinction between them and slaves, as in former times, was lost in some cases (Kapteijns 1985:48); in any event, constituents, clients or slaves all added to the power and prestige of the ambitious.

It appears that a large portion of the immigration was by Masalit and was conducted in terms of indigenous patterns of mobility, such as marital residence choices, relocations with kinsmen in crisis periods and recruitments to join new settlements; harsh French policies added to these factors to alter the balance of local mobility and cause a substantial net migration to Sudan. Many clans had territories on both sides of the border which also facilitated resettlement. Thus, it was not surprising that the maliks and furshas of the Native Administration were not willing to try to prevent immigration, especially of Masalit (Darfur 3/1/5, correspondence 1928–29). This extended to the sultan, and to his 'open-door' policy; in this respect it may be particularly significant that Arabs were incorporated under sheikhs—later called "omdas"—who were directly responsible to him (Darfur 1/34/175, 1938 report). The sultanate was also engaged in geographical expansion, including extension into areas on the entire length of the eastern border, especially in the south on Wadi Azum where Sir Harold MacMichael had observed a no-man's land two day's journey wide in 1916 (Intel 2/12/102). Immigration of a population to settle these areas and be incorporated under his authority was clearly to the sultan's advantage. The vacant no-man's land no longer exists (compare Haaland 1978).

The French resented the loss of the emigrant population, and a number of officials posted near the border demanded British efforts to block this movement and repatriate emigrants (Darfur 3/1/5; but see DeCoppet quoted in Balamoan 1976:346 for a more relaxed attitude). Complaints from French officers recurred throughout the Dar Masalit records of the 1920s and 1930s. The British responded on a number of occasions but certainly not all, and the French did not complain about every case. In 1929 the British burned a number of refugee houses and one whole village, but record with regret that the immigrants were always warned in advance and able to escape (Darfur 3/1/5). In one nine-month period, they repatriated two hundred twenty-three people (Darfur 3/1/5). This must have been a small fraction of the migrants; the British were not capable of reversing the immigration that they invited by their system of taxation, and by their support of a hierarchy where power was drawn from numbers.

In fact the British had little enthusiasm for the task, since they believed the Dar to be underpopulated; the resident Pollen in 1924 observed that "the increase in population [from natural increase] is slower than might be desired" (Darfur 3/3/21), while the Governor of Darfur wrote in 1937 that "the steady flow of population from French territory is economic and so long as better conditions prevail on this side of the border accretions are inevitable" (Darfur 1/34/175, comment on 1937 Dar Masalit confidential Annual Report). This comment also reflected the recurring theme that emigration from French territory was the fault of French administrators. The British felt that their efforts to respond to French complaints were unappreciated and fruitless; consider, for example, this "note on immigration from French Equatorial Africa." After pointing out that the English do not ask the French for the return of *their* refugees, the author states: "Our DC's have tried really hard and spent a lot of time at it this year and we got little thanks from the French. It is also apt to clash with NA [Native Administration] in Dar Masalit since it is always a cause of possible friction with the Sultan. Also it appears endless." (Darfur 3/1/5)

So far this prediction has proven true. Conditions on the Sudanese side of the border have deteriorated in recent years, but conditions in Chad have become worse still. However, the capacity of Dar Masalit to absorb new population has been exhausted. Rangeland and forest resources, as mentioned above, are under heavy pressure, while sufficient agricultural land is no longer available to support fallowing. Analysis of census data from 1955–56 and 1973 indicates that the sedentary population of the Dar reached a plateau by the time of the first census, with population increase apparently balanced by emigration after that time. The nomadic population has continued to increase, perhaps because of drought to the north.

There are two bodies of census information on Sudan including Dar Masalit. The most recent of these is the 1973 census, which is still officially subject to revision. This is a *de facto* census using complete enumeration—thus, everyone has been counted in their location at the moment of the census. Unfortunately, although data has been collected by districts within Dar Masalit and then has been aggregated to Dar Masalit as a whole, very little of the local-level information has been reported or preserved. Almost all of the data have been further aggregated to the provincial (Darfur) level, only the gross population numbers being reported for Dar Masalit. Thus, for information on the internal population structure of Dar Masalit, one must return to the 1955–56 census.

The 1955–56 census was a *de jure* census, which allowed temporary emigrants to be counted if they were present for six of the preceding twelve months. This would mask some labor migrants, but since emigration from Dar Masalit was usually for periods of years (especially at that time) it probably did not hide much of the emigration. The 1955–56 census was also a sample census, sampling in each omda or fursha's district, and relied heavily on tax rolls. (There may have been some underenumeration on this basis.) Use of the 1955–56 census required revision and analysis of the data provided. In it, Dar Masalit was divided into three sections with geographical overlap. Since statistics were not calculated for the Dar as a whole, those provided here were calculated from the data given for the districts. More importantly, in order to calculate figures by regional, ethnic and sedentary-nomadic distinctions, it was necessary to go back to the raw numbers given by the omda or fursha. In combination with a recent tax list and data gathered on the furshas when in the field, it was possible to locate and determine the adaptation of all but 3 percent of the population. These were then grouped into more relevant and convenient categories, as discussed below.

In table 3.4 are shown the raw population figures by adaptation for 1955–56 and 1973. Although the population has grown from 323,621 to 385,956, there are some unusual features of this growth shown in the breakdown. Geneina has tripled in size in a matter of seventeen years. The nomadic population has nearly doubled. But the population of villagers is nearly the same; in fact it shows a growth rate of only 0.3 percent per year. This is in spite of the fact that indicators of fertility and population growth from the 1955–56 census indicate a high fertility population. The child-women ratio is seven hundred seventy-eight, and the average complete family size is 4.7.[6] The most likely explanation is that all of the natural increase of the sedentary population in these years, as well as all immigration to rural areas, has been balanced by emigration.

While it is true that the 1973 census was taken at a very bad time for Dar Masalit, when migration was high because of the low rains of 1972, this would only partly explain the low rate of growth. Apparently, the rural sedentary population exhausted its capacity to expand locally in the 1950s or earlier.

As for the nomadic population, the figures confirm what the omdas and furshas report—increasing numbers of nomads immigrating from Chad, the northern areas, and Southern Darfur, due to war, drought, and population pressure respectively. There may also have

Table 3.4
Populations and sex ratio by adaptation in 1955–56 and 1973

	1955–56			1973		
Adaptation	Population	Percent. Total[a]	Sex Ratio	Population	Percent. Total	Sex Ratio
Sedentary	263,631	84	0.80	278,304	72	0.81
Nomadic	39,003	12	0.97	72,228	19	0.81
Urban (Geneina)	11,817	4	0.82	35,424	9	0.88
Unknown[b]	9,165					
Total	323,616	100	0.83	385,956	100	0.84

Source: *Republic of Sudan,* (1960) *and Republic of Sudan, Central Office of Statistics records.*
a. Excluding population of unknown adaptation
b. See note 6

been an undercounting in 1955–56, due to the lesser participation of the nomads in administrative affairs, and their greater success at avoiding administrative incorporation at that time.

The masculinity ratio in table 3.4 should be noted. The low number of men relative to women is indicative of labor migration, since a higher number of men than women migrate, leaving their families at home. If one assumes equal numbers of men and women in the total population, and assume that no women emigrate, the sex ratio indicates a minimum figure for the rate of male emigration. That is, a sex ratio of 0.80 indicates that *minimally* 20 percent of the male population is absent. The figure is a minimum because women do emigrate as well; for example, if one in four emigrants were female, a sex ratio of 0.80 would indicate that 27 percent of males are absent. Note that in 1955–56, migration had hardly touched the nomadic population; but by 1973, their sex ratio became equal to that of the villagers.

Emigration rates were higher in particular age groups. The age structure of Dar Masalit in 1955–56 is shown in table 3.5. Comparable figures are not available except at the provincial level in 1973, but the Darfur figures, grouped to correspond as closely as possible to the 1955–56 figures, show a similar structure (table 3.6). The masculinity ratio is higher in the province as a whole, possibly reflecting more female or whole-family migration from parts of Darfur that are closer to the Nile Valley. Statistics for 1973 at the province level are available for a fine age gradation (table 3.7), which show clearly that the absent males are primarily from the 15–39 age group, especially 20–29.

Table 3.5
Age and Sex Structure of Dar Masalit Population, 1955–56

	Males		Females		Sex
	Number	%	Number	%	Ratio
Age Group					
Over Puberty	73,301	23	105,924	33	0.69
5 - Puberty	42,307	13	39,080	12	1.08
1 - 4	24,622	8	24,704	8	1.00
Under 1	6,563	2	7,115	2	0.92
Total	146,793	45	176,823	55	0.83

Source: *Republic of Sudan* (1960)

Table 3.6
Age and Sex Structure of Darfur Population, 1973

	Males		Females		Sex
	Number	%	Number	%	Ratio
Age Group					
Over Puberty	501,251	24	630,086	30	0.80
5 - Puberty	299,651	14	287,268	14	1.04
1 - 4	157,464	8	154,966	7	1.02
Under 1	23,182	1	22,865	1	1.01
Total	981,548	47	1,095,185	53	0.90

Source: *Republic of Sudan, Central Office of Statistics records*

Table 3.7
Sex Ratio according to Age Group, Darfur, 1973

Age Group	Sex Ratio	Age Group	Sex Ratio
15–19	0.88	45–49	1.08
20–24	0.60	50–54	0.93
25–29	0.59	55–59	0.87
30–34	0.72	60–64	0.87
35–39	0.86	65–69	0.96
40–44	0.94	70 +	0.91

Source: *Republic of Sudan, Central Office of Statistics records*

Information on tribe or ethnic affiliation was not collected in the 1973 census. However, in Dar Masalit, these groupings are still of considerable importance. Further, grouping by ethnicity will help us to see the regional distribution of the population. The 1955–56 census did ask individuals about their 'tribe,' but for Dar Masalit the categories are rather hard to use. While it is reassuring that the majority of the population consists of "tribes of western Darfur," one must make some effort to realize whom the "Moru-Madi" or "Bongo-Baka-Bagirmi" categories might comprise in Dar Masalit—much less "other western southerners." And the twenty-four thousand "Fung tribes" people remain a mystery.

Similarly with language, the categories sometimes can be understood in terms of linguistic classifications used in that period, but it still is quite an effort to imagine 10 percent of the population speaking Nilotic "southern Lwo" languages. Instead of attempting to interpret these statistics, I have compiled data from the omda and fursha listing in the census, for rural sedentaries only, according to the ethnic group of the ruler. Within each fursha's territory, usually the large majority of the population belongs to his ethnic group, if not his own clan. There are, in addition to the listed groups, numbers of Tama, Borgu, Daju, Fur and others settled within these territories, but their numbers cannot be known from published census data. The rural sedentary population is listed according to the ethnic group of the fursha in table 3.8.[7]

Table 3.8
Rural Sedentary Population Grouped by Region and Ethnicity of Fursha or Omda, 1955–56

Ethnic Affiliation	Population	Sedentary Population
North		
Gimr	23,328	8.8
Jabal	20,706	7.9
The Goz		
Erenga and Awra	41,829	15.9
Arabs	19,799	7.5
Marasi	1,354	0.5
Masalit	76,244	
South		57.9[a]
Masalit	76,326	
Sinyar	4,050	1.5

Source: *Republic of Sudan* (1960)
a. Total

As of 1955–56, the Goz was the population center of Dar Masalit, with 53 percent of the sedentary population. The Masalit themselves were about equally divided between it and the south. The sedentary population density was about seventeen persons/km^2 in the Goz compared to ten in the north and twelve in the south. The south contained large areas of forest and non-arable land; the ratio of persons to arable land in the south probably approached or exceeded that of the Goz at this time. The north was already showing signs of a high rate of emigration, with a masculinity ratio of 0.74, compared with 0.82 in the Goz and 0.80 in the south.

As I have indicated above, great changes have taken place since 1955–56, in both climate and market penetration. This has resulted in a shift in the population of Dar Masalit from north to south, as well as out of the Dar entirely. The north, which already has the lowest population density in 1955–56, is now even less populated; the Goz population is reduced in most areas, while the south is becoming more heavily populated. These trends cannot be quantified with the data available.

As a very poor surrogate, one might note that while the size of the sedentary population of the south was only 57 percent that of the Goz in 1955–56, by 1979 they were paying 90 percent as much in livestock taxes as the Goz. The government was also aware of these shifts, and was hastening to open new rural councils, cooperatives and Sudan Socialist Union branches in the south, more proportionate to their population.

The Research Site

Subsequent chapters are more concerned with processes occurring at the village level than I have been so far. No localized study could do justice to the variety of processes which are occurring throughout Dar Masalit. Yet a study of Dar Masalit as a whole could not fully comprehend any one of the many faces worn by the world economy interacting with the rural villages. Therefore, while general information for other parts of the Dar was collected from furshas and government officials, intensive data collection was undertaken in a restricted area, and it is this area that the following chapters are directed to analyze and describe. The processes appear to exemplify not only those taking place elsewhere in Dar Masalit, but also some that are taking place or have taken place in many rural areas of the Third World.

The area studied was the vicinity of Masterei, about thirty miles southwest of Geneina. While no area could be considered typical of Dar Masalit, perhaps Masterei could be considered average. It is neither close to nor far from Geneina; it has a moderate level of government services; it is a growing, but not thriving, commercial center. Being in the south, it supports the cultivation of export crops, especially groundnuts. Being almost in the Goz, it also partakes somewhat of the characteristics of that area.

Masterei, to outsiders, is the name for a town that is known locally as "Buga." To the people of the area, however, Masterei is a *furuʃiyya*, the domain of the fursha of the Masterei clan. It is a large furushiyya with one hundred twenty-eight sheikhs, including a number of villages near Wadi Kaja, far from Buga. It has much goz soil, but also much forested area.

After three months in Buga—to which I continued to come often for visits and markets—I spent nineteen months residing in a Masterei village, working closely with its people and those of another nearby village, as well as their camps and satellite settlements. Comprehensive studies of two villages rather than sample surveys over a large number of villages were chosen in order to identify processes at the community level. Thus, my analysis of conditions in Dar Masalit is based on significantly more intimate knowledge of these villages than other villages, towns, or Geneina. It was in these villages and settlements that the majority of the detailed agricultural information, household budgets, social organization data—in short all data that require continuous participant-observation—were collected.

At the time of village selection I was only able to gather information on village size, distance from town, and available wadi lands as variables that might differentiate them. Neither town nor bush, the villages chosen were about average in being an hour or less from Buga by foot. Many people went each Monday and Friday to the Buga markets, and prayed there at the mosque on Fridays. Yet, the people of these villages did not have to buy water or wood, and had as little as possible to do with Buga merchants. While the village I lived in was a bit larger than average and the other study village was quite small, they were well within the range of commonly found sizes. A few Masterei villages had large expanses of wadi land, but those studied were more typical in having only a bit to supplement goz farming.

If there is an atypical feature, it is one that I came to understand later. The larger village is strategically located between Buga and the more rural settlements, as well as the forested areas used by Arab nomads. This location has been beneficial to its merchants who act as intermediaries to the more rural people. Similar intermediate villages exist in all directions from Buga, so it is not unique in this respect. Rather, it is perhaps a luckily chosen village for study because of its role in commerce.

Summary

In this chapter, I have considered the position of Dar Masalit in terms of broad tendencies of environment, population and ecology. The growth of towns, increasing exports, declining rainfall and increased population are placing serious stress on natural resources throughout the region and both forest and farmlands are in decline. Part of the population has responded by emigrating as shown by the census figures.

In the following chapters, I shall draw on data collected at the village level to understand what these trends mean in terms of community and family life, and as harsh realities confronting individuals who must find ways to cope. I shall analyze the role that these large-scale trends play in bringing the world market to the local level.

4. *Production and Exchange*

Introduction

People must adapt with the techniques at their disposal to the physical environment in order to meet their needs. The preceding chapter has been devoted to the ecological context of the Masalit. In addition to the influence of the physical environment, the economic activities that people undertake are constrained by the availability of capital, labor, and land, and are affected by their goals and expectations. At this stage, the questions of resource availability and economic strategies are postponed as much as possible; these topics are discussed in the next chapter. In the present chapter, the major economic activities are described in terms that are as comparable as possible without loss of important detail. This chapter includes their labor and capital requirements, the income available through them, and their place in the overall socioeconomic system. I also consider who engages in various kinds of activities, their seasonality, their history, and how they are valued within Masalit culture. This done, the issues of the distribution of productive assets, access to resources, consumption levels, and class formation can be treated in a way that is more meaningful and palpable.

The universal productive activities are domestic and agricultural, and these are discussed first. Then, economic activities that supplement or draw upon these are analyzed: animal husbandry, crafts, services, trade,and labor migration. Data used throughout this chapter have been collected at several levels, the most important of which are the sample villages, the large sample, and the small sample.

The *sample villages* include all people residing in the two villages selected for intensive study as described at the end of the last chapter. They also include those living in bush camps who consider themselves members of these two villages, and temporary emigrants from these villages.

In 1978 the sample villages included 705 people in 190 families. Families were of the following types: ever-married women, with or without a husband and/or children (184); ever-married single men (5); and one case of three teenaged girls in a compound with no adult. Family membership was defined by co-residence, except in the case of temporary labor migrants. Of the 184 ever-married women in the sample villages, one was a temporary emigrant. Only one woman over twenty-five had never been married; she was listed with the family of her brother and sister-in-law, with whom she resided. There were 129 men married to these women, of whom seventeen were temporary emigrants, and there were five ever-married male bachelors. Since thirty-one of these men had other wives outside the sample villages, this overstated the number of men present. Weighting for polygyny; that is, counting only one-half of men with one other wife outside the sample villages, and one-third of men with two other wives outside them, the total number of men that are effectively members of the sample villages was 118.

In the sample villages, information was collected for all families concerning age, sex, marital status, household composition, and a number of other matters that do not concern us here. Ages were corrected in some cases by comparison of the time of birth of children in these families with those of the children of my assistants and others whose ages were well-known, and by interviews with reliable informants concerning the relative ages of adults. At a later stage, interviews with crafts or service specialists were carried out that included the enumeration of all other specialists in each activity in the sample villages, and in a similar manner other sorts of public information were used to supplement or check interview or questionnaire data at various stages of the research.

Within the sample villages, a detailed economic questionnaire was administered from September to December, 1978. This covered field areas, land use, livestock ownership, and other matters. Twenty-one families or 11 percent chose not to participate; the 89 percent who agreed to this interview are herein called the *large sample*. Those declining to participate included three of the eight village merchants; this may reduce the count of livestock more than proportionately to the sample size, and may have an effect on farming and land use information. The large sample included one hundred sixty-four ever-married women, including one absentee, and one hundred and seven ever-married men, of whom fifteen are temporary emigrants.

Based on the data collected in the large sample study as well as the demographic information on the sample villages, a subgroup called below the *small sample* was selected for more detailed study. Information collected from the small sample included labor allocations and household budgets over the course of 1979 (which are only partly analyzed in this work), land use and harvest yields for 1978 and 1979, and various details concerning the intra-household division of labor, minor agricultural activities, household finances, and other matters. The small sample included thirty-one women's families or 17 percent of women in the sample villages; single men were excluded because bachelorhood was usually a transient state for males. Although there were always some single men in the villages, no representative of them planned to stay single for a year.

The small sample was stratified on the basis of family type, field-consumer ratios, age, and a three-category "perceived wealth" ranking based on my two principal assistants' estimates.[1] Since the relevance of co-residence was uncertain, I decided that all families in any joint compound must agree to participate for any of them to be included, in case the compound emerged as a significant economic unit (it did not). For men with two or more wives in the villages, both were included in the small sample, but wives outside the sample villages were not included.

The small sample was not chosen randomly for two reasons. First, the number of stratifying variables left little possibility of choosing from reasonably sized pools of eligible families in each category. Second, due to the small size of the sample and the subtlety of the processes under investigation, the quality of data collected was considered of paramount importance; poor data from a random sample would be of little use. With no previous knowledge of this type of research and no expectation of reward, members of the small sample were asked to reveal the most intimate economic information, and to take the time to do so each week for one year. I decided that this could best be done with people who would be willing and cooperative. Often these were relatives or neighbors of my two main field assistants or myself. For these people, cooperation in data collection was a smaller part of a friendly overall give-and-take, and the more intimate knowledge that my assistants and I had of their circumstances made accurate data collection easier. However, a possibility of bias was introduced by this decision.

To properly evaluate the information obtained from the small sample, it was necessary to know of any major differences between it and the population of the sample villages. For this reason, several factor analyses and multiple regressions targeting sample membership were carried out with all usable variables in the sample villages and large sample data. These included demographic variables such as age and family size, participation in trade, crafts, services, etc., ownership of the five major animal species, existence of absent migrants, field size and areas planted to each crop, and areas fallow or manured. A number of composite variables were also included, such as ratios of producers to consumers, field areas to producers and consumers, and manured area to total area. Variables that made a statistically significant contribution to the explanation of variance in sample membership, over the entire population or a subset of it, and other variables suggested by factor analysis, were subjected to one-way analyses of variance. The results of these operations on significant variables are listed in table 4.1.

Table 4.1
Nonrepresentative Characteristics of the Small Sample

	One-way Analysis of Variance			
	Sample Mean	Overall Mean	F-Ratio	Probability of Chance
Variable				
Farmhand in Family	0.65	0.25	16.8	0.01
Family Size	5.10	3.80	14.2	0.01
Groundnut Area	0.94	0.61	11.0	0.01
Tailor in Family	0.13	0.04	7.1	0.01
Leatherworker	0.13	0.04	7.1	0.01
Camels Owned	0.31	0.17	4.8	0.03
Joint Compound	0.23	0.39	4.5	0.04

Notes: Overall means for farmhand, groundnut area and camels are based on the large sample; for other variables they are based on the census of the sample villages.

The small sample appeared to differ from non-sample families on several variables. Small sample families have reported more sale of labor by some member of the family; however, because this is somewhat shameful, the high rate in the small sample was most likely a result of greater rapport and knowledge by interviewers of family activities. Another substantial difference was in family size; small sample families were significantly larger than non-sample families. Large families were overrepresented and small families are underrepresented (table 4.2). I have no explanation for this. Family size may influence the frequency of certain activities discussed below, such as dry season gardening, which are largely undertaken by children.

Table 4.2
Number of Families by Size in the Small Sample and in the Entire Population of the Sample Villages

	Small Sample		Sample Villages	
	Number	Percent	Number	Percent
Family Size				
1–3	9	29	101	53
4–6	11	35	61	32
7–9	11	35	28	15
Totals	31	100	190	100

The small sample also planted a larger area to groundnuts in 1978 than other people in the large sample, and had more tailors and camel-owners. These differences may be important, since sewing and camel-transport are the major high-capital services in this area, and have higher economic returns than low-capital crafts. In combination with the more extensive groundnut cultivation, these occupational differences indicated that sample families may have had a greater tendency to engage in cash-producing activities, and, thus, higher incomes than the general population.

However, with respect to groundnut area, tailoring and camels, a considerable amount of the small sample deviation can be traced to the two merchants (with three families) in the small sample. While the small sample does not differ significantly from the rest of the sample villages in terms of the proportion of families with merchants, these two merchants happen to be tailors, to own camels, and to plant substantial groundnut areas with hired labor. On the other hand, three of the six sample village merchants who are not in the small sample declined to provide information on camel ownership or groundnut planting in 1978, which would have increased overall means. Therefore the small sample is probably more representative on these variables than it would appear. In any event, because merchants are treated separately in the analysis of incomes and economic strategies,their possible distorting effect on the small sample is eliminated.

Makers of leather rope were also overrepresented. However, this occupation differs little in economic terms from other low-capital occupations. In terms of the overall category of low-capital occupations, which also includes tanning, hemp-rope making, brewing, and making doors, the small sample did not differ significantly from the non-sample populations. Finally, small sample families were less likely to live in joint compounds; this is due to the fact that it was difficult to find compounds made up of two or three families that would all agree to participate *and* that fit the requirements of stratification, and since all families in a compound were included or none, joint compounds were underrepresented in the final sample.

Information was collected within the three samples discussed above by interviews structured by questionnaires, conducted by myself or one of my two principle assistants. In addition, information on a number of activities, for example, crafts, trade, and manuring was obtained through interviews with specialists (usually three or more per activity). Direct observation supplemented interviews for domestic activities and some other pursuits. Labor inputs in agriculture were drawn from observations and reports of both hired and non-hired labor on measured plots. Information concerning the background of the various activities was obtained through interviews with older men and the use of the colonial records.

The Domestic Economy

In terms of the amount of time expended over the entire year, domestic labor is comparable to agricultural labor. Domestic activities are here defined as those that are immediately related to feeding, sheltering and raising the family. Because there is a substantial overlap between domestic activities and the use of forest resources, I have found it convenient to include hunting and gathering activities in this section as well. As discussed above, Masalit families are variable in size and composition, including single women with or without children, monogamous couples, and polygynous arrangements. However, extended families as economic units are rare. Almost invariably, ever-married women cook and carry out domestic activities independently, without taking turns or pooling. This is true even though women frequently help each other in other kinds of work, or do their domestic activities side by side; it is true even though sisters, mothers and daughters, or (very rarely) co-wives may live in a joint compound.

Likewise, a man's domestic activities are directed particularly to his own wife or wives and children. However, the more occasional and intensive male tasks are often done with extra-familial labor. Male domestic tasks can also be done more easily by hired labor, and thus in a sense men can be replaced by cash much more easily than women can. Further, male tasks are more discretionary, and less closely tied to the basic daily survival needs. Thus, women without husbands are numerous and may stay unmarried, but men without wives almost always remarry quickly.

Women's Daily Domestic Activities

Without respect to season, people require food and water, and the provision of these is primarily the responsibility of women. Certain tasks of this nature, such as gathering wood or making oil, are occasional; some, such as making beer or special foods, are discretionary; while the essential tasks of bringing water, grinding grain and cooking must be done every day. In the agricultural season, village life starts an hour before dawn with the sound of women grinding grain on flat stones; at night, the same sound closes the day. At the first light, women and girls walk to the wadi with pots on their heads; in the late afternoon, when the heat sometimes eases, they go again. Their agriculture and other economic activities must coexist with the demands of female familial responsibilities.

WATER. Women carry water to their houses on their heads, in clay jars of about ten liters each. Water is available throughout the year in the wadis; in the wet season it is usually near the surface, but in the dry season the wells may be one to two meters deep. There are seasonal wells in the small wadis of the outlying areas, used by bush camp residents and herders, which may dry up or produce only a meager supply of water in the dry season. The trip to the well and back takes about fifty-five to seventy-five minutes from the central village, depending on house location, water supply, and the number of women waiting. For a single woman, or a woman whose husband is away or with his other wife, one trip per day may suffice; women with husbands and children usually go twice. In the bush settlements, the trip takes about half as long in the rains, but if the well dries up in the dry season, and the family does not return to the village, a woman may have to go extra distances for water. Finally, in the agricultural season women often take their pots to their fields, and reduce the time required by getting water on their way home at the end of the day.

In Buga, women with cash purchase water from the *xarra:ji*, boys who bring water from the wadi in skins on a donkey (the going rate in

1979 was 10–15 PT per *xuruj* of about 70 liters). However, in the sample villages no one purchases water (except myself, and that was a difficult negotiation) and water is rarely brought by donkey. Some boys might help their mothers in this task, which requires a sort of pack-saddle adapted to carrying two clay jars, and men use this method to bring water in the period of their wife's postpartum seculsion. But few women use a donkey in this way except in situations of special need. One reported that others considered her to be putting on airs when she used a donkey. Donkeys are also rather difficult to load and unload without help, because the pack becomes unbalanced when one jar is removed, they are somewhat intransigent, and they often interfere in the conversations that are an important part of going to the well. Thus, most women consider that at these distances, the pluses of using a donkey are outweighed by the minuses.

GRINDING. Grinding millet is perhaps the most arduous female task, and the most sex-specific; in gossiping about a man whom he considered shamefully dominated by his wife, one villager applied the *coup de grace*: ". . . and they say he even grinds grain!" It is frequently recounted how prisoners of a former fursha, in addition to being in shackles, were forced to grind their own grain; male tellers of tales consider this particularly illustrative of the harshness of that ruler (compare Kapteijns 1985:269–270). But for women, grinding is a daily necessity. Ground millet or sorghum is the basis of asida (*ʿasi:da*, porridge) that is the staple food of Dar Masalit. Grinding is done with a quern, consisting of a large, flat stone, which becomes conveniently curved after long usage, and a smaller stone that is pushed and pulled over it repeatedly. The first grind is usually reground. Overall the process takes about fifty minutes per *kora* (the standard measure, a bowl of 2.5 kg). The amount of time this takes per day depends very much on the size of a woman's family. A woman alone uses about one third of a kora per day, but a woman with a family may use about one kora per day,and the wife of a man who offers a great deal of hospitality may grind half again or twice that.

In Buga, there was a Russian-made mill at which one could grind grain for 3.5 PT/kora in 1979, but it broke down; due to the changes of national alliance from the time the mill was installed to 1979, it was unlikely that spare parts could be had for repairs. But even before its breakdown, it was rarely used by women of the sample villages, except in the case of a festivity where much flour was needed. Most found the quality less than they produced themselves. They also were discouraged by the changeable procedures used at the mill and the Arabic spoken there; for village women, the mill was not a congenial place.

COOKING. Cooking is a subject on which a great deal of research could profitably be done. While every woman in the villages makes asida (and some make flat panbread, *kisra*, considered by the villagers to be elite food), the choice of moulah (*mula:H*, sauce) is very much dependent on the situation of the cook. Oil and butter are unavailable to many village women after their cash needs force them to sell the last of their groundnuts,and fresh meat depends on ready cash. Dried meat (used beaten to a powder), onions, garlic, red pepper and other spices usually must be purchased, and therefore many do without them. In the rains, many greens can be gathered; leaves of melons, pumpkins and wild greens, such as *tamle:ka* (*Amaranthus graecizans* or *Gyandropsis gyandra*) are available to all. But in the dry season, those without money flavor their bland asida with less tasty greens, dried okra, or *kawal* (a pungent fermented product of *Cassia* spp. or *Cleome viscosa* leaves). Some of these greens require simmering for a full day to be edible.

Thus, the labor required for cooking is highly variable. Starting with flour and powdered ingredients, times of meal preparations varied from sixty-seven to eighty-three minutes for asida and moulah. The types of moulah that require many hours of preparation were not timed; however, most of the work merely involves maintaining a low fire. Women with families cook at least twice per day, but a woman alone may well restrict her evening meal to leftovers from the morning, or vice-versa. A husband would not accept this, in general, but women who have the choice can reduce their cooking in this way. Again, wives of husbands who provide high levels of hospitality cook more.

Food preparation is an activity that is only slightly monetized. Men without wives cannot obtain food on any regular basis, even in Buga, except through special arrangements with female relatives or neighbors. There are women in Buga who cater to the travellers on the market lorries that stop for dinner twice per week in season; they offer kisra, roasted chickens, hard boiled eggs and roasted nuts. On market days, women in Buga sell a variety of prepared foods, especially kisra, which can be eaten with *ro:b* (buttermilk). There are also nuts, fruits, locusts, and other seasonal foods. A few village women, who do not make beer for religious reasons, occasionally sell kisra or kawal in the Buga market to get a little money. However, by and large, food preparation is a domestic, nonmarket activity. Men occasionally cook; caravans, for example, must eat between Masterei and Geneina. The asida produced at these times is usually inferior to that of women in their homes, although the stews are comparable. Men also roast meat, especially in groups on market days; this is particularly favored by beer drinkers, but non-drinkers also delight in a male style meal of dry-cooked meat. Aside from meat feasts and the demands of travel, however, cooking is a female activity.

These daily chores of women, which include a few other minor activities, make up a substantial workload. However, it is highly variable depending upon the size of a woman's family and its consumption level. The daily labor involved is summarized in table 4.3. A woman by herself or with a child or two can take care of her daily needs in about two to two and one half hours, depending on location, but a woman in the village with a family may spend five and one half hours per day on these necessities. If she is poor it may be more, because of labor intensive food preparation; if she is wealthy it also may be more, due to higher levels of hospitality. Women can reduce these time demands in some ways. The help of daughters is most important and useful to a woman with a growing family, while increased skill and simultaneous performance of more than one task also may reduce the time required. Nevertheless, the daily family obligations are clearly an imposing demand on women's labor, and in the agricultural season they conflict with her farming activities.

Table 4.3
Time required in Minutes per day for Women's Daily Domestic Activities, according to the Woman's Location and Family Size

Family Size	Small		Large	
Location	Bush	Village	Bush	Village
Activity				
Water	30	65	60	130
Grinding	17	17	50	50
Cooking	75	75	150	150
Total[a]	122(2.0hr)	157(2.6hr)	260(4.3hr)	330(5.5hr)

a. Child care is excluded.

CARE OF CHILDREN. The care of children is also very much the sphere of women. Although the men feel responsible for the moral well-being of their children as well as their physical needs, and although they often like to play with their children, they rarely take an active role in the time-consuming aspects of child care. When boys are seven or eight, a religious father may start teaching them to recite the

Qur'an. In their teens, a father may take a more active role in discipline and supervision, and fathers are considered primarily responsible for guiding and assisting in the marriages of their children. However, on a day to day basis, child care does not make a major time demand on most men. It is also difficult to quantify its time requirements of women. Mothers rarely are engaged specifically in child care, although their children are with them most of the time. Babies are carried in the course of other activities, and older children help in these same activities. As will be described below, the labor of children is valuable to women in agriculture. They also help their mothers in daily or occasional household activities, and in fetching and carrying. In addition, a girl of five or more may take considerable responsibility for an infant sibling. Thus, although child care places an additional demand on women's attention, its addition to her schedule of tasks is mixed and variable, and it would require additional research to properly evaluate the net effect.

Women's Occasional or Discretionary Activities

In addition to the above daily tasks, women perform a number of economic activities that permit some flexibility of timing, and that may present a greater or lesser time demand depending on the situation and choices of the woman. Some of these activities are opportunities for women to produce marketable goods, such as beer and oil. They are all, it will be noticed, tied to food production either directly or indirectly.

GATHERING FIREWOOD. This is of course essential to cooking, and most women gather wood about once per week. This is less when family size is very small, and is increased if a woman has a large family, is brewing, or is feeding many guests. The time required shows clearly the effects of deforestation near the village. Women living in the village require about four and one-half hours for a full ras (*ra:s*, head) of wood, while women in the bush settlements need only an hour. Men with camels, as will be discussed below, sometimes sell firewood in Buga; a camel carries about five ras, which sell for LS 1.50–1.70. Although no women in the sample villages were observed buying wood, some men who owned camels did bring part or all of their families' firewood needs, which required somewhat less than one day's work per month. Men also gathered firewood for their own needs in cattle camps.

OIL. Oil is desirable in food, but is not essential, so it is often lacking in the stews of the poor who cannot afford the onions and spices that go along with the oil. Hence,the amount of labor expended in oil production is variable, but most women make one to three bottles per month. Several families in the small sample do without oil entirely for a few months before the harvest, either because their groundnuts are exhausted or because they are saving them for seed. Very likely, when the price of nuts doubled in the preplanting season of 1979, many farmers decided to plant their groundnuts instead of using them for oil. It is also possible that the women do not wish to take the time to make oil in the farming season. A bottle of oil takes about five and one half hours to make, but of this time 80 percent is required to shell the nuts, which is easily done in spare moments at a leisurely pace. The remaining time involves cleaning, roasting, beating, grinding and pressing, which are laborious tasks. The seedcake is usually sold but may be used in stew.

Some oil is sold in Buga by women of the sample villages, but little was sold during the research period. The rate of return for doing so compares favorably with many low-capital occupations (see below). In November 1979, a profit of 55 PT/bottle (subtracting the value of inputs) or about LS 1.00 per day's labor was possible. Several households purchased oil in the course of the year, and the demand for oil was such that Buga merchants imported oil into the Masterei district from Geneina. It was not certain why more women did not make oil to add value to their groundnut production, but it may be that women in 1978, because of poor rains, only harvested groundnuts in sufficient quantities for family use. With the increased plantings and good yields of 1979, perhaps more women were producing oil for sale in the dry season after the survey ended.[2]

BEER. Millet beer (*marissa*) is the most important manufacture in economic terms for women, although many will not make it due to their own or their husband's religious convictions. Brewing is an exclusively female activity, and continues to have much importance even though alcohol consumption in Dar Masalit has fallen. Beer is produced for home consumption, but is also made in sufficient quantity for the purposes of sale, gift, hosting a work party, or occasionally a simple drinking party. It is an activity where skill is needed and appreciated by the consumers, and techniques and trade secrets abound. Hamid Ahmed Ddirar (1976) considers marissa a more sophisticated product than other African grain beers because of its special treatment of the starter. With the multiple processes of malting grain, wetting and redrying various batches of grain, portions of which are pounded, ground or cooked into porridge, the process requires attention to several simultaneous activities, and takes three to seven days to complete. It also requires substantial amounts of water and wood, and then the beer must be carried to market if it is to be sold.

Economically, beer is significant in several ways. It is a food, with certain nutrients enhanced by "biological ennoblement" in the brewing process (Platt 1955:121). It is traditionally the major food offered to guests at work parties as well as a commonly shared food among neighbors and friends. In these capacities, it is also a way in which women's labor can be used by their husbands and male relatives—both directly in consumption, and indirectly as gifts, hospitality, or payment to others. Although men cannot oblige their wives to work in their fields, they can make legitimate requests for beer, which they can use to feed helpers in agricultural labor. Women themselves, of course, also can brew beer for their own work parties.

In addition, brewing holds a special place for women in the market economy; it is the female task that can most easily be turned to a source of cash. While oil is also produced at a Geneina factory, and wood and water are now brought to market by men, beer production remains local and female. From the beer-makers' point of view, it is an activity that adds cash value to their crops, while simultaneously producing beer for themselves and their friends, who will reciprocate at some later date. It is also a way in which grain is made into clearly defined women's property; a woman can be criticized for selling grain in large quantities, but beer is her own affair. As Dorene Reynolds (1982) has suggested, transformations of household property may be used for the purpose of establishing personal rights over it (compare Saul 1981). Selling beer is considered a bit immoral even by many drinkers, and so a man may wish that his wife did not sell beer; however, when she brews beer for sale, he appreciates that there is also beer to drink and to give to visitors. Thus, brewing can be a source of cash for women, which pleases both them and their husbands. In addition, many of the regular producers of beer are single or married to emigrants, which means the full production is theirs to dispose of as they wish. In the large sample, 30 percent of women in these categories brew regularly for sale, compared to 14 percent of women with husbands present.

Beer is made in batches of two to six jars, each about eight liters. Equipment includes special jars and strainers worth LS 1–3, in addition to normal cooking utensils. A typical batch of three jars requires ten to twelve hours of direct labor over several days, including hauling wood and water, as well as longer periods of waiting for grain to malt, soak or dry. Roughly, one kora (2.5 kg) of millet is used per jar. (The respective market prices of the millet and the beer were 25 and 60 PT in November, 1979.) Thus, a woman brewing three jars for sale can add 35 PT to the value of each kora of grain, repaying her labor at LS 0.85–1.05 per day. Typically, at least one of the jars would be consumed in the village; in this case, the woman still gets LS 1.20 for two jars (instead of 0.50 for the millet) and the beer that is consumed at home partly offsets the millet and cooking labor she would use to feed the family anyway.

However, the marketing of marissa has become more difficult. In 1979, the various Sunday markets in Masterei district were closed by order of the rural council; these, like the Wednesday markets, had as much a social as an economic function, and much beer was consumed there. As for the major Monday and Friday markets in Buga, beer is no longer allowed for sale. Police have broken beer pots on several occasions when women were found selling near the market. Drinkers, at last observation, occupied suitable shady spots in a circle about twenty minutes walk from the central market; this made arrangements between them and brewers more difficult. The fursha hopes to prohibit beer entirely in the future, which would impose a great hardship on the women who depend on it as a source of income. This was presumably accelerated by the national prohibition on alcohol enacted in 1983.

AJINA. Brewing has considerable social and symbolic significance; in the past, when drinking was nearly universal, it probably had a role as important as its role in Uduk society, as described by Wendy James (1972; compare Netting 1964). As a form of reciprocal exchange and an expression of good will and sharing in the good life, beer drinking strengthens Uduk society. Masalit drinkers express these sentiments, but abstainers consider beer a sinful and disruptive force. Nevertheless, some of the uses and symbolism of beer have been retained by abstainers, and invested in a nonalcoholic substitute called ajina (*ᶜaji:na*, dough). It is uncertain whether ajina existed before the calls for abstention from alcohol in the late nineteenth century by Ismail Abd al-Nabi, but it is certain that its importance has grown in symbolizing the fraternity of pious nondrinkers. (One section of a nearby village separated from the drinkers and called itself "Ajina"). Like beer, it is made exclusively by women, and is consumed by groups of friends and neighbors at work parties, on holidays, and just for the pleasure of sharing. It is a major form of hospitality for the pious elite, among whom women prepare considerable amounts for visitors.

Unlike beer, it is not sold or consumed in the marketplace, and so it is not a source of cash for women.

Ajina is a thick grain infusion, like beer, but it is unstrained, and drunk with a large spoon. This, and its consumption from clay pots (*burma*) rather than jars makes it evident to passersby what a crowd is drinking. The production of ajina requires pounding the millet to remove the seed coats, cleaning, washing, and drying, beating again one or more times, and then boiling the pounded grain with water and spicing agents (wood of the *moxe:t* tree, *Boscia senegalensis*, is commonly used, as well as tamarind fruit, various leaves, fenugreek, and lemon). It is then allowed to sour (probably by the action of lactic acid producing bacteria), but not to ferment. Production of a typical batch of two and one-half pots from six kora of millet requires fifteen hours of labor, including hauling water and wood. Like beer, it is a substitute to a certain extent for other cooking.

DAMIRGA. A discretionary female task that is carried out by some women is the processing of millet into a form called *damirga*, which is then ground and cooked like ordinary millet. In this process, the millet is pounded and winnowed to remove the bran layer, then soaked for some days and redried. The average time involved was 20 min/kora. Damirga produces a finer quality of asida, and some husbands oblige their wives to make it frequently, complaining when ordinary millet flour is used. Women are much less likely to make damirga if they have no husband present, and they make it less in the agricultural season. Damirga is also less used by poorer families, since it reduces the quantity of food (although the bran or *kamfu:t*, which is removed by the process is not discarded; it has a small cash value, and is used as a millet substitute in animal food and beer). The wet-processing also may reduce the nutritional value of the millet by extracting water-soluble proteins, including lysine which is already deficient in millet (Hulse et al 1980:25). This is presumably offset in the higher-income families by the greater amount of millet available, and the consumption of milk, meat or other foods. Men with higher incomes are also in a stronger position to demand that their wives carry out this labor.

MARKETING. Marketing is done both to buy the family's needs and to sell one's goods. Both men and women may go to Buga, where there are markets on Monday and Friday, as well as to a nearby Wednesday market. Although some men insist on doing all marketing themselves in order to keep their wives at home, in most families wives go once every week or so to buy small amounts of spices, onions and other necessities. Women who sell beer may go more often. Usually they spend the morning in the village, leaving about noon to get to Buga before the sun becomes too hot. After the heat of the day is broken, they return. In the agricultural season, they try to limit their trips or go for shorter periods of time. This is especially true for women in the bush camps, who may have to walk for two hours in each direction.

GATHERING. Gathering of food is currently of little importance in the villages studied. In the rainy season, there are greens which are used in stews; these grow throughout the area and are collected with little effort. Women or girls in outlying areas sometimes collect *jakjak* (fruits of *jumme:z, Ficus sycamorus*), hime nuts (*hime:d Sclerocarya birroea*) or mohet fruits (*moxe:t, Boscia senegalensis*), and occasionally these are brought to market. Other formerly important fruits, such as *nabak (Ziziphus mauritiana*), and lalob (*lalo:b*, fruit of the *hajli:j, Balanites aegyptiaca*) are rarely gathered in any quantity. Lalob pits are still very occasionally used as a source of oil, but the process requires considerable labor. Edible locusts are also gathered when available, and they may be sold in the market. In addition, there are a number of plants and trees that are only used in times of famine; Kapteijns (1985:28) states that her Masalit informants claim superior survival skills in such circumstances. One journalist observed these Masalit techniques being used again in the recent famine (Dickey 1985).

Aside from locusts, the availability of gathered foods has been much reduced by deforestation and increased population. Thus, gathering is much reduced, both as a contribution to the diet, and as a portion of the female workload.

In the past, I was told many times, lalob oil was used much more than groundnut oil, and jakjak and nabak were gathered in basketfuls. Informants were nostalgic about the large cakes made out of sweet nabak flour and water, baked in underground ovens, in the days before they had sugar. One informant stated that the wornung opened the season on jakjak and nabak in the early dry season, and women with some men went out in groups to harvest them (compare with Tubiana and Tubiana 1977). They spent a month picking every day. As for himed, lalob, and mohet, they were picked late in the dry season, or with the first rains. Thus, in the past, women's contribution to the household economy included some fairly important food gathering and processing activities, which took work, but did not conflict with their agriculture. Also gathered food was sold, in some cases. But these resources are no longer available.

MISCELLANEOUS. Some tasks have not been recorded. From time to time, perhaps in the religious holidays, women make special foods. They occasionally weave a food cover or a basket; some very few of these are sold for cash. As stated, a few women make kisra or kawal to sell in the market, especially those whose religious convictions do not permit them to sell beer. The labor and cash returns for these activities are not major or continual considerations in the economic activities of any sample village women.

SUMMARY. This category of occasional female domestic tasks has included a number of disparate activities. Some are obligatory, though not daily; some are at the discretion of the woman who does them, while others are more accurately at the discretion of the husband. In practice, the time demands on women from discretionary activities, in total, are approximately thirty to ninety hours per month, or one to three hours per day (table 4.4), but most of these can be somewhat reduced in the agricultural season. In combination with daily tasks, women's domestic labor requires approximately three to eight hours per day, depending on season and circumstances.[3]

For both discretionary and daily domestic activities a woman's family situation is highly relevant to her workload, in that the presence of a husband or children increases the demands for domestic labor. To effectively require his wife to increase her work on discretionary activities, however, a husband must be able to provide cash goods, such as meat, sugar and clothing, at a fairly high level. He may also take over some female tasks—by bringing wood, hiring labor for her fields, and marketing—which leaves his wife more time and responsibility for domestic discretionary activities. Women with a husband of low income perform less discretionary activity for their husbands' sakes and more for their own—especially making and selling marissa. As for women without husbands present, their domestic workload is the lowest of all women. However, they must meet their own and their families' cash needs alone, which may require more marissa brewing, hiring out as agricultural laborers, or selling crops.

Men's Domestic Activities

Besides food production, a man's most demanding responsibility to his family is that of providing for its cash needs. To meet these needs men sell crops and engage in a number of activities that perforce take them outside the household. In addition to these cash needs, a man is responsible for housing his family. He also may engage in hunting, and many do some or all of the domestic marketing, wood hauling, or other activities. He has considerable discretion with regard to both

Table 4.4
Women's Occasional or Discretionary Domestic Activities and their Time Requirements

Activity	Labor Time	Frequency	Hours per Month	Factors Affecting Hours per Month
Collecting Firewood	1-4.5 hrs/ras	3-6 ras/mo	3-27	Family size, bush proximity, husband's help
Making Oil	5.5 hrs/btl	1-3 btl/mo	6-17	Consumption level, butter available, groundnut supply, purchase or sale
Brewing Beer or Making Ajina	3-5 hrs/jar 6 hrs/pot	0-6 jars/mo or 0-5 pots/mo	0-30	Cash needs (beer), husband present, hospitality, work parties
Making Damirga	20 min/kora	0-30 kora/mo	0-10	Millet supply, husband present
Marketing	3-6 hrs/visit	1-6 visit/mo	3-36	Cash needs, other economic activities, distance to Buga, husband's help

timing and determining the necessity of his domestic tasks, but the expectations of his wife and the community also compel him to maintain a certain standard of housing for his family.

HOUSING. A typical house in Dar Masalit is round, about 4 meters in diameter, with a conical roof rising from the walls, 1.3 meters high, to a point about 3.5 meters from the ground. Houses can be made smaller or larger according to need and resources. The roof is composed of grass, carefully thatched over a frame of straight poles bound with bark rope, and tied at several levels with circles of flexible green sticks. The roof is raised onto or built upon uprights of strong, termite-resistant wood that is forked at the top; these are inserted into holes dug directly in the sand. A house is then walled with grass or stalks, and a door of woven sticks is attached (currently using wires from the tea crates of the merchants). The last step in the making of a house is the floor; this is typically done by teenage girls who bring clay, direct from termite mounds, and water to make a plaster-like raised surface, which they then cover with fine sand from the wadi. Aside from being somewhat permeable in a sandstorm, a newly built house is comfortable and quite pretty.

Actually building a house, once the materials have been gathered, is not a very time consuming activity. Most houses constructed in the sample village during 1978 and 1979 were finished in a few hours by groups of 10–30 men, while some were built by two or three men in one to three days, depending on the type. If a work party is used, then the major domestic labor involved is the brewing of beer for the group, not the actual building. However, the labor of gathering the materials is many times greater than the labor of construction. In table 4.5 are shown the approximate time requirements to gather the materials for an average-sized village house. These times, which assume the builder has a camel, range from ten to twenty days, depending on the quality of the house. Of this time, travel is three to five days of the total; a man with only a donkey makes perhaps four times as many trips, thus increasing his labor to 19–35 days. On the other hand, to build a house in a bush camp less labor is required since travel time is reduced, perhaps by half.

The range of times required also reflects two major choices a man makes about the quality of the house; how to make the roof and the walls. The roofing grass of choice is a perennial called "marhabib" (*marHabi:b*, *Cymbopogon nervatus*), which formerly has been so abundant and near that it has been taken for granted; however, much has been destroyed to make fields. Currently, most of it is found in distant uninhabited areas. In addition, two to three times as much work is required in the actual construction of a roof of this grass. However, it

Table 4.5
Labor or Cash Requirements to Build a House of Average Size

	Travel Hours	Total Hours[a]	Market Cost (LS)
Materials			
Vertical Roof Struts (*korki*)	4	10	1.90
Horizontal Struts (*matarik*)	14	45	2.75
Roof Stalks (*gasab*)	0.5	2	0.38
Door (*ba:b*)	1	7	0.68
Bark Rope (*Habl*)	3	10	1.00
Uprights (*ʃa^{c}b*)	3	10	2.55
Roofing Grass[b]			
(*andafufu*	5	14	4.55
or			
marHabi:b)	14	64	9.75
Walls[b]			
Millet Stalks (*gasab*)	1	4	0.75
or			
Mats (*ʃarganiyya*)	14	50	7.50
Total Materials	29-52 (3-5 Days)	102-198 (10-20 Days)	14.48-26.43
Construction		2-6 Days	(No Cases)
Total		12-26 Days	

a. Total time includes travel time, assuming use of a camel.
b. Only one type of material will be used; the higher quality materials need more time.

is extremely durable, and several houses over fifteen years old have their original marhabib roofs in good condition. The other grass used is an annual called "*andafufu*," which is more easily gathered. Roofs of andafufu are vulnerable to weather and termites, and often look frayed after three to five years. However, they are the most common type made now. The other major quality choice a man makes concerns the walls. A man can gather enough millet stalks to 'clothe' the house in a few hours, and tie them on in the rest of a day. This type of wall is very susceptible to termites and usually stays in good condition for only one or two years. The better walls, like the better roofs, require a perennial grass that is now only found in the distant forest areas. From this grass are made large thick mats (*ʃarganiyya*s), which are very durable. To make six of these to fully wall a house, a man must go to the forest in the appropriate season and spend four days, working hard.

This description should make clear the problems that deforestation creates for men in fulfilling the duty to provide shelter for their wives and children. While formerly all of the ingredients could be gathered locally with less labor and perhaps in shorter periods of available time, the materials are now fairly hard to get. Without a camel, the job takes even more time, and many more separate trips. This illustrates another way in which the forest is becoming a resource that the poor cannot easily exploit.

On the other hand, the forest is becoming a source of income for those who have camels. All of these materials can be purchased, and are brought to market by the camel owners. As shown in table 4.5, the market cost of materials for a typical house ranges from LS 14 to LS 26, again depending on the type of roof or wall. Some of these materials are brought by truck from Chad border towns, and appear to be cheap compared to the local labor required to gather the same goods. Most men who build rely on some combination of purchase and gathering, and possibly hiring a camel owner, to complete the accumulation of materials.

A man first builds a house when he marries; this is in his wife's mother's compound, and belongs to her if the couple moves out. Most compounds have at least two houses, and a man with two wives usually has two compounds. One may also have a house in a bush camp in addition to a house in the village. Thus, the number of houses that a man must build is quite variable.

In 1979, fifteen houses were recorded raised by work groups, and a few houses were built by individuals, in a population of one hundred thirty-four ever-married men (including temporary emigrants). If we proportionately reduce the contribution of thirty-one polygynists with wives in other villages, this indicates one house being built per year per 6.7 men: that is, the average man builds a house about every seven years.

In addition to the houses, compounds in the villages must be fenced. Fences are made of millet stalks tied with bark rope on a line of thin poles placed in holes in the sand. This is not done in the bush camps where the small numbers of families tend to treat each other as kin, but in the villages it is considered that one should be protected from the eyes of strangers who might pass through, or even other villagers. This was not so commonly done in the past when villages were smaller and more voluntary of composition like the bush camps, but nowadays people are obliged to continue living where their fields are no matter what they think of their neighbors.

The size of a compound perimeter is quite variable, but, to give an idea of the size of the task, I have estimated the labor or cost for a 100 meter fence in table 4.6. At twenty-four days or about LS 20, it is comparable to the job of building a house. Again, a man must have a fence for each wife's compound, and again, the man without a camel has more work to do.

Table 4.6
Labor or Cash Requirements to build a 100 Meter Fence

	Travel Hours	Total Hours	Market Cost (LS)
Materials			
Stalks (*gasab*)	6	24	4.14
Poles (*arow*)	24	43	10.50
Total Materials	44	137	17.14
Construction		50	2.50
Total		187 (19 Days)	19.64

Besides houses and fences, there are a number of other structures in each compound. There are one or two structures (*raku:ba*) that provide protection from the sun (two days or LS 2–3) and there may be granaries, resembling little houses raised up on stilts. (Grain is also stored in sacks or in large clay jars, in which case it is kept inside a house). Finally, all of these structures need to be maintained, which means occasionally replacing damaged or worn out sections of grass or stalks, or replacing wooden sections weakened by termites.

Construction activities typically are done at the end of the dry season. A man who is building gathers materials through February and March, and builds in April or May in order to have a solid house in time for the rainy season. This does not conflict with agriculture. Because these activities are so intermittent, it is difficult to estimate the overall labor demand of men's domestic activities from the small sample of thirty-one families, and these data have not been collected in detail for the whole village. Very roughly, working from the above estimate of a house every seven years, if one fence is built per two houses, and if maintenance and small structures require an additional 10 percent labor input, then the average man spends about five days per year in providing housing, or pays others for equivalent work (plus transport for non-camel owners).

However, this labor burden is not evenly spread, and for young men with new wives and growing families the demands of construction are more substantial. This is especially true for those who do not own a camel, and cannot afford to hire one or to buy materials. For them, construction may place a large demand on labor that they cannot then use for cash-generating crafts activities; alternatively, it places a very significant claim on their possibly meager cash resources. Thus, the poorer families tend to live in older or more worn-out houses, have fewer structures, and use the lower quality building materials. From the point of view of city dwellers, a grass hut is a grass hut; but there are significant differences in comfort in the cold of winter, in sandstorms, and in the rains. Deforestation has thus increased even this inequality.

As for women without husbands, the quality of their houses has much to do with how long they have been unmarried. Those without cash resources tend to have the most limited housing, and less ability to maintain it. However, a woman can usually recruit neighbors or relatives for small maintenance jobs, possibly but not necessarily offering a little beer or food to her helpers. Also, women may do some repairs of fences or houses themselves. Although this work is customarily male, there is no prohibition on women engaging in construction.[4]

This was made quite clear at one of the more spectacular beer parties of 1979, thrown by a man to move a house from one village to another. Men and women carried the roof together, the men on their shoulders and the women on their heads. In addition, girls are responsible for making the floors of houses.

HUNTING. The other male domestic activity of any importance is hunting. This is comparable to women's gathering in two important ways: it is a dry season source of food, and it is much reduced from former times. Also, like gathering, hunting was a source of cash within living memory. Commonly in January and February, large groups of young men or teenagers gather under a hunt leader and fan out over large territories, armed with dogs, throwing sticks and spears. The yields to the group are a few guinea fowl, rabbits or hares, and occasionally a small gazelle; mostly it is reduced to an unproductive sport these days.

Older informants stated that in the past, hunts were carried out two times per week in season, under close organization; game was the main source of meat. According to Gunnar Haaland (1980) there was considerable social pressure on young men to engage in the hunt, and it acted as training for warfare. Giraffe, antelope, and lions were found in the forest.

With increases in cultivated area, deforestation and desiccation, there is less for wild animals to eat and drink, and those that exist are hard put to stay away from humans (Wilson 1980). Thus, like gathering, hunting is an activity that is now largely defunct. Occasionally, a rat, *worl* (monitor lizard?) or python is killed by an individual; some people eat all of these meats, and the skins of the latter two are valuable. But in this region, hunting is a very minor part of the local and domestic economy.

Agriculture

Without question, the most important nondomestic economic activity for the Masalit is agriculture. Every person who is capable farms. Farming provides the vast majority of the calories in the Masalit diet, and of the cash in the Masalit market. Even those with well-paying nonagricultural skills do not neglect their farms, and of all the craftsmen and merchants interviewed only one—a man with a shop, a sewing machine, and limited fields—considered agriculture his second most important economic activity.

In this section, agriculture will be discussed in terms of its simple economic inputs—labor, crops, soils—and its ecological effects and economic returns. Agricultural wage labor as a source of cash will be compared to other activities. The pattern of wage labor relations, as well as the distribution of land and the role of agricultural activities in market integration, will be explored in chapter 5.

Crops

Bulrush millet, also called pearl millet (*Pennisetum typhoides*; Ar. *duxn*) is the main crop, occupying over 80 percent of the land under cultivation. It is considered by agronomists one of the most drought tolerant of cereals, and is important throughout the Sahelian zone. For the Masalit, millet is the basis of every meal, ordinary or festive; millet porridge is the staff of life. In Masterei, millet is produced primarily for family consumption, although a certain amount is sold. On the goz, where groundnuts do not grow well, more surplus millet is grown as a source of cash. However, this is consumed primarily in Dar Masalit by city and town dwellers, nomads, and fellow villagers whose stores are insufficient. Export of millet from Dar Masalit is restricted by law, and, although smuggling occurs, this limits the amount leaving the Dar.

Sorghum (*Sorghum bicolor*, Ar. *Dura*) and maize are minor grain crops. Sorghum is said to require more moisture than millet, as well as soil of higher fertility; this limits it to clays and manured areas. In the large sample only 4 hectares are grown in open fields, and at most an additional 20 hectares are grown in the small garden plots next to houses (*jubra:ka*), which are fertilized by household animals and cooking refuse. In more remote villages where animal numbers are higher, these house-side plots are larger and sorghum appears to be somewhat more important. The most popular type of sorghum is *kor-nyang*, a short, early yielding variety which can be a source of food before the millet harvest. There are several taller varieties called *mare:g*, some of which are grown for their sweet stalks as well as their grain. *Ankolib (Sorghum saccheratum*) is a variety grown in wadi plots solely for its sweet stalks. Maize is often grown in the jubraka and also ripens early; it is something of a luxury, fresh roasted and eaten from the cob.

Groundnuts (*ful suda:ni, Arachis hypogaea*) the second most important crop in the Masterei area, became a major cash crop in Masterei in the 1950s. A creeping variety known as *baladi* (local), long in use, was cultivated in small plots by women as a source of oil and as a stew ingredient. According to a medical officer stationed in Masterei in 1954–1956, the government brought new seed and encouraged more production at that time. The seed was probably the upright variety, known in Masterei as *taja:rab* (experiment), which now predominates. Several Geneina merchants stated that they got their start in trade by buying groundnuts in Masterei and other areas of the Dar in the 1950s, and shipping them to El Obeid merchants. Currently, nuts are still exported whole to oil merchants in Nyala, Abesher, El Fasher and elsewhere, while in recent years an oil factory in Geneina has absorbed much of the production and increased the demand.

Other crops are far less important than millet and groundnuts, except insofar as they provide variety in the diet. Sesame, hibiscus (*karkade*) and cotton are seen in occasional plots less than 10 meters square. (Formerly these were export crops, and when prices were high they were cultivated in larger quantities.) *Lubia* (cowpeas?) and a single-seed groundnut called *ful abun gowi* are grown in similar patches; since both are eaten fresh, only small amounts can be used and none are exported. Cucumbers and melons are frequently sown mixed with millet seed. The vines grow primarily in the cool season as the millet is drying out, requiring no extra labor except collecting the harvest; if the yield is good, the extras may be sold. Vegetables are also grown in many people's jubrakas (table 4.7) and sometimes in a small patch of wadi land called a hudar (*xuda:r*). The most important of these is probably okra (*bamia* or *dara:ba*) which can be grown in sufficient quantity to dry and eat in later months, saving the cost of purchase. Some families also grow red peppers, tomatoes, pumpkins and cassava, as well as utensils in the form of gourds (*gara*) and scrubbers (*li:fa*).

Table 4.7
Numbers of Families Growing Crops in Various Types of Fields

	Field	Jubraka	Wadi Garden
Crops			
Millet	31	5	
Groundnuts	31	1	
Sorghum	7	23	
Maize		9	
Okra		17	5
Chilies		3	1
Tomatoes		1	1
Ankolib			1
Cucumbers	21		
Melons	20		
Abun gowi	19	1	
Karkade	6		
Lubia	6		
Sesame	2		

Notes: Based on the small sample. (N = 31). Data from the 1979 rainy season

These crops are appreciated as sources of variety as well as some nutrition and cash. However, their place in Masalit agriculture is very small compared to millet and groundnuts. The provision of sorghum in the jubraka before the main harvest is nutritionally important for some, and a sweet melon is certainly a pleasure on a hot afternoon; the Masalit diet is not just millet and groundnuts.

However, because the subject of this research was the social and economic organization, I concentrated quantitative data collection on the major crops. In discussing crop economics at the end of this section, field sorghum is merged with millet, while sorghum and vegetable production in jubrakas is omitted. Wadi gardens receive further attention with orchards in the next section of this chapter.

The Labor Cycle

The agricultural season in Dar Masalit usually lasts from April to March, but the point of most concentrated effort is the central two months of the rainy season. These vary somewhat from village to village. The timing of the rains also varies from year to year. Compare, for example, the years 1978 and 1979 in Masterei (figure 4.1). In 1978, the first rains came in June and people were planting into the first part of July; while in 1979, rains began in April and millet planting was finished by mid-June. In 1979, central Masterei was weeding about two weeks earlier than regions a few miles south, west and north, due to earlier rains.

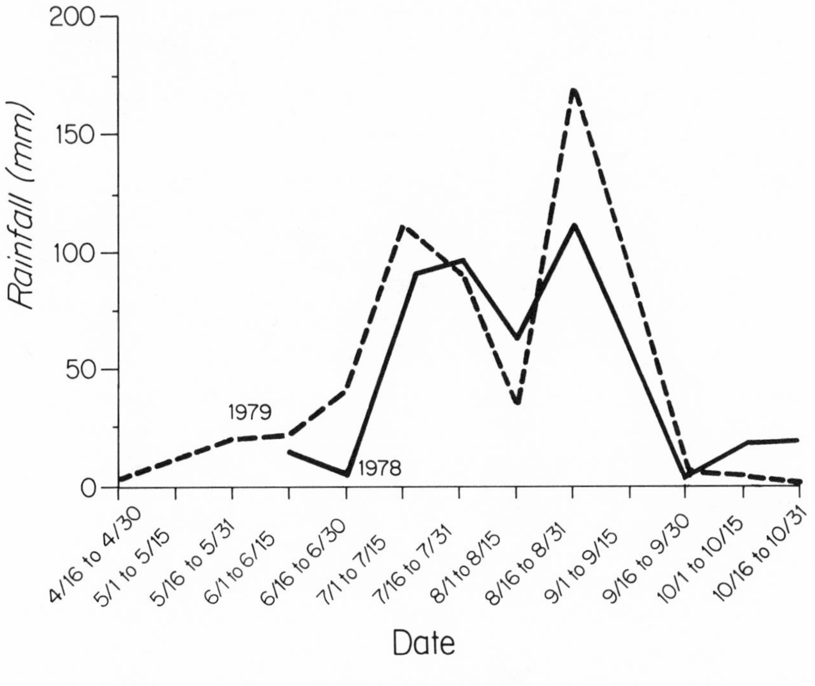

Figure 4.1. Bi-monthly rainfall totals at Masterei, 1978 and 1979 (mm)
Source: Masterei dispensary records.

Therefore, the labor cycle is described in terms of the rains rather than calendar months, and is based on my observations of two such cycles. The reader may follow the timing of the seasons and the various agricultural activities as they occurred in 1979 in figure 4.2.

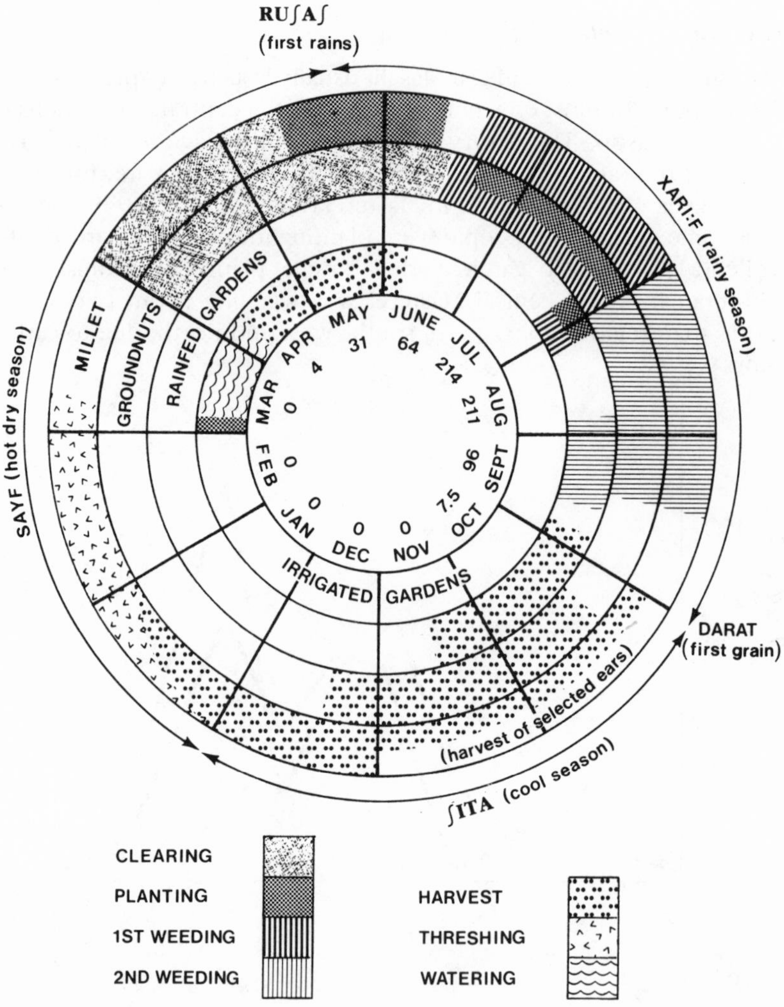

Figure 4.2. Timing of agricultural activities by season. The central circle shows the months in which these seasons occurred and rainfall in 1979. The dominant activities for each crop are represented, but in practice there is considerable overlap.

The first job is actually a dry season task, the *nada:fa* or cleaning. This involves chopping down any bushes that have grown up, and takes very little work. There is not much remaining of millet stalks at this stage, thanks to the termites, and the stubble is left on the field. It is at this time also that one might clear bush land for cultivation, which requires considerable work; however, as little uncleared land remains few people were involved in this task in 1979.

With the first rain (*ruʃa:ʃ*, showers), some people rush off to plant millet, while others wait and speculate over whether the rainy season has truly begun. Thus, the planting (*tayra:b*) of millet is spread over a month or more, but not because it is a demanding job. In fact it is considered relatively easy. Usually, after a rain when the ground is soft, the farmer walks in lines across the field, swinging a *to:ria* (an iron-bladed, bent-handle hoe) to make a series of shallow holes in the earth. A child or another adult usually walks behind, dropping a few seeds in the hole and using a foot to cover the seed. Two people can finish half a hectare in a morning, and, since there is plenty of time and the season is still hot, farmers usually quit by noon. In this season there is also a rush of last minute building projects, as the beginning of farming marks the end of building materials, and friendly assistance rapidly becomes scarce. Farmers who intend to plant groundnuts also use this time to prepare seed. Shelling is easy but time-consuming; enough for one hectare (about 50 kg) may take sixty hours to shell, and these hours are hard to find once weeding starts. Visitors, including inquiring anthropologists, are always welcome in houses where shelling is going on, since conversation and extra hands make the work go faster.

The next step in millet farming is the first weeding, (*Haʃa:ʃa*), ideally done when the crops are 7–25 cm tall. It is carried out with a long handled push hoe called a *jara:ya*, whose sharp, flat blade is passed just under the surface of the entire field, cutting off the sprouted weeds. Then the millet is thinned, close weeds are pulled, and the sand is brushed off by hand in a process called *guhu:r*. At roughly this same time, the first weeding is carried out on fields that are to be planted in groundnuts, but this is somewhat easier because there are no sprouts to watch for and the guhur is not required.

Groundnut weeding is followed within a maximum of three days by planting on the bare soil. (This was rated the most laborious agricultural job by the farmers I interviewed, corresponding to my observations.) Although groundnuts are planted with the same procedures as for millet, the nuts are more closely spaced, the digging is thus more frequent, and the work somehow does not have an easy rhythm. It may also be considered unpleasant because it is so time-consuming in a period when time is very short. Weeding millet, weeding groundnuts, and planting groundnuts are all best carried out at the same time, and late sowing or weeding reduces yields. Replanting failed millet or nuts also must be done at this time.

Thus, in this period—the first five weeks of heavy rain—people work very hard, and there is little marketing or other nonagricultural activity. Men and women work from about seven until two; men usually spend the hot period in the fields, and weed for another one or two hours before sunset, while women often come home to get water, prepare dinner, and work in the jubraka at that time. An adult man or woman can weed a hectare of millet in about seven days, although it takes longer after the first three weeks when there are more weeds, and hard soils also take longer. Weeding a hectare for groundnuts takes only six days since there is no guhur, but planting takes eight days. Thus, using a piece of land for groundnuts involves a commitment of twice as much labor in this season as millet.

After about four weeks, there is a feeling of relative ease on the part of those who are nearly finished. Cooperative labor parties begin, in which a host invites neighbors and kin to help and to share in meals or beer. Those who are nearly done help out those who are behind. This is also the time at which a wadi garden may be planted.

Approximately five weeks after the beginning of the first weeding (August 1 in 1979), the second weeding or *janka:b* begins, and this goes on for another four or five weeks. For millet this is somewhat easier than the first weeding because the crop canopy inhibits weed growth, but groundnuts sometimes require more effort. Generally the jankab requires five to seven days per hectare. It was done in short days during 1978 and 1979 because in both years the month of fasting, Ramadan, took place in this season. People tended to come home and sleep or do light work until sundown when they could drink and eat. In spite of this, in the small sample more than 95 percent of fields weeded once were also weeded the second time. There continued to be work parties in this period, indicating that some farmers had time to spare.

After the second weeding the rains ease off, and for about a month there is a lull while waiting for the crops to ripen. Some sorghum, maize and vegetables are ripe, and there is time for visiting. Craftsmen and traders are at work again, although money is scarce at this time and buyers are few.

This period of relaxation is brought to an end when the groundnuts are ripe (about October 10, in 1979). The groundnut harvest goes on for two months; the nature and amount of the work is quite variable. In 1978, the rains tapered off slowly, so nuts could be uprooted from moist earth fairly easily. In 1979, high yields of groundnuts were experienced, with much to be harvested. However, the rains stopped abruptly that year, which caused the green plants to dry out and the ground to harden. The ground in most fields had to be struck with a club over each plant, and great care was taken not to detach the nuts. In many fields, farmers had to pass their fingers through the soil to gather the last nuts, a few at a time.

Thus, harvesting labor varied from seven to nine days per hectare for green plants on moist earth, to as much as fifty days per hectare in the case of dried plants on hard earth. All family labor was mobilized at this time, as well as hired labor and work parties. Groundnut harvesting was considered boring and frustrating work, but it had the benefit that the fruits of one's labor were immediately seen.

After harvesting nuts, if they are green they need to be dried; dried nuts must then be separated from the stems for sacking and sale. This is light work, and an adult can separate about eighty to one hundred kg of nuts in a day. Thus, this task requires eight to twenty days per hectare, depending upon the yield.

The end of the groundnut harvest overlaps with the beginning of the millet harvest. Ripe ears of millet are harvested in October and November by those who need food, and also by some people in bush camps who wish to return to the village. At this stage the heads of millet need to be cut off. However, most millet harvesting takes place in December and January, after the plants are well dried out. It involves simply breaking off the heads of millet and piling them up, leaving the stalks bent for animals to eat. Harvesting requires seven to fourteen days per hectare, depending on yield, and is considered moderate work.

Harvested millet can be left in the field to continue drying on the ear even as late as May, but most of the harvest is threshed by the end of February. Threshing is hard work, and is done by repeatedly beating a pile of millet heads with a large club. Eventually the cobs are removed and the grain is winnowed. Actually beating for four hours, then winnowing about three, one can process about 75 kg of millet per person; this is a typical work day for this type of labor. Thus, this step requires approximately four to twelve days labor per hectare, depending on yield. This task, because it is so laborious, is frequently done by work parties. On a smaller scale, relatives help each other and work in small groups. There are also traveling groups of women, including many Zaghawa from the north, who thresh in exchange for 10 percent of the harvest. If people make *zaka:*—the Muslim tithe which is sometimes applied to yields above a certain size—they often consider the portion given to hired threshers or to members of the work party to be appropriate forms of this offering.

All forms of agricultural work are done by both men and women; however, there are some slight specializations. Winnowing is most often carried out by the women of the family. If there is a harvesting work party, the men often cut grain while the women gather and pile it after they are gone. In a weeding work group, women usually do the guhur on the area hoed by the men, although they may also weed a section themselves. By and large, however, men and women do the same tasks and carry out their agriculture independently if they desire.

Children are capable of assisting in most tasks. They are very helpful at planting in dropping seeds in holes and burying them; without their assistance an adult would have to do this job. Children over ten are capable of weeding, and some fifteen year olds can weed as fast as adults. Children assist in the most time-consuming tasks of groundnut farming—shelling, harvesting and separating the nuts—and in these tasks, two ten year olds can sometimes do as much as one adult, though rarely as persistently. Women have the primary right to the help of their children, who usually hoe with their mothers in the weeding season. However, they often assist their fathers in jobs such as planting, where they can take the place of an adult, and harvesting groundnuts, for which task their fathers often need more assistance than their mothers.

This description of the agricultural labor cycle has neglected two related factors: travel time to fields, and transport. Travel time is highly variable; some farmers commute as much as two hours each way to some of their fields. On the other hand, many fields are within a half hour's walk of the village. Frequently, farmers with fields over one hour away set up camp in them for days or weeks at a time, particularly for harvesting groundnuts after the rains, to save this traveling time. Others prefer to commute, sometimes in darkness but often at the expense of weeding time.

These time expenditures were not collected in a large number of cases, but in general I estimate that travel absorbs 10 percent of agricultural labor time. On the other hand, it does not take much energy, and it is probably the case that a farmer working close by does not weed proportionally more in ten hours than a commuting farmer does in nine. These details require a more exhaustive research project. As for the transport of harvested crops to the home, this again varies with distance. Nearby, it can be done with one's own donkey, but at a distance camel owners must be hired, at a rate of approximately 5 percent of the load that they carry.

Labor requirements of millet and groundnuts are compared in table 4.8. In 1978 and 1979, groundnuts required a great deal more labor per hectare than millet. The high end of the range in groundnut labor was increased by the sudden end of the rains in 1979, which was not typical. However, with high yields, even without this effect groundnuts required approximately 60 hours per hectare. Perhaps of greater importance with respect to farmers' planting decisions was the peak period labor demand. This work must be done as an investment in a future harvest of uncertain size; it requires almost as much labor when rains are poor as when they are not. Because these labor demands are in competition, and timing affects yields, farmers must consider the labor available in their decision to plant a certain area to groundnuts. This includes personal, family, and hired labor.

Table 4.8
Typical Labor Requirements for Agricultural Tasks

	Millet	Groundnuts
Task		
Cleanup	0.5	0.5
Seed Preparation	0	6
Planting	1.5	8[a]
First Weeding	7[a]	6[a]
Second Weeding	6	6
Harvest	7–14	7–50
Processing	4–12	8–20
Total	26–41	42–97
Peak Period Total	7	14

Notes: Labor in adult days per hectare.
a. Peak period tasks.

All parts of the labor cycle may be carried out by hired labor, although hired workers are a small part of the total labor force. The pattern of farm labor relations is discussed in the next chapter; at present only wages in agricultural labor are needed for comparison with other economic activities. Before the peak period, labor is usually employed for cleaning or sowing at a daily rate, which was 35–50 PT/-day in 1979. However, this is usually a limited day in terms of total labor time; six or seven hours at an easy pace is considered normal.

Groundnut seed preparation is occasionally done by hired labor in this period, at a rate of 15 PT/per *rayka* (bushel of approximately 13.5kg), which is an extremely low daily rate.

With the beginning of the peak season, labor is almost unavailable for about two weeks, while everyone weeds their own fields, and there is considerable speculation and discussion of the wage rates that will obtain. Weeding labor, when it begins, is almost always on a contract rather than a daily basis. Standard prices per mahammas (*maxammas*, 0.57 hectare)[5] emerge for millet and groundnuts; these may be increased or decreased according to the state of the fields (hardness of soil, amount of weeds) and the personal relationship of employer and employee.

In the 1979 first weeding season, the wage per mahammas of millet was LS 4, moving to LS 5 as the weeds grew tougher; for groundnuts, the wage was LS 3–4. Planting of groundnuts was rarely done by hired labor; farmers considered it a task requiring some care, and almost invariably chose to do it themselves. However a few contracts were recorded at LS 6/mahammas. In the second weeding, workers were paid LS 3–4 per mahammas.

In contract labor of this type, adults usually work continuously and hard, as they would on their own fields, since they are anxious to finish and go back to their fields. Weeding the fields of others is considered a sign of poverty for adults, and it is assumed that one only does it due to lack of grain to feed oneself and one's family. Working hard for eight or ten hours per day, adults are able to earn approximately LS 1.00 per day throughout the weeding season. Although considerably below the returns experienced on one's own field, it is better than the returns to labor in most low-capital manufacturing activities, and there is no time spent marketing. Furthermore, there is little market for crafts at this time of year, because most people do not have extra cash. Thus, for those without grain, agricultural labor is more rewarding than manufacturing activities at the peak weeding season.

In the season of harvesting groundnuts, there were many contracts on a per sack basis, (approximately 57 kg/sack), with the separation of the pods from stems sometimes included and sometimes a separate job. Wages varied from 25–70 PT per sack, depending on how rarified the nuts were by previous harvesting in these fields. Workers in this job were usually children or mothers working with several children, so it was difficult to estimate daily wages for adult laborers. However, in these cases and in a few contracts with adults for harvesting groundnuts, it appeared that the daily return to adult labor had dropped to 50–90 PT. This probably corresponded to shorter workdays, since workers were not under the same pressure as in the weeding season, and children did not work long hours easily. In the harvesting of millet, the few cases recorded showed a wage that was again 80 PT–LS 1.00 per day. This was primarily an adult activity. As for threshing, assuming 75 kg threshed per day (threshing days were usually short because the work is strenuous), a worker earned millet worth 70 PT per day.

Agricultural Soils

Land use, productivity and ecological effects of farming all depend substantially on the nature of the soils under cultivation. In the Masterei area, agriculture is carried out on the clay soils of the wadi, and far more extensively on the sandy soils of the plains. These soils, primarily aeolian in origin, are very low in clay, silt and nutrients, but they are fairly free of stones and are easy to cultivate.

In order to understand locally used soil categories and land use patterns, and also to compare Masterei soils with other savanna agricultural soils, samples were taken from the surface of Masterei fields, and analyses of particle size, nutrient levels and other characteristics were undertaken. The following discussion of soils in terms of their importance to agriculture draws on M. J. Jones and A. Wild (1975) unless otherwise stated.

Ninety-three percent of the cultivated area in the large sample is of a type of soil known in Sudan as *go:z*. It is of the ferruginous or iron-containing family, and has a sandy composition that reflects its origin in mobile desert dunes. Thousands of years ago, increased rainfall produced vegetation that fixed the dunes, and since that time sandiness has been further increased by the downward eluviation of clays. The quantities of clay and silt remaining are thus low, but differences in their amount result in different soil properties, which lead Masterei farmers to distinguish a type of soil known as azaz (*aza:z*) from the rest of the goz. (This term was not known to Geneina agricultural staff whom I interviewed). Azaz soils are said by farmers to have more *ti:n* (clay). This is confirmed by analysis of the particle size distribution in three goz and three azaz soils (table 4.9). The percentage of sand varies from 87 to 95 percent, goz being sandier, with a slight overlap in samples three and four. Azaz is defined by its hardness, and there are further gradations within this category. (Samples four, five and six were described to me as soft, hard and very hard azaz, respectively. I found this to be all too accurate when digging trenches in these fields.) Hardness increases as expected with larger silt and clay fractions in the soils. Clay also increases the water holding capacity and reduces permeability, and these effects are considered by farmers to be characteristic of azaz.

Table 4.9
Characteristics of Seven Soil Samples from the Masterei Area

	Sand %	Particle Size[a] Silt %	Clay %	Organic Matter[b] %	N (ppm)[c]
Goz Soils					
1	95.0	5.0	0	0.91	490
2	92.8	7.2	0	0.79	420
3	91.8	5.9	2.3	0.68	360
Azaz Soils					
(soft) 4	91.6	7.0	1.4	0.84	450
(hard) 5	87.9	9.7	2.4	0.90	484
(harder) 6	86.6	10.7	2.7	1.05	560
Tin Soil					
7	70.9	24.3	4.9	2.99	1600

a Determined by hydrometer. Sand: 0.06–2mm; silt: 0.002–0.06mm; clay: <0.002mm.
b Measured by loss on ignition.
c Estimated from organic matter assuming carbon to be 59 percent of organic matter and a C/N ratio of 11. *Source*: *Brady* 1974:154–156.

It is to be expected that a soil with a higher clay content has a higher cation exchange capacity (CEC), which increases the ability of a soil to maintain nutrients and to slow leaching losses. This parameter is measured on mixed samples composed of equal parts from the three goz and three azaz samples (table 4.10). As expected, the cation exchange capacity of the azaz mix is higher than the goz mix. However, CECs of both goz and azaz are still low in terms of ferruginous soils generally, and ferruginous soils as a group are very low compared to other agricultural soils. In addition, the effective CEC of the azaz may be reduced by the higher acidity of azaz soil.

A third soil category is that of tin (*ti:n*, clay). Because tin soils represent a small fraction of field area, they have been given less attention. Only one sample of tin from Masterei has been taken, and its composition is listed in table 4.9; other samples from other wadis may be quite different. All are very hard when dry, which is the sign of high

Table 4.10
Characteristics of Mixtures of the Goz and Azaz samples

	Goz Mix	Azaz Mix
Cation Exchange Capacity	2.2	2.6
pH	6.1	5.6
Potassium (K)	0.45	0.34
Calcium (Ca)	1.20	1.05
Magnesium (Mg)	0.70	0.57
Total Phosphorus (P)	22	18

Source: *Soil and Plant Laboratory Inc.*, (Bellevue WA).
Notes: Cation exchange capacity, potassium, calcium and magnesium in meg/100g; phosphorus in ppm.

clay content, but they are not cracking clays like those of the Nile Valley, and they do not swell up when wet. They are considered fertile but hard to work, and some tin fields have been turned into orchards in recent years.

In combination with soil composition, levels of nutrients are an important determinant of agricultural productivity. Organic matter is one of the most important soil components, and values for this substance are listed in table 4.9. Organic matter ranges from 0.68 to 1.05 percent, with azaz soils testing somewhat higher; this is likely to be the result of the fact that samples five and six have not recently been cultivated.

Organic matter is valuable for several reasons: it contributes to the cation exchange capacity; it improves infiltration, water holding, soil structure, and resistance to erosion; and perhaps most importantly, it is a source of nutrients. Nearly all nitrogen for crops, in the absence of fertilizers, comes from the mineralization of organic matter. Given sufficient water, nitrogen availability is the major determinant of millet growth (Olsson and Stern 1981:22). Assuming that organic matter is 59 percent carbon (Brady 1974:154–6) and a carbon-nitrogen ratio of 11, the average nitrogen content of these soils is 0.046 percent (462 ppm).

Organic matter is also one source of phosphorus, which is, however, primarily derived from inorganic soil constituents. Total phosphate has been tested on the mixed samples. Goz soils have slightly higher levels, but both goz and azaz are extremely low in this nutrient. It is likely that the amount of this phosphorus which is available to crops is lower in azaz soils, since availability rapidly declines below pH6 (Brady:388).

In addition to the major nutrients, sulfur, potassium, calcium and magnesium are important elements in agriculture. Levels of these nutrients are low throughout the savanna, but are not usually limiting with traditional cropping practices. Where fertilization with nitrogen or phosphorus has led to increased yields, or where continuous cultivation of export crops takes place these elements may become deficient (Nye and Greenland 1960:116–119; Anderson 1970). The mixed samples of goz and azaz have been tested for potassium, calcium and magnesium, and the goz is somewhat superior in these elements (table 4.10).

To understand the significance of these measurements of soil characteristics, it is best to place them in context. M. J. Jones and A. Wild have compiled data on some characteristics of a broad range of ferruginous tropical soils. Their mean values and ranges are presented in table 4.11, compared with mix values or mean values for goz and azaz. Masterei soils fall on the less desirable side of every mean, and towards the low end of every range. Phosphorus appears to be particularly deficient. In view of these facts, one must consider how the limited fertility of these soils is or is not maintained under current farming practices, and the effects of increasing groundnut cultivation. This point will be considered after discussing the uses to which these soils are put.

Table 4.11
Comparison of Characteristics of Goz and Azaz with other Ferruginous Tropical Soils

	Goz	Azaz	Other Ferruginous Tropical Soils	
			Mean	Range
Percent Clay	0.8	2.2	9.2	0–34.0
Percent Organic	0.79	0.93	1.24	0.18–5.68
pH	6.1	5.6	6.2	4.8–8.2
Exchangeable Bases (meq/100g)	2.4	2.0	3.1	0.7–11.8
Phosphorus (ppm)	22	18	125	13–560

Source: *Jones and Wild*, compilation of data from two hundred forty-five soils for pH, organic matter and exchangeable bases, one hundred ninety-five soils for clay percent, and one hundred eighty-one for total P (1975:29). Figures for goz and azaz derived from tables 4.9 and 4.10. Exchangeable bases are sums of Ca, K and Mg, plus 0.05 to approximate sodium.

Land Use According to Soil Type

By comparison with other soils, goz and azaz have many similarities. However, the higher levels of clay and silt in azaz have effects that are important to local farmers, and affect their decisions as to what crops to plant, and whether to use a field at all. To a large degree this also depends on rainfall. As documented in the last chapter, rainfall levels in this region have been dropping since the 1950s, and this fact has altered the relative desirability of the various soils. In the higher rains of the past, the hard azaz soils were considered very desirable, in spite of their low permeability. Many of them have to be worked with a *kadanka* or short handled hoe, rather than the push hoe, and furrows (*ula:m*) are sometimes required to hold water and allow it to penetrate the soil. However, with enough water they are said to yield well. Goz, on the other hand, is said to yield poorly in high rains, with the millet leaves turning yellow. This may be due to the fact that sandy soils release their nitrate with the first rains in an early flush, which may be rapidly leached away in goz soils, when moisture is high; on the other hand, the low penetration in azaz probably permits the nutrients to remain available.[6]

Thus, in the wetter 1950s, azaz soils were preferred and soft goz areas were abandoned. With the recent drop in rainfall, the situation was reversed. Water has become scarce, and goz soils which absorb it well are better producers, while crops on azaz get insufficient water. Thus, in the current environment goz soils are favored, and goz areas were reopened in the 1960s, while hard azaz areas began to be abandoned.

Sample six comes from an area which has not been cultivated in at least ten years, while sample five is from an area that is now only used in small parts, through formerly heavily cultivated. The kadanka is rarely seen in the current low rainfall conditions. This change is reflected in reported field use: of the land reported as owned, 89 percent is under cultivation, of which 21 percent is azaz. Of the so-called fallow, 73 percent is azaz, much of it in the areas of hardest soil. There is undoubtedly additional land which is not reported as part of landholdings because of its presumed uselessness and long abandonment.

Softer azaz continues to be cultivated, and many farmers prefer to have both azaz and goz fields to ensure reasonable yields in any rains. However, goz is preferred for groundnuts; they have been planted on 20 percent of the goz land in 1978, compared to 11.4 percent of the azaz (table 4.12). This preference may be due to different nutrient levels; in addition, it is easier to harvest groundnuts from soft soil. Another difference is related to the area left unweeded, which usually happens when the sowing does not sprout well. Only 8.8 percent of goz planted to millet was not weeded in 1978, compared to 13.9 percent of azaz. (Since groundnuts are weeded before planting, unweeded areas in table 4.12 are all millet).

Table 4.12
Area planted to each Crop by Soil Type, and Areas Unweeded

	Goz Area	Goz Sown %	Azaz Area	Azaz Sown %	Tin Area	Tin Sown %	Total Area	Total %
Crop								
Grain	335.7	80.0	106.9	88.6	37.1	84.9	479.7	82.1
Nuts	84.0	20.0	13.7	11.4	6.6	15.1	104.3	17.9
Total Sown	419.7	100	120.6	100	43.7	100	584.0	100
Unweeded	29.4	7.0	14.9	12.4	1.7	3.9	46.0	7.9
Weeded Area	390.3	93.0	105.7	87.6	42.0	96.1	538.0	92.1

Area is calculated in hectares. 1978 large sample

As for tin, it continues to be valued for agricultural purposes. Although it is hard, it usually gets sufficient water due to the fact that most of it is in wadis. In 1978, 9.8 percent of tin lay fallow, but since this comprised only four fields, the statistic probably does not indicate its relative desirability. Of cultivated tin, 84.9 percent was planted to grain, of which only 3.9 percent was not weeded, indicating a high success rate in sowing. Approximately 10 percent of the grain sown on tin was sorghum, which does well in fine-textured soils (Cocheme and Franquin 1967:83). Fifteen percent of the tin cultivated was sown to groundnuts and a bit of sesame. Other areas of tin soil have been converted to orchards or irrigated vegetable gardens, which will be discussed separately; these areas are not included in the above calculations.

Exact crop areas were not collected on the jubrakas or garden plots beside houses. General information was taken from the small sample, representing thirty-one of one hundred eighty-four women's families. Of these, twenty-five had a jubraka, with a total area of 4.9 hectares. If the small sample was representative, the large sample should have had approximately 27 hectares of jubraka land in addition to the 584 hectares of cultivated open fields. As mentioned previously, this land was primarily used for fast ripening grains and vegetables, as well as millet. Small sample use of this land is listed in table 4.13 (compare table 4.7).

Table 4.13
Use of Jubraka Land by Members of the Small Sample

	Number of Cases	Total Area (ha)
Reported Use		
Grain only	6	1.2
Grain with some Vegetables	18	3.4
Vegetables with some Grain	1	0.3
No Jubraka	6	
Total	31	4.9

Notes: N = 31

Other Factors

FIELD VARIATION. Farmers with experience in their fields take into account other factors that influence yields. The slope may have important effects on water penetration or susceptibility to waterlogging—usually a gentle slope is preferred to a flat or steep one. Light exposure may also be a factor. Another aspect that farmers frequently comment upon is the 'coldness' of a field, which is evidenced by the survival of vegetation well after the rains have stopped. Since millet continues to ripen for several months after the rainy season, this is obviously important. Coldness probably reflects the water storage capacity of a field, and this very likely includes deep strata of the land, since groundnut and millet roots can penetrate deeply. In ferruginous soils, it is common to find redeposition of clays from shallow to deeper strata, which may restrict deep drainage (Cocheme and Franquin 1967:15) and perhaps lead to waterlogging in high rains. On the other hand, this clay-rich layer can be a valuable repository of moisture and perhaps of nutrients.

In trenches dug in the same six fields discussed above, a reddening of the soil was apparent within 15–35 mm, and in four of these trenches increasing redness was apparent down to 60 mm. In one goz field noted for coldness and high yields, a very distinct red layer was reached at 54 mm. I was told that 'clay' could be found anywhere by digging deeply enough.[7] The depth and nature of this clay-rich layer is probably an important contributor to variations in yields among different fields, but a proper agronomic study would be required to evaluate the relative importance of these soil factors.

PESTS. Another factor affecting yields is the affliction of various sorts of pests. A chronic problem is that of locusts, which may attack crops at any time, from sprouting to ripening. There are numerous types of locust which vary with the season. In 1978 and 1979, there were chronic low-level locust problems, and a few fields were extensively damaged. I was told that in 1974 and 1975 there was a locust plague of greater intensity, and other periods of locust plagues in the more distant past also left strong memories with many villagers.

Locust control is basically done by hand; they are battled by killing or burying them. Poisons are occasionally available in Buga, but they are far from sufficient for the region, and villagers rarely get access to them.

Also reducing yields is a millet pest called "*du:d*" (worm) that I did not identify. There may be other insects or diseases of importance as well. Birds sometimes attack the ripening millet, but this seems to be much less of a problem than it has been in former times when fields adjoined forests. However, birds and mice do eat groundnut seeds. Ripe millet and groundnuts are also sometimes eaten by termites, and the farmer who observes this in his field must harvest early.

Finally, one of the more serious problems is that of livestock; animals are especially dangerous to young groundnuts, since merely treading on a plant may kill it. Millet is apparently quite tasty to cows and goats as well, and fields that abut herding routes, grazing areas and waterholes usually suffer some damage. About three weeks into the weeding season, the fursha (or the wornungs, in his absence) decides that his ceremonial drum should be beaten to indicate that livestock owners must control their animals; they are then liable for damages until the drum is beaten again, after most of the millet harvest is complete, and the animals are released into the fields. However, damage still occurs.

All of these pests, as well as the other factors mentioned, affect yields; they make cultivation that much more risky, and increase the difference between low and high yielding fields in any given year. These factors all play a role in producing the average yields to be discussed later in this chapter. They also contribute, in ways that have not been measured, to the labor required of farmers. Trips to monitor fields for pest or animal damage, replanting because of lost or spoiled seed, and locust control are all factors that take extra time. Labor estimates understate the total labor required of farmers; they only reflect the total measurable labor for routine tasks. Proper measurement of these minor labor inputs would increase the average labor input per hectare, although in practice the labor requirements from these causes are highly variable from one field to another.

The Maintenance of Fertility

The use of agricultural land in Masterei has changed in the colonial and postcolonial era. In the nineteenth and early twentieth centuries, Masalit had sufficient land to fallow some fields and cut new ones from forest, while growing millet for subsistence, trade and taxes; the latter partially fed the ruling elite, and also supplied public granaries maintained for emergencies (Kapteijns 1985:42). Forest products supplemented agriculture in the diet. However, the higher population, together with the diminution of forest resources, has increased pressure on the land and has resulted in continuous cultivation. The cultivation of groundnuts has added to this pressure, and also introduced the problem of exporting nutrients from the region. These practices have presumably had effects on the soil, and will continue to do so in the future. To understand these effects, it is relevant to consider other savanna agricultural areas that have undergone similar changes.

In stable, low intensity agriculture, even poor soils can be maintained in a productive state by returning nutrients and organic matter to the fields. Humans, animals, crops and soils are part of an ecosystem which is nearly self-contained. As M. J. Jones and A. Wild aptly describe it:

> Under true subsistence farming there is considerable recycling of nutrients. Little, if any, of the harvest is exported from the neighborhood of the farm; crop residues are burned on the field; and ash, household refuse, and animal dung are returned to the field. By using manure and domestic residues in those areas immediately adjacent to the homestead, there is some transference of fertility away from the outlying areas, but in the long term the shifting of village sites has a leveling effect (1975:141).

The return of crop residues in one form or another is the key to the system. Millet seeds make up a very small proportion of the total millet plant, most of which remains on the field. "Leaf litter, other debris and root residues are rapidly consumed by insects, fungi and other organisms and thus converted partly to carbon dioxide and partly to colloidal substances which become intimately mixed with mineral matter (sand, silt and clay) in the topsoil." (Vine 1968). In Masterei, by the end of the dry season the root structure of the millet plant has disappeared except for the base, consumed by the numerous termites. The millet stalks are partly eaten by termites as well, but livestock plays a greater role; after the harvest is complete, animals roam freely over the fields, eating and breaking up the stover: "Probably their main benefit to the farmer is that they convert into dung the bulky crop residues which are otherwise difficult to incorporate into the soil" (Jones and Wild 1975:141). Dung beetles further the process of incorporation.

In such a system, nutrient levels and yields can be maintained for fairly long times compared to African soils generally; older farmers have reported cultivating for five to ten years in a row even when forest land was available for new fields. In a somewhat more arid Darfur location, Holy (1974:37) has reported that Berti farmers cultivate millet for fifteen or more years without fallowing, even though other land is abundant. Similarly, Kassas (1970:129) reports a traditional rotation pattern in Kordofan with cultivation for a period of four to ten years. These cases imply that yields on savanna soils can be maintained for fairly long periods of continuous cultivation. This is supported by H. Vine (1968:109) who reports a mere 25 percent drop in yields over nine years in a savanna case in Ghana. These slow declines in fertility may be due to the low offtake or to the fact that deep-rooted crops like millet can overtake leached nutrients and bring them back to the surface. Nevertheless, fallowing has a beneficial effect on nutrient levels, especially in the first few years as leached nutrients are brought to the surface by fallow growth. Periodic resting of fields is also important in the long-term maintenance of soil fertility (Vine 1968:101; Jones and Wild 1975:126–30).

Fallows of two to four years, which have been practiced in the past, might improve nutrient levels, but they would not restore soil physical properties; savanna soils, unlike forest soils, attain only weak structure under these conditions, and the "native systems of cropping savanna soils rapidly destroy any small improvement promoted by fallow" (Nye and Greenland 1960:81–85).

The main reason fields were fallowed, according to farmers, was weed growth, particularly the appearance of parasitic weeds. The main one appeared to be *Striga hermonthica*, which may reduce yields by 70 pecent or more (Bebawi 1984). "When the *bude* weed came up in one man's field all the surrounding fields were abandoned as well" (Kapteijns 1985:27). Supplementing the short fallows were longer periods when entire agricultural areas were abandoned and village sites moved. Although villages are relatively permanent now, many of the agricultural areas have fertile zones within them called "*dungus gadi:m*" (old dung heap) from the days when small villages existed on those spots.

Manure is also an important contribution to maintaining the agricultural productivity of soils. In addition to the deposits of free roaming livestock mentioned above, Masalit corral livestock on fields at night to produce *daya:r* soil. In current practice, it takes years to manure a field, moving corrals over the surface of the field every ten days or so (this will be described in more detail in the section on livestock). The resulting higher yields are said to last for seven to ten years, which indicates that the soil character is profoundly changed by the process. Hans Van Raay (1975:18) found doubling and tripling of organic carbon levels under a similar Fulani practice, although the numbers of animals are not given. However, the existing animals are not sufficient to manure all of the fields, and only 14 percent of the cultivated fields have been manured within the last ten years.

In the early part of this century, dayar was also made; in fact it was considered particularly valuable when rains were high, especially on goz.[8] Since houses, fields and forest were in close proximity, animals would naturally be corralled on the fields at night, which transfered organic matter from forest to fields and increased soil nutrient levels. However, in the absence of sound information on livestock numbers and field-animal ratios, it is difficult to judge whether animals played a greater role in maintaining soil fertility in the past than now.

In addition to the fertility effect of manure, there may be an indirect effect related to the parasitic weed problem discussed above. It appears that the incidence of *Striga* is reduced in the presence of high levels of nitrogen (Bebawi 1984; Parker 1984). This might have had an important effect on settlement patterns, because it suggests that settlements with high ratios of animals to cropped land would have been viable for extensive periods. The importance of this factor in terms of precolonial population movements needs to be evaluated.

With the current pressure on land, continuous cultivation is the norm, and fallow is no longer a routine part of agriculture. Many fields have been cultivated for over thirty years. Thirteen percent of agricultural land claimed was fallow in 1978, but as mentioned above most of this was poor land, abandoned in fact rather than resting. Only three percent of goz soils were fallow. People who idled good fields did so because they had no time, or they were too far—not because of weed or fertility problems.

Without fallowing to control weeds, people must hoe more intensively; a second or even a third weeding is the norm under current conditions. Further, with continuous cultivation, declining fertility over the long term is a real problem. Masalit farmers complain of declining yields, and this is sure to be due partly to reduced rainfall. However, the consensus of agronomists is that soils also lose fertility under continuous cultivation, even though this process may take longer on savanna soils. Without manure, yields "decline rather gradually, and decreased supplies of nitrogen, phosphorus or potassium are much more important than other factors" (Vine 1968:92). On well weeded savanna soils, Nye and Greenland believe that declining yields are usually related to declines in phosphate availability (1960:75). John C. DeWilde (1967a:16–17) and M. J. Jones and A. Wild (1975:69–72) note the serious loss of organic matter under continuous cultivation, due to its exposure to mineralization and oxidation. Continuous cropping also can lead to acidification, decline in cation content, and declining cation exchange capacity (Jones and Wild 1975:157). Thus, it is likely that the low fertility levels of soils tested are in part a result of their continuous use in recent decades.

The problem of nutrient loss is aggravated by cultivation of export crops such as groundnuts. The amount of animal fodder produced by nuts is small, and is removed from the fields at the harvest. The pods themselves form a large proportion of the plant matter produced, and these are not only removed from the field; they are taken out of Dar Masalit and out of the Sudan. Each 1000 kg of nuts that are exported removes 30–50 kg nitrogen, 2.7–4 kg phosphorus, and 9 kg of potassium (Jones and Wild 1975:165).[9] Since this amount might be harvested from one or two hectares, it makes a substantial impact on the nutrient content of these fields. The nutrients lost can be staggering in regional terms. Consider a comparable case: "It has been estimated that exporting 500,000 tons of groundnuts and groundnut oil from Northern Nigeria means a loss of 23,000 tons of phosphorus in the form of superphosphate for the nut-growing areas. At the same time, the total consumption of fertilizers in Northern Nigeria in 1964 was only 12,000 tons. Any agricultural export means the loss of a certain amount of valuable soil constituents" (Svandize 1968:320).[10]

G. Delbosc (1968) argues that moderate applications of nutrients can maintain yields, although results have been mixed. Even if true, it is unlikely that the farmers of Dar Masalit will be able to buy inorganic fertilizers in the foreseeable future. If farming comes to depend on fertilization, those with money will have increased control over agriculture, while those without will continue to mine the nutrients of their land. At the present time, there is absolutely no use of fertilizer by Masterei farmers that I could discover, so the question is academic.

Based on European and American experience, groundnuts have been considered a useful rotation crop due to their presumed ability to fix nitrogen, and add to the level of this nutrient in the soil. However, it has not yet been demonstrated that groundnuts form nitrogen-fixing nodules under African conditions (DeWilde 1967a:37; Jones and Wild 1975:83). If this could be achieved, it would still leave the problem of the removal by groundnuts of scarce phosphate from these soils. However, groundnuts do have a positive effect on yields of millet in the following year. Farmers attribute this to the 'cleanness' of the land after groundnut cultivation, which reduces weeds and perhaps pests. The worst weed, according to farmers, is the parasitic *bu:da* (*Striga hermonthica*) that attacks millet. According to F. W. Andrews (1948:403), groundnuts can stimulate the germination of buda, which then dies due to the lack of an appropriate host crop. In this respect it may be a useful rotation crop, serving the purpose formerly served by fallow, although it is costly in terms of valuable and scarce soil constituents.

In addition to these considerations of soil nutrients and composition, one must consider the conservation of the agricultural soil itself. As L. Berry points out, "soils need to be assessed not only in terms of their fertility, but also in terms of their vulnerability . . . the highest rates of soil loss potential [in sub-Saharan Africa] are found in the Sahelian zone in ferruginous soils; over 200 tons per km^2 may be lost each year in this zone" (1975:14). The erosion hazard is greatly increased by continuous cultivation, and sandy soils erode particularly easily. The eroded material is usually richer in the precious clay, silt and organic matter than the soil left behind (Jones and Wild 1975:62–64), leading to lost fertility and poor soil structure. Over the long term, gullying or repeated sheet erosion may render large areas totally unsuitable for agriculture (Nye and Greenland 1960:90–91).

Fouad N. Ibrahim (1978) considers millet cultivation the main cause of desert encroachment in this area due to wind and water erosion that results and the loss of natural vegetation. Whatever the extent to which millet cultivation contributes to erosion, groundnut cultivation is clearly a greater hazard. While millet is planted amidst the litter of the previous year, and only weeded when it has begun to grow, groundnut fields are weeded and cleaned, left with a surface of unprotected loose soil at the high point of the rains. Due to the cost of seeds, they are planted at a relatively wide spacing, and vegetative growth never covers more than 50 percent of the soil surface; in most of the rainy season 80 percent or more of a groundnut field is directly exposed to the sun and raindrops. At the harvest, the field surface is again disturbed, and the field is left stripped bare of vegetative cover during six months of direct sun and wind. These aspects of groundnut cultivation would seem to make its large-scale production unwise on these soils, although the present level (18 percent of cultivated soils) may not be excessive. Since there is considerable economic pressure for expanded groundnut cultivation, the area planted to nuts will probably increase with possibly grave consequences. The results can only be predicted by thorough study of the soils and fertility losses under local conditions, which may also discover techniques to mitigate the problems of groundnut cultivation. However, there does not seem to be any research effort directed at this issue at the present time. Therefore, the results of increased groundnut cultivation will be discovered by the farmers through their own, possibly disastrous, experience.

Yields and Economic Returns

Information on the harvest yields of groundnuts and millet was collected for fields cultivated in 1978 and 1979 by the members of the small sample, with the exclusion of jubraka and hudar plots. Fields were subdivided each year into plots with pure stands of millet or groundnuts, except for the minor crops discussed above. Harvest data were obtained for two hundred twenty-eight such plots, from a total of two hundred thirty-nine. In tables 4.14 and 4.15 mean yields based on these plots are tabulated by soil type for these two years. Aggregation of the data in this manner ignored variation from field to field based on timing, pests, and other factors, which produced a wider range of yields than that recorded here. However, this table illustrates the importance of two factors—rainfall and soil type—in determining yields.

Mean annual rainfall in Masterei, based on recordings at Buga of fifteen years between 1959 and 1979, was 595 mm with a range from three hundred thirty-one to eight hundred nineteen. In 1978, 488 mm

Table 4.14
Mean Yields of Millet by Soil Type in 1978 and 1979

	1978 Yield[a] (kg/ha)	1979 Yield (kg/ha)	Increase over 1978 Percent
Soil Type			
Goz	417	565	35
Azaz	285	439	54
Tin	394	581	47
Manured	709	990	40
Overall Mean	393	593	51[b]

a Based on the area weeded by small sample families, excluding jubraka and hudar plots.
b An increase in manured area from 7 percent of the millet area in 1978 to 14 percent in 1979 is partly responsible for the increase in overall yields.

Table 4.15
Mean Yields of Groundnuts by Soil Type in 1978 and 1979

	1978 Yield[a] (kg/ha)	1979 Yield (kg/ha)	Increase over 1978 Percent
Soil Type			
Goz	1094	1810	65
Azaz	740	1291	74
Manured[b]	1171	918	-48
Overall Mean	1117	1639	47

Notes: Tin omitted as only one plot was recorded.
a Based on the area weeded by small sample families, excluding jubraka and hudar plots.
b Manured area planted to groundnuts is 2.9 ha (16 percent of nuts planted) in 1978 and 1.1 ha (5 percent) in 1979; these small areas are in different fields each year and are probably not comparable.

were recorded, while in 1979 rainfall totaled 626 mm. Thus, these two years were examples of fairly low and moderately high rainfall levels. In general, water availability is a more complicated matter than the total rainfall; the timing of humid periods and the water surplus may be more significant factors (Cocheme and Franquin 1967). However, in these two years the distribution of the rain over the season was rather similar (figure 4.1).

The result of higher rainfall in 1979 was markedly higher yields. Millet yields were 35–54 percent higher according to soil type in 1979 than in 1978, and groundnut yields were 47 percent higher.[11] If rainfall is decreasing, as suggested in the last chapter, then yields for both millet and groundnuts can be expected to decline.

Tables 4.14 and 4.15 explain the local preference for goz soils over azaz. Yields on goz were 28–47 percent higher than yields from azaz plots. The farmers' contention that azaz yields better in higher rains was given some support; millet yields improved 54 percent on azaz soils in 1979, while yields on goz only improved 35 percent. Possibly in higher rains the azaz would overtake the goz, but in the observed range the goz was still superior. As for tin soils, they appeared to be comparable to goz in millet yields. Only one tin plot was cultivated in groundnuts in each year, so one can say nothing of significance about it.

The value of manure in increasing millet yields is dramatically illustrated in both years, with average yields 68–70 percent higher than plain goz. These figures are based on a set of fields ranging up to ten years since they have been last manured; several recently manured fields had yields exceeding 1500 kg/ha. The yields for groundnuts on manured soil are not conclusive. Although the data appear to indicate a decrease in 1979, relative both to goz and to 1978 yields for groundnuts on dayar, this represents only three plots. Further, these are different from those planted with nuts in 1978. Thus, the value of manure in groundnut farming is unclear. Farmers rarely use fresh dayar for groundnuts, and in 1978 only 14 percent of the manured land of the large sample (compared to 21 percent of plain goz) was planted in groundnuts.

The overall mean groundnut yield of 1366 kg/ha is quite good compared to yields obtained under similar conditions elsewhere in Africa. In table 4.16, millet and groundnut yields from a variety of sources are listed for comparison; Masterei mean yields of nuts exceed or approach the high end of other reported yields. Millet yields do not compare as favorably; Masterei mean yields are near or below the low end of these ranges. This may be a result of the deleterious effects of continuous millet cultivation, discussed above. Groundnut yields also decrease with continuous cultivation (Anderson 1970, Delbosc 1968), but Masterei fields have spent little time under groundnut cultivation at this point. The land may have relatively high levels of available phosphorus in spite of low total phosphorus, and it may still be relatively free of pests and diseases that attack groundnuts.

The data also permit a comparison of yields obtained by men and women in their fields. Eliminating manured fields, which were not

Table 4.16
Comparison of Small Sample Mean Yields in 1978–79 with Yields reported in Other Sources

	Rainfall	Millet	Groundnuts
Small Sample Mean	488–626	495	1366
Jones and Wild	unknown	430–1070	400–950
Nye and Greenland	858	284–823	288–906
DeWilde	400–600	600–700	500–1000
Anderson	391–810	—	743–1624
Delbosc A	420	200–250	700–900
Delbosc B	725	500–650	1000–1200
Cocheme and Franquin	796	670–1770	—
Ross	unknown	586–602	345–1033

Sources: Jones and Wild (1975:50) cite national statistics for 1969–70 from thirteen West African countries. Nye and Greenland (1960) give 5-year means from 1931 to 1955 at Kano, Nigeria. DeWilde (1967b:345) reports on nonexperimental plots in Bokoro, Chad. Anderson (1970) reports results from a sandy loam in Sambwaa, Tanzania over a four year period; the crop is closely spaced with no fertilization. Site A of Delbosc (1968) is the sandy zone of Louga, Senegal while site B is the ferralitic area of Darow, Senegal. Cocheme and Franquin (1967) report data from Bambey, Senegal over an eleven year period. Ross (1982) reports data from 1976 and 1977 in three villages of the Groundnut Basin of Senegal.

equally distributed, it appeared that women obtained yields comparable to those of men in millet cultivation in both years (table 4.17). However, women's yields in groundnut plots were substantially less than men's. This could be due to the greater domestic labor commitments of women, which were previously shown to amount to several hours per day. Groundnuts required twice as much peak season labor as millet, and I was told that they are considerably less forgiving than millet with respect to timing. Women were possibly not able to schedule their agricultural work as effectively as men to meet the labor and timing requirements of groundnuts. In addition, as is shown in the next chapter, men made greater use of hired labor than women, which may have enabled them to carry out groundnut cultivation with better timing and more thorough weeding.

In order to compare agriculture to other economic activities, one can estimate typical returns to labor and money invested in agriculture, based on these yields and the above information on labor inputs. The figures used to make these estimates are summarized in table 4.18. Yields for millet and groundnuts that are slightly below

Table 4.17
Yields in kg/ha for Men and Women by Crop and Year

	Year	Men	Women	F/M Ratio
Millet	1978	347	395	1.14
	1979	592	472	0.80
Groundnuts	1978	1408	807	0.57
	1979	1908	1417	0.74

Notes: Manured soil is excluded to eliminate the effect of men manuring new lands between the 1978 and 1979 seasons.

average 1978 yields and slightly above average 1979 yields on unmanured goz are used to represent low and high yields. Millet value is calculated at 23 PT/kora (2.5 kg), the price that prevailed from May to December, 1979. Groundnut prices varied in 1979, and are calculated at LS 5/guntar (45.5 kg) at planting time and LS 3.70/guntar at harvest. Early labor includes sowing, seed preparation and weeding; it does not vary according to harvest. Harvest labor is estimated according to the yield. Labor costs are estimated based on contract prices given above in the section on the labor cycle. Labor inputs and costs in groundnut harvesting assume a moderate degree of soil hardening, and labor costs of 40 PT/sack, bagged.

Table 4.18
Inputs and Outputs per hectare of Millet or Groundnuts under Differing Yields

	Millet		Groundnuts	
Preharvest Inputs	Amount	Value	Amount	Value
Seed	15 kg	1.38	50 kg	5.50
Labor	15 days	16.23	27 days	24.24
Total Value or Cost		17.61		29.74
Harvest Labor, Processing				
Low Yield Case	13 days	16.40	16 days	7.02
High Yield Case	19 days	23.70	31 days	14.04
Yields				
Low	400 kg	36.80	1000 kg	64.67
High	600 kg	55.20	2000 kg	129.33

Notes: Based on figures for unmanured goz soil and nonextreme conditions

If we assume no use of hired labor, the returns to labor vary by crop and yield. Millet cultivation produces a harvest with a value of LS 1.27–1.58 per day's labor while groundnut cultivation returns LS 1.14–2.15 per day (table 4.19). However, groundnuts require the investment of LS 5.50 per hectare in seed, as opposed to only LS 1.38 for millet. These rates of return to labor are greater than those recorded for low-capital manufacturing as will be shown below. It is also clear from these rates that working as a hired laborer (at rates of LS 1.00 or lower) is less rewarding than working in one's own fields.

Table 4.19
Returns to Labor in Groundnut and Millet Cultivation

	Millet		Groundnuts	
	Low Yield	High Yield	Low Yield	High Yield
Net Harvest Value (LS)[a]	35.42	53.82	59.17	123.83
Labor Days	28	34	42	58
Return per Day	1.27	1.58	1.41	2.15

a Equal to harvest value minus seed value, per hectare

If we assume that all labor is hired, we can estimate overall rates of return excluding land. In table 4.20 net profits are shown for millet and groundnuts with low and high yields. Clearly groundnuts have greater profit per hectare using both yield assumptions. Based on the costs of early inputs (since harvest and processing labor is often paid out of the crop and is not really an investment), groundnuts also have very high returns to capital, more than tripling invested money in a high yield year. As will be described in the section on trade, these rates of return have attracted the attention of merchants, who invest considerable amounts of money in agriculture labor. Hiring is not carried out over the entire agricultural cycle at the same intensity, but is used to supplement (and increase the value of) personal and family labor.

These estimates are very sensitive to market prices of millet and groundnuts, and there is no reason to expect them to be stable. In the last half of 1978, millet prices ranged from 8 to 13 PT per kora, while groundnut prices varied from LS 1.50 to LS 2.20 per guntar. In the first half of 1979, millet rose continuously to 23 PT, where it stayed until December; groundnuts reached LS 8 for a brief interval in August, dropping again at the harvest to LS 3.50–4.00. It is in part because of this instability that a duality persists in farming decisions; millet is

Table 4.20
Profits per hectare of Groundnuts and Millet if all Labor is hired, and Rate of Return

	Millet		Groundnuts	
	Low Yield	High Yield	Low Yield	High Yield
Harvest Value (LS)	36.80	55.20	64.67	129.33
Costs	34.01	41.31	36.76	43.78
Profit	2.79	13.89	27.91	85.55
Pre-Harvest Costs	17.61	17.61	29.74	29.74
Rate of Return[a]	16%	79%	94%	288%

a On the basis of pre-harvest input costs; that is, seed and labor

grown primarily for consumption, since it may become too expensive to buy. Groundnuts are considered the best chance for making money from agriculture at the present time, although millet can also be profitable. Farmers take these uncertainties into account, as well as their labor and cash resources, in determining how much of each crop to plant.

Orchards and Wadi Gardens

In addition to cultivation on open fields, people of this area use the clay soils of the wadi for the cultivation of vegetables and tree crops. Previous studies of the neighboring Fur (Barth 1967a; Hunting Technical Services 1977) stressed the importance of wadi cultivation in their agricultural economy, both as a means of producing export crops, and also as a dry season activity smoothing the labor cycle. For this reason, particular attention was given to wadi cultivation in the initial phase of the research, and the villages selected for study were partly chosen on the basis of the fact that they were approximately medial for the region in their access to cultivable wadi land. Further study indicated that wadi cultivation is a minor aspect of Masalit agriculture in the Masterei area, although it is important to small numbers of people. However, wadi cultivation is of greater importance for farmers along the major wadis of Dar Masalit, particularly in the south.

As mentioned above, rainy season gardens are planted after the first weeding of millet and groundnuts. This is partly because of the slight pause in field cultivation at this time, and partly because the wadi tends to ease in flow once the crops and grasses have grown enough to reduce the rate of runoff. Gardens planted earlier would be likely to be washed away.

In 1978, sixteen of thirty-one small sample families had wadi gardens in the rainy season; nine were planted by women, four by men, and three were joint. Rainy season gardens tended to be small, about 0.05–0.2 hectares; however, these small areas required considerable labor, because the soils were hard and the weeds were tall and thick by this time. Weeding a small plot took three days or more, depending on the soil as much as the size.

The major crop is okra, present in fifteen of the sixteen gardens; tomatoes and chilies are each grown in five gardens as well (table 4.7). These crops may be recent introductions; some older informants said they did not use them when they were young. It is possible that they existed, but that the demand for them has increased with the elimination of forest products and other supplements to the millet diet. Production was limited and I recorded no case of sales from a rainy season garden, although a few fresh vegetables were available at this time in the Buga market. Production was oriented to home use, and in this capacity, it saved a family money. However, in April 1979 only four families had okra remaining from gardens harvested six months earlier.

Wadi gardens cultivated in the dry season (*sawa:gi*) are of a different type. They must be irrigated, which requires digging a well, and they must be fenced, since animals are at large at this time. For this reason they are usually made by groups of people who share these labors, and divide up the land within the fence.

In 1979 they were begun in March, after the last threshing was finished and people had rested a bit. Of the thirty-one small sample families, nine had a dry season garden; five of these were made by adolescents (two boys, three girls), three by mothers jointly with one or more child, and one by a woman alone. Only three men in the sample villages had irrigated vegetable gardens. The gardeners each made a number of basins (10–50 in gardens of the small sample), one-half to one meter square, and a system of small canals by which they directed the water to each basin in succession. Every three or four days they spent the morning, or sometimes a full day, drawing water for their crops and pouring it through the canals. For the young, this was primarily a pleasant way to pass time with their friends, but in large gardens the work was tiresome. Gardens began to yield after about forty days, and continued until the rains came and the wadi washed them away. Thus, there were two to three months of production, depending on the timing of the rains.

Okra dominated in these gardens, and tomatoes and chilies were also popular. In addition, ankolib, green onions, pumpkin, radishes, and a cooking green called "*moloxiyya*" (*Corchorus olitorius*?) are grown.[12] As with the rainy season gardens, most crops were grown for home use, but sometimes a surplus was sold. The highest sales recorded were by a woman with forty-four basins who sold vegetables worth 10–20 PT twice per week, at the height of the season. In Buga and a few villages with particularly good situations for gardening, vegetables were produced on a larger scale by some people, and tomatoes and other crops were usually available by the box. Nevertheless, it was clear that wadi cultivation in this part of Dar Masalit did not approach the importance that it had for the Fur, and exports were limited.

Wadi land was also used for fruit trees, primarily mango, as well as guava and lemon. Mangos were brought to Masterei in the early 1940s by Amin Ahmed, a representative of the sultan living in Buga. He and other political notables established orchards, which continue to bear well at the present time. In the 1950s, a few residents of the sample villages planted mangos in the local wadi, but only one tree survived that decade. In the 1960s it appears that mangos began to fetch a good price, and were in demand by traders to export as far as Khartoum. Numerous young men of the villages again planted trees in the local wadis, and many of these were successful and are still bearing fruit. By the 1970s, little land was available and few additional trees were planted. However, at this time mango prices began to drop and the export market became somewhat reduced. It may be that areas nearer to Khartoum also responded to the high demand of the 1960s thus cutting off the Dar's market; in any event, Masterei farmers said that the quantity of mango exports in 1978 and 1979 was relatively low.

The major work in establishing an orchard is the watering while the trees take root. This must be done every day at first, then tapers off to once per week after about three years. Most owners interviewed said that they would not do it again, stressing the labor and the problems of continuously being present in the village for a period of years. In addition, thorn fences must be made to keep out livestock, and bushes for fences are no longer easily gathered. In spite of these efforts, about half of the trees are lost to animals, termites, the wadi, or other causes. However, a few owners with good locations are still planting, particularly lemon. Once the trees begin to bear fruit, after two to six years, there is little to be done except picking the fruit and, if there is enough, selling it. Since mangos bear in the dry season, there is little problem finding a few hours to pick and transport the fruit. Men usually pick their own trees, but in some families the children—the main beneficiaries—do this.

Forty-five people have trees in the village wadis, while twelve have trees in other villages (usually where they have other wives). Of these fifty-seven owners, three are women, who either purchased or inherited the trees. As shown in table 4.21, the ten largest owners have 71 percent of the mango trees, 34 percent of the guavas, and 67 percent of the lemons. Two men in this group have eighty and sixty-two mango trees, while the rest own 9–20 trees. Most holdings are small, and fourteen people have only one mango tree apiece.

Thus, for the majority of owners, fruit production is only sufficient for family consumption. Those with four or five trees may sell a box or two per week in the market at the peak of the season, earning LS 2–3 in total; many owners in this category leave the picking and selling to their children, who keep the money. However, among the large owners there is more income. Three men interviewed with nine or ten trees each earned LS 7–20 in the 1979 season, while the largest owner with eighty trees earned LS 220. Owners of this magnitude sell to merchants by the truckload, while small owners sell by the mango in the Buga market.

Table 4.21
Fruit Tree Ownership by Residents of the Sample Villages

	Mango	Guava	Lemon
Trees Owned by[a]			
All Villagers	357	82	30
Ten Largest Owners	252	21	20
Two Largest Owners	142	10	13
Mean Holdings of Ten Largest Owners	25.2	2.1	2.0
Mean Holdings of Other Owners	2.3	1.3	0.2

a These figures slightly overstate village tree ownership, because they are not weighted to reduce the contribution of men with second families outside the sample villages.

Thus, wadi cultivation takes various forms in Masterei agriculture. While it is clearly not as important as it is to the Fur, various people take advantage of wadi land to grow vegetables or fruit that add variety to their diet, and a few earn substantial income from fruit sales.

Summary

In the preceding sections, I have tried to describe Masalit agriculture as an economic activity, but I have given weight to various subjects according to my estimation of their relative importance in the overall socioeconomic system. Thus, the main crops, the main soils, and the main practices have been the focus of this section, but I have provided qualitative information about minor subjects to give an idea of their place in the system. This analysis provides a basis for comparing agriculture with other economic activities, and for understanding its role in subsistence, trade and ecological change. This section is also drawn upon in discussions of inequality and the changing social organization of the rural economy in chapter 5.

Livestock

The use and care of animals in Dar Masalit is easily as complicated as the agricultural system. There are several varieties of animals, each with special care requirements. They are used as savings, investments, sources of income, and luxuries; their labor has its season and a calculable return; and they are affected by market fluctuations, risks of loss, diseases and other factors. In addition, they play diverse roles in the economic strategies of the farmers and merchants of the Dar. Thus, understanding economic activities concerning livestock in this area requires at least as much study as field crop production. Sufficient data has been collected to show the rough outlines of asset and income distribution related to livestock, and to describe the roles of the various species in the local economy. Additional study would be extremely useful.

Domestic animals include cattle, sheep, goats, donkeys, horses, camels, chickens, dogs and cats. No quantitative data were collected on chickens, dogs and cats, but a few observations can be made.

Chickens are kept in perhaps one third of families, by men, women and children alike. They usually fend for themselves within the compound and are sometimes fed grain. An enclosure or shelter may be made for them, but is not required. Eggs are very rarely used by villagers; the purpose of keeping chickens is to raise more chickens, primarily to eat and occasionally to sell. A chicken was worth about 50 PT–LS 1.00 in 1979, but there were very few because a disease killed nearly every chicken in Masterei in February.

As for dogs, they are kept by approximately one-fourth of the families. They are primarily watchdogs, but a few are considered valuable hunters. They usually eat the leftovers of the family food, and few are fed enough to grow large. Cats are rare and are passed around among people with mice problems.

The numbers of other livestock are listed in table 4.22. Goats and sheep are listed together because they are often aggregated by villagers in giving information. (Based on my observations there are at least three times as many goats as sheep.) The transport animals—donkeys, camels and horses—are few compared to the herding animals. Goats and sheep are greater in number and are owned by the largest proportion of families; however, cattle predominate in terms of total economic value, for cattle are worth about six times as much as goats.

Table 4.22
Livestock owned by the Large Sample

	Number[a]	Percentage of Families Owning any
Species		
Cattle	549	66
Sheep and Goats	1035	79
Donkeys	115	52
Horses	20	26
Camels	30	21

a Animals owned by men with other wives outside the sample villages are given reduced weight proportionate to the ratio of wives in the sample to their total number of wives.

The various species play different roles in the local economy. Camels in the village herd are not reproductive and are used primarily for transport, although they increase in value as they grow. Horses are a luxury item, ridden by and almost always owned by men. They are the preferred means of travel, and have played an important role in the days of warfare. However, they are expensive to keep; the typical small horse will eat 2.5 kg of millet per day, which is comparable to the grain consumption of an average family, plus grass. A few large horses, apparently bred from stock brought to Darfur by the British, are present in Buga, and these easily consume three times as much. Horses also require expensive riding equipment, and a sword is considered an obligatory part of the accoutrements of the rider. A horse may increase in value as it grows, but it costs more to raise than it can return; thus, it is primarily a consumer item for the well off, especially those with surplus grain.

It is not surprising, then, that donkeys predominate as riding beasts. (They are also useful in hauling). Their food needs are considerably less than those of a horse, and they can be turned loose to graze during much of the year. Saddles and gear for a donkey are of the utmost simplicity, minimally, a gunny sack for its back and a heavy stick for communicating one's wishes. They also reproduce themselves and the offspring can be sold. However, as for all transport animals, building a herd is not the goal; only 5 percent of large sample families owned more than two donkeys, and the maximum number owned was four.

Cattle, goats and sheep are the main savings and investment media in this area. Livestock prices appear to have wide fluctuations; they more than doubled, and then subsided, in the course of 1979. In the drought years of the early 1970s, there was a glut of animals for sale, which depressed prices. However, the overall price trend, at least for the last twenty years, has been upward at a rate that appears to exceed the inflation rate. In addition, one can expect one's herd to increase, although there is always a risk of starvation, disease, theft and other loss factors.[13] In the case of cows and sometimes goats, one can also obtain an income from the sale of dairy products. Thus, owning livestock is an attractive form of savings and investment for the Masalit. It is also relatively accessible—only fourteen families in the large sample (eight percent) owned no animals at all. On the other hand, most animals are concentrated in few hands.

The labor involved in herding and milking varies according to the number of animals involved. As shown in table 4.23, over half of the small stock and cows are owned by 13 percent and 14 percent of the families, respectively; the other half are distributed thinly over the majority of the population. For the latter families, the herds in question are small, comprising up to six cattle and/or ten goats. However, animals from these small herds are frequently grouped into larger herds under the care of farmers living in bush camps or manuring fields, and sometimes they are entrusted to nomads.

Bush camps are small settlements outside of the main villages, at distances of ten minutes to two hours' walk. In 1979, forty-five of one hundred ninety families in the sample villages had bush camp dwellings in the rainy season, (ten of them occupied by one member only), and of these, 24 had been occupied through the dry season as well. These camps were primarily for the purpose of agriculture. Many were located in field areas that were a long commute from the village, often lacking water in the dry season, and so some people moved to them

Table 4.23
Distribution of Cattle, Sheep and Goats in the Large Sample, and Sizes of Family Herds

Herd or Flock Sizes	Number of Families	Percentage of Sample	Number of Animals	Mean Number
Goats and Sheep				
0	36	21	0	0
1–10	111	66	505	4.5
11–20	22	13	530	24.0
Total	169	100	1035	6.1
Cattle				
0	57	34	0	0
1–6	89	53	266	3.0
7–50	23	14	283	12.3
Total	169	100	549	3.2

seasonally. The rural location of these camps made them preferable for livestock, due to better grazing and the greater distance from the majority of village fields.

At any given time, some camp residents can be found in the process of manuring their fields, which requires penning a large herd onto the field at night over the course of several years. This is the usual reason for spending the dry season there. Few people have enough animals to manure their own fields, and so camp residents agree to tend livestock belonging to villagers, accumulating herds of 25–110 cows and 20–100 goats (based on interviews with owners of twenty-four manured fields).[14]

In 1979, the vast majority of village herding stock was being kept in camps by sixteen families manuring fields. Villagers usually kept riding beasts with them as well as a few goats or cows.[15] These were mostly kept within the compound, where they manured the jubraka. Large animals were tethered while goats or cows had a pen within the compound. Only one villager with numerous cows had a separate kraal next to his compound.

The herder usually gets the benefit of the milk as well as the manure. Although owners try to keep milk cows at home, herders negotiate for at least one milk cow when they accept animals. However, in the case of camps near the village, owners often go to milk their own cows, and in exchange they take over the herding from time to time. Most herding arrangements are made among relatives and friends, although owners of large herds may entrust some of their animals to Arab nomads who take them further afield, again keeping the milk.

Caring for livestock involves watering them, supervising their grazing, milking them, and occasionally tending to health problems. A fair amount of time also seems to be spent looking for lost animals. Horses and camels are grazed with some care, usually by an adult who tethers or hobbles them while carrying out other tasks nearby. For part of the year, goats, sheep, cattle and donkeys are usually set loose in the morning and find their own way home at night, especially those kept in villages. However, in the cultivation season after the first weeding is under way, usually in the second half of July, the fursha orders a drum beaten that signals that animals must be restricted. After this time, farmers can obtain damages from herders if animals damage their crops. The animals are not free to roam again until the millet harvest is nearly complete, when the drum is beaten again, approximately in mid–January. Thus, for approximately half of the year during which crops are vulnerable, herding is something of a problem, especially near the village where fields are dense. The number of animals in the camps increases in this period.

Grazing also varies with the season. No pasture is specifically set aside, and no hay is grown. Nevertheless, during the rains there is abundant fresh grass on nonfarm lands, and cows are said to give their best milk yields. After the harvest, millet stover is plentiful. However, after this and the dried grasses are gone, there is an annual period of near starvation while waiting for the rains to come. This is especially problematic near the villages where pasture is scarcest. The animals become weak; some starve, while others fall over cliffs in their dazed state, and many animals get lost as they wander about looking for food.

In June 1979, at a minor market where normally a handful of goats met the demand for meat, seven cows were slaughtered on the point of starvation. It was considered the responsibility of every man to slaughter any animals he found at the point of death, in order that the owner would be able to sell the meat. (Muslims cannot eat meat from unslaughtered animals). This duty was carried out with some frequency in this season.

It was obvious that there was insufficient grazing available, and Masalit usually blamed the increased numbers of Arab nomads for that. However, informants were also consistent in reporting that the absolute number of animals owned by Masalit (although probably not the number per capita) had risen over the last few decades. As previously noted, during this period the expansion of cultivated land reduced the available pasture. Whatever its origin, the shortage of grazing land has led to a seasonal cycle of herding labor. The work load involved in supervising animals becomes high before the rains as the animals are in danger of starvation, loss or accident, stays high while the animals threaten crops, and then is greatly reduced for a few months after the harvest.

Perhaps because much herding labor is required in the cultivation season, adults do not usually participate in herding stock. A man or a woman may help in watering the livestock, but when they are supervised it is usually by a boy or girl in the 9–16 year age range. In the case of small herds, a few children may herd together or take turns. The lack of children capable of herding is another reason that some animals are placed in camps, especially in the cultivation season. No adult would neglect his farming to herd. However, some men personally supervise animals in the late dry season, and they usually take them into relatively distant pastures.

Adults who are tending large herds, be they their own or others', have additional labors. Men usually take responsibility for guarding the animals. Many men sleep by the herds, warming themselves with a fire. The large logs required to burn all night must be brought from a distance. They must make a thorn fence for the animals, and move it every seven to ten days so they can manure the entire field; this requires several hours each time. They are also responsible for watching over the health and safety of the animals and informing the owner when they see a problem; they are liable to accusations of mismanagement. Many men complain about the fact that they have to be continuously present for three to five years while they manure the field, which interferes with travel for marketing or visiting, as well as labor migration. In addition, most men and women find the isolation and the distance from the village social life difficult.

However, the benefits are considerable. The income from milk can be substantial, but the fact that herders near the village let owners milk their animals indicates that it is not the main consideration. Increased yields of millet are the primary purpose of manuring.[16] The data do not permit a quantitative analysis of the returns to manuring labor, but the pattern is clear: labor over the course of the entire year is being invested in improving fields, which increases the marginal productivity of peak season labor. In addition, this process makes use of the labor of children to increase agricultural output, and the improvements made in the field continue after there are no children of appropriate age in the family. Thus, two forms of labor—dry season and children's—are used to enhance the returns to adult labor in the agricultural season.[17]

Women's work is also changed by camp life. As mentioned earlier, the gathering of wood, water and greens is usually easier in the camps, and this is appreciated. Women also play important roles in the tending of livestock. They may water the animals and herd them at times, but their most important labors are probably milking, which some men do, and making butter, which is exclusively female. These are, of course, also done by women with milk cows in or near the villages. Milking takes approximately five minutes per cow, and is done once per day while a calf is nursing, twice thereafter. A herd of thirty cattle may have three to six lactating females in it, and, if they are next to the house, milking is quickly done; for village women with a cow or two in a nearby camp, the process may take 30–60 minutes including travel. In November 1979, I recorded milk yields of 0.9–1.1 liter per cow per milking, but this was generally considered half of the best yields of the rainy season.

Some milk is consumed whole, especially in the camps when it is abundant, but most of the milk is used to make clarified butter (*samn*). Butter is preferred to oil by many people, and it can be readily sold, especially due to the town and export markets for it. To produce butter, 4–6 liters of milk are placed in a gourd suspended by leather ropes from a frame or sunbreak. The milk is churned with repeated, sharp shakes for 45–60 minutes. The butter is accumulated from three to five churnings until there is enough for a bottle. Then, it is heated—sometimes with an onion—until it clarifies. A bottle of butter requires approximately four hours of labor, compared to 5.5 hours for a bottle of oil. It is also worth more, 75 vs 60 PT, and the buttermilk is worth approximately as much as the butter itself. Some men claim a portion of the income of the cows belong to them, but others leave it all to their wives, with the understanding that it should mostly be spent on food for the household. Thus, the production of butter is a fairly well paid labor for those women who own cows or have access to cows, especially compared to beer or oil making.

Livestock are significant elements in the export economy as well. Animals were collected as taxes in the precolonial period, and were the basis of most tax assessments in colonial and post-independence periods; owners have been expected to raise more cash than others, if necessary by selling some of their animals. Animals have been purchased by townspeople to feed traders, soldiers and the political elite in Geneina at least since 1922. The urban demand for meat increased with the growth not only of Geneina, but also of small towns such as Buga, where merchants, police, civil servants and local elites added to the demands of local people.

In addition, itinerant livestock traders regularly buy animals for export to El Fasher, Nyala or Chad as well as Geneina. Traders prefer large males of all species for export, because they travel better, which has led to a depletion of these, and an increase in their price relative to other animals. (Elders speaking of festive or religious celebrations in the past during which animals were slaughtered almost always specify 'big' bulls and rams, but currently cows and young males are often consumed at these times.) The export market for animals, as well as for animal products such as hides and butter, has probably contributed to the maintenance of high values for livestock.

All informants considered the absolute numbers of animals to have risen over the course of this century.[18] Based on interviews with thirteen men concerning the period 1925–1950, at that time the distribution of livestock was comparable to the present one in shape: many people had five to twenty cows, a few had fifty or more, and a few had none. However, better data are needed to estimate the relative inequality, as well as the ratio of livestock to humans or to cultivated area, in the past for comparison with the present.

Due to the greater dangers of theft and wild animals in the past, adults herded in that period, so herding may have been a choice which involved some neglect of agriculture. Livestock diseases were much more widespread, and veterinary services are considered by many to be the reason for increased livestock numbers. However, grazing and water were also more plentiful. As described in the last chapter, grazing and even water have been under considerable pressure in recent years, due to the increased population of people and animals, the expansion of cultivated land at the expense of forest, and reduced rainfall. Thus, while the livestock health has been improved, in terms of disease, their nutritional situation has become more difficult.

Clearly, economic activities involving livestock are diverse and complicated. Horses, camels and donkeys can be ridden, which is a form of consumption, but camels are also used in hired hauling while donkeys are used in transporting family crops or goods. Cows and sometimes goats can provide an income through sales of dairy products. All of the species provide a reasonably secure form of savings, by maintaining their value in the face of inflation, and possibly increasing in number or size. Finally, livestock play a vital role in improving the soils that feed the expanding population. Although the direct contribution of milk and meat to the total caloric intake of most Masalit is relatively small, animals are a crucial element of the local economy.

Manufacturing and Service Activities

Although the Masalit are farmers and everyone in the sample villages cultivates, there are many other specializations, both in manufacturing and service activities, which are economically important. The importance of beer, which is regularly brewed for sale by at least thirty-five of the one hundred eighty-four women in the sample villages, has already been discussed. In addition, women sometimes sell oil, roasted nuts, kisra, kawal, or food covers; but the combined importance of these is much less than that of beer for village women. Most other manufacturing and service activities are carried out by men. Some examples of activities that require little money are discussed first, and then two new specializations with higher capital requirements are considered.

Low Capital Activities

A wide variety of specialized tasks requiring little capital are carried out by members of the sample. These are listed in table 4.24 with the number of ever-married men currently engaged in each activitity for money. Of one hundred seventeen men present, fifty-two performed one or more of these activities for cash in the fieldwork period. Others have some skills but did not use them. In addition, boys and young men are active in some crafts or service activities. For them and for some men, nonagricultural work of this sort is an occasional source of spending money. However a number of men, usually with several specializations, are dependent on these activities for cash to meet family needs. Several of these activities are seasonal; for example, bushels are in demand just before the harvest, and straw mats are made around January when the grass is available. Those that are not seasonally determined tend to be done in the dry season, when time is available. If one needs cash in the rains, agricultural labor usually pays better than any of these crafts. However, when Ramadan falls in the rainy season, many men spend the afternoons on some physically undemanding craft, after working in the fields in the morning.

Table 4.24
Numbers of Males engaged in Various Manufacturing and Service Occupations in the Sample Villages

	Numbers of Men Involved: Ever-Married[a]	Never-Married
Low Capital Occupations		
Tanning Goat Skins	18	4
Tanning Cowhides	9	
Making Leather Goods (rope etc.)	8	
Carving Wooden Goods	13	
Religious Specialization (*faki*)	13	
Making Hemp Rope	11	
Making Saddle Girths	7	
Making Grass Mats (*ʃarganiyya*)	6	
Making Sleeping Mats (*fanga*)	6	
Butchering	5	
Making Bushels (*re:ka* or *domayya*	4	
Making Skullcaps (*tagiyya*)	3	
Making Doors	2	7
Being Sheikh	2	
Giving Injections	2	
Making Horse Saddles	1	
Making Baskets or Hats	1	
Making Sheaths for Knives	1	
Making Cloth	1	
Making Mattresses	1	
High Capital Occupations		
Tailoring	5	
Transport	18	5

a N = 117, unweighted for polygyny and excluded absentees

Most nonagricultural occupations require little training, but to be a feki, a sheikh or a saddlemaker requires some special knowledge. Saddlemaking is quite profitable since these craftsmen are few, and the one in the sample charges apprentices (from elsewhere) LS 4.00 to learn to make saddles. The fekis also work hard and pay money to receive their training, although this is not mainly for the purpose of acquiring a profitable skill; genuine piety seems to be more common. The most respected ones have been studying with many teachers since childhood, and some have made the pilgrimage to Mecca. As for the two sheikhs in the villages, one has been to school, and both are sufficiently literate and mathematically competent to carry out tax collection as well as other administrative duties. Again, the money is only part of the motivation to become a sheikh.

The other occupations in this category can be learned free of charge by anyone with the interest. The 'clean' occupations, such as woodcarving, basketry, and ropemaking, are commonly carried out in one of the village masiks (*masi:k*, a cleared area used for prayer as well as other male gatherings), where the craftsmen chat; the techniques are visible to all. Similarly many tanners work side by side in a special place near the wadi, where they share equipment and conversation with each other and help newcomers. Thus, many specialists, when asked how they learned a skill, merely stated: "I watched, then I did it."

Since it is not practical to discuss each occupation in detail, a few of the most important and illustrative ones found in Masterei are described:

TANNING. By far the most popular of the low-capital occupations is tanning, done by twenty-two men and boys in the large sample. All twenty-two tan goat skins, while nine of these also tan cowhides, and eight make leather goods from the tanned cowhides. Some of these men also tan on order in a manner that preserves the animal's hair on the hide, and some also have a technique for preparing oiled hides. Most of the hides are simply tanned and sold to traders who export them to Geneina, and from there to West Africa or Khartoum. Darfur produces a large number of untanned, dried hides, which are usually exported to Europe, but it seems that the tanned hides of Dar Masalit largely supply Sudanese and West African shoemakers. Sudanese leather slippers made from these hides (*marku:b*) are considered part of the male national costume, and the market is quite large in urban areas. They are too costly for most villagers, however, who usually wear plastic shoes or thongs.

Hides were used in the nineteenth century for clothing, bags, shields, and sandals (Kapteijns 1985:27) and were exported across the Sahara from the sultanate of Wadai (Cordell 1977). Tanning is done using local materials and a process that predates colonial occupation. The chemical processes are potent, and the hands of tanners tend to be thickly calloused and cracked, with fingernails broken and stained. For simple tanned goat skins, the process is as follows. After buying fresh hides from the butchers, one soaks them overnight in a caustic solution made with ashes from the Sihab tree (*siha:b, Anogeissus leiocarpus* or *A. schimperi*). The hair is then scraped off and the skins are washed and placed in a softening solution called *ᶜaffa:na*, ("rottenness"), made from the leaves of the usher bush (*uʃar, Calatropis procera*). After one half to one day, the skins are placed in a solution of pulverized *garad* (*Acacia arabica*) seed-pods in water and worked. This solution is changed two or three times over one to three days with continued working. Finally, the skins are removed, washed in very hot water and spread to dry; in the course of drying, the skins are folded and beaten for a few minutes, then respread and stretched, four or five times. This final step is particularly laborious if one is tanning several skins.

Equipment costs for tanning goat skins are minimal, since the mortars and pestles are shared and the vessels are often castoffs. One needs to have the money to buy raw skins at an average of 40 PT, and garad that costs about 5–10PT/skin. One also must gather the wood for ashes. Overall, tanning four skins costs about LS 1.90 in raw materials, uses permanent equipment worth LS 1.00, and requires ten hours of labor, not counting the time spent buying and selling the skins. The selling price of the tanned hides is about twice their raw price. Thus, the return to labor for tanning is approximately LS 1.30 per day. At this rate, it is not surprising that it is so popular. However, as one of the tanners pointed out, it is poor man's work; with all the foul smells and pain, he only does it because he is in need. Returns also are less in the dry season, when the harvest is complete and the groundnut money is spent. At that time tanners are most active and profit margins drop.

Cowhides are processed by a similar technique, but they use larger containers, longer soaking and drying times, and additional steps with a tar called "*butra:n*" extracted from melon seeds. Most men who tan cowhides also produce some goods from them, such as leather rope, stirrup ropes, hobbles for horses and camels, or feedbags. The labor input (three or four days) is spread over two to three weeks, in which one's money is tied up in the cost of the skin (LS 4–5), and the chemicals; most tanners cannot afford to do this, and so they process far more goat skins than cowhides. At September 1979 prices, income for making rope was about LS 1.00 per day. However, high prices occasionally obtain. In November a man could earn LS 3.00 per day's labor by tanning and making rope. Sudden price fluctuations such as this are common in the small Masterei market, and tend to profit those with some money to invest—even those, as in this case, doing "poor man's work."

CARVING. Thirteen men make objects from local woods, including donkey saddles, mortars for pounding grain, throwing sticks, writing slates, bed frames, and stools. At least the last two of these are introduced needs, probably of the last century, but all of these objects may be made by the same carvers. Wooden bowls were more commonly used in the past and had specialists of their own. In general, the work of carving involves searching for the right species of tree with the right shape for a particular object, and cutting it out with an axe. For most objects the tree is not killed, according to my informants. The luck of the search had much to do with the time required; if one is willing to make a variety of products, or keeps in mind many possibilities from previous searches, this effort can be reduced. Once cut out, the object is shaped with axe, adze or chisel (equipment worth less than LS 1.00) into the desired form, and in some cases further assembled. Over a wide variety of products and carvers, the average return to carving work was 66 PT/day, not counting marketing time.

FEKI. There are thirteen fekis in the large sample. The feki (*faki:*, from Arabic *faqi:H*) is a religious specialist who, in the course of his religious studies, has acquired certain skills with economic value. He may have one or several pounds worth of sacred books as well, and his personal reputation also has considerable importance in determining his income. Fekis can play a role in political events or dispute settlement, and one may be the village imam, who maintains the mosque and presides at prayer on religious holidays. The fekis are called upon by individuals or groups on many occasions. At a funeral, a feki may be asked to preside over a recitation of the Qur'an, or a set of litanies. Fekis may be called in for curing, to protect the village from locusts, or to curse a thief who has not been caught. Most commonly, fekis are asked to prepare hijabs (*Hija:b*, amulet of written talismans from sacred scripture) or mahayas (*maHa:ya*). A mahaya is prepared by writing prayers or texts on a board with an ink of soot and water, and washing the writing into a water solution each time the board is full. The water is drunk or otherwise applied. They are prepared for protection from illness, accidents or weapons, to increase fertility, to make someone loved, and for many other reasons.

Mahayas and services are not exactly sold, but a feki is given a donation that has some relationship to his labor and degree of training. One man regularly writes the simple "bismalla"—"by the name of God, the Merciful, the Compassionate"—twelve thousand times; this limited task, which takes him about four days, earns him a donation of about LS 2.00, or 50 PT per day. A more learned feki, who has made the pilgrimage, has a number of mahayas that he can write. He is usually given LS 1.00 or more per day. One feki, who presided over a recitation of the Qur'an at a wake, received LS 2.70 in donations, but this is not a frequent occurrence. The fekis do not earn a great deal of money, but their occupation is prestigious and satisfying. Most fekis are disdainful of trade and other highly capitalized work; they consider riding a camel inconsistent with their piety and humility. Modest consumption and comfort levels are part of the image of the feki. Perhaps this is general in Sudan; it is interesting that the Sudanese plural of feki is not the standard Arabid *fuqaHa:* ', but rather *fugara:* ' (poor men).

HEMP ROPE. Making hemp rope is another common craft, practiced by eleven men in the sample villages. The plant used is *karkang* (*Sansevieria sp.*?), which grows wild and may also be planted around the edge of the compound. It is soaked in wet dirt or scraped to remove the bark, which is twisted into ropes. Once bark is removed, one can make two ropes per day, for an income of about 60 PT per day's labor plus the time of marketing.

BUTCHERING. Five men in the sample are butchers. These men go to market one to three times per week and buy animals, then slaughter them and sell the parts and the skin. In addition to knowing how to butcher an animal, they must be able to judge the meat on a goat or cow before they buy it, as it is their own money they are putting at risk.

Butchering is considered somewhat disreputable, and is almost exclusively the domain of drinkers in Masterei. This is probably due to the high demand by drinkers for meat on market days, and the aversion of the pious to dealing with them; it is also likely that the drinkers make life difficult for any non-drinker who tries to join them. Typically, a butcher slaughters one to four goats per market day, with a profit varying from nothing to LS 2.00 per goat. A butcher in the small sample, over the course of a year, averaged an income of LS 1.01 per market day.

OTHER CRAFTS. The numerous other activities practiced by a few specialists in the sample are usually comparable in income to the above. Manufacturers of articles, such as bushels, doors, skullcaps, and sleeping mats, earn 60 PT–LS 1.00 per day's labor, not counting marketing time. The least practiced crafts, such as basketry or sheath making, have very low returns of about 30 PT per day. Thus, they tend to be done for diversion, very occasionally, by very few people. One of these poorly-paid crafts, weaving cloth, deserves special mention for its historical importance.

Formerly, weavers clothed the people, producing strips of rough cotton that were sewn into garments. This cloth was used for trade, taxes and tribute as well. Nowadays, only one old man in the sample villages weaves, while a few other old former weavers sit by and watch. The cloth now has only one specialized use, as the lining of the leather covers of horse saddles. Clothing is currently made of Pakistani cotton, Japanese and Korean polyester, and other mostly imported fabrics.

Another economic activity that has been formerly of much greater importance is that of locust charming (Kapteijns 1985:28). Protection of crops is now largely in the feki's hands. Other charming, divination and magic are also much reduced (though specialists still exist) except insofar as they have been incorporated into an Islamic idiom. Herbalists still practice, but they are few and probably reduced in number from precolonial times.

The sample villages do not include several other crafts and services that still are of some importance. Blacksmiths and potters are the men and women respectively of a despised caste in Dar Masalit. They include both Masalit and non-Masalit speakers. My informants are divided concerning whether a smith could actually be a Masalit. They live throughout the area in villages or quarters of their own. They are of considerable importance in the economy as providers of agricultural and cooking tools, and to some extent still, of weapons. Currently, many of them simply farm and do not practice their traditional crafts; since smiths no longer have to smelt the iron, this activity does not require a large communal effort, as it used to. But many smiths and potters are still active and seem to make an income comparable to other low-capital crafts (compare Doornbos 1984a).

SUMMARY. The distribution of people over occupations appears to be very responsive to the going rate for these crafts, in that the most popular occupations are the best paid, while the least popular are the worst paid. If one looks beyond the individual decision, it is clear that the prices of various manufactures and services are largely determined by their place in the larger economy. Locally consumed goods, such as carved objects, bushels etc., have a limited demand if the price goes up very much, due to the general shortage of money locally. However, hides have an external market, and are relatively high in price. Likewise, leather goods are mostly used by those involved in transport, so the increase in the export trade has also raised the demand and thus the price.

There are some features in common among the crafts discussed so far. They have low capital requirements—about LS 1 in equipment, and zero to LS 5 in 'variable capital'—which is not to say these requirements are insignificant. Many craftsmen described seasonal price fluctuations for their goods; the relative abundance of money after the harvest appeared to increase local demand while reducing the supply of manufactures. Income to labor, defined as actual work at about ten hours per day, was approximately 60–100 PT/day for most tasks in the post-harvest season of 1979; at the prices estimated for the middle of the dry season, income was closer to 40–70 PT/day. Irregular price fluctuations were also common. Those with several skills and money for inputs took advantage of the most profitable opportunities at any given time.

Tanning was the craft with the highest income, about LS 1.00 in the dry season and 1.30 after the harvest. This was perhaps a reflection of the unpleasant nature of the task, and also of the relatively high amount of cash required to buy raw skins and chemicals. Since the tanners were almost always poor, the few pounds needed was a serious constraint.

Besides low prices, other factors limit the income that these craftsmen can make. First, since there are many specialists, sales or orders are spread rather thinly, except in the brief periods of high seasonal demand for certain goods. Most craftsmen carry out less than one day's craft labor per week. Second, the labor for many of these tasks cannot be carried out intensively, but rather involves periods of waiting. This is especially true of tanning. Third, in most cases much time is taken up with marketing. Unless one is working on order, one must go to Buga and sit with one's wares on display; they may or may not be purchased. For tanning, one must also go to seek out raw skins at a reasonable price; many tanners return with less than a full batch of four or five, and so must tan at a lower profit margin and lower total income for the process. And fourth, in the case of butchers, the price of meat is administered by the rural council, while the price of livestock is not. Their profit margin, therefore, reflects their ability to influence the political process.

High Capital Activities

Two occupations in the villages studied stand out from those discussed above due to their higher capital requirements and higher incomes. These are tailoring and transport. Five men own sewing machines and make clothing; two of these are also merchants, while none of them perform any low-capital activity. Of the eighteen men who work camels in transport, only three do any low-capital activity at all. Thus, this group is rather distinct from the craftsmen. Their occupations hold a key position in bridging the gap between villagers and the world market, and they receive high incomes in consequence.

TRANSPORT. In the sample villages, eighteen men with families regularly work transporting goods by camel. Fourteen own their camels, while four camels belong to fathers, a wife's father, and a sister's husband. Two unmarried young men do a little transport work; three camels are used occasionally by children of their owners, and a few other men also know how to use camels and may borrow one from time to time, giving the owner a share of the profits. However, in this section I am concentrating on the eighteen regular transport workers. Camels are also owned by six merchants who use them only for their own commercial goods; these are to be considered below. Two men own camels solely as investment livestock; one of these uses his from time to time to transport his own crops, while the other "doesn't even ride it," as his brother complained.

Camels are fairly new to the Masterei area, and were first owned in numbers by Masalit in the 1960s. With desiccation, the area became healthier for camels, while the increase in trade made transport work a profitable occupation. Deforestation also made the transport of forest products from distant bush a very important job.

The Masalit do not breed camels, but buy them from their Arab neighbors. All camels in the village are male except one sterile female, because the Arabs rarely sell breeding stock. Most of the camels are bought about two years old, and they are broken in with small loads soon afterward. They are able to carry a load of 200 kg after about their fifth year of age, increasing to as much as 300 kg by age ten. They frequently live more than twenty years. Fifteen of the eighteen camels worked in transport are in the 200–300 kg load range.

Camels increase in value as they grow. In 1979, five men bought two year olds for LS 75–100, while fully grown camels were worth LS 400–500.[19] Camel prices have also increased over time; for example, young camels in the late 1960s cost LS 8–10.

In addition to the costs of the camel, transport workers must have leather ropes, pads and saddles worth about LS 12. The care of camels is fairly easy and inexpensive; they are tied out or hobbled to graze, and are fed millet worth about LS 1.00 per month. They must be guarded from thieves, however, and occasionally treated for sores or other problems. They should get enough work to keep fit, but overwork can reduce their weight and value.

There are three main jobs that these jammala (*jamma:la*, camel workers) perform: local transport, long distance transport, and wood cutting. Local transport is seasonal, since the majority of this work is the transport of people's threshed millet from their fields to their homes, or groundnuts from their stores to market. In some ways this is a newly needed job, for in the past people built their villages where land was available and farmed near their homes. Now, with large permanent villages and scattered fields, transport is more difficult. Payment is in kind for millet transport, approximately 5 percent for a typical one hour haul; at November 1979 prices, the owner of a grown camel could earn approximately LS 3.50 transporting millet in a full day.

Bringing wood to market is a more continuous source of work for jammala. Buga women cannot find wood nearby, and thus must buy it constantly; there is always a strong demand, and selling wood takes very little time. Cutting a load can be done in two hours in outlying areas; thus, this job is particularly easy for those who live in the bush settlements. A load of wood brings LS 1.50–1.70 in Buga; counting two hours transport time, labor is repaid at a rate of LS 4.00 per day. Several wood haulers also cut and bring building materials on order, at a similar rate of return.

Twelve of the jammala also transport over longer distances, primarily between Buga and Geneina. This is especially profitable in the rainy season when the roads are washed out for three or four months, and lorry traffic is stopped, but they work all year long. The jammala travel in caravans of five to twenty, including people of other villages and usually one or more merchants. They leave in late afternoon and usually travel until midnight, sleeping outside Geneina; they enter the city by morning and leave in the afternoon, sleep on the way, and arrive home the next morning. This is done with good spirit and friendship, but it is also recognized as hard work, and in the rains it interferes with agricultural activities as well. Ideally, a camel worker is hired to carry a full load each way, groundnuts or millet to Geneina, and sugar and other trade goods returning. In total, he can make LS 10 or more in the rainy season, and about LS 7.00 in the dry season when he competes with the lorries. In addition, nine of the jammala who transport over long distances increase their incomes by small trade that exploits price differences; this is discussed in the next section.

Thus, hauling provides a fairly high income per labor day expended, about LS 3.50–5.00. The timing of this income is also beneficial. While throughout the year, jammala can earn LS 3.00 per week for less than one day's labor—by bringing two loads of wood to market, for example—they can actually earn larger amounts of money in the rains, when most other crafts are in little demand. In the harvest season, when others are selling their groundnuts to raise money, jammala can live on their income from hauling, and then market their groundnuts later when prices rise. They also save the cost of hauling their own crops, and they can take their groundnuts to the Geneina market themselves to sell them for the best price. Added to these factors is the value of camels as an investment, and as a preferred means of transporting oneself in the sandy trails of Dar Masalit. With these advantages, it is not surprising that only three jammala practice any low-capital activity at all, and these three—a butcher, a giver of injections, and a feki—do not depend on those occupations to any significant extent.

TAILORING. The five tailors in the sample villages sew garments by order on pedal-operated machines. Two tailors keep their machines in Buga, and go in to sew every day if they have orders. Two who are also traders work mostly in their homes, and sometimes take their machines to the Buga market. The fifth tailor only works on market days. All of them learned to sew by apprenticeships in the town of the Nile Valley, as did almost all Masterei tailors. Indeed, tailoring is one of the target occupations for Masalit migrants, and my observations in Khartoum and Gedaref indicate that Masalit comprise a substantial proportion of the tailors of eastern Sudan. In 1979, thirteen emigrants from the sample villages were tailors, and in addition two nonworking tailors were in the village temporarily for family reasons, anxious to get back to their jobs in the East.

The five locally active tailors were able to buy sewing machines and return to Dar Masalit some time after completing their training, and they were pleased with the economic rewards to their trade in the Dar. They said that the income was lower than in the cities, but costs were also low, and they were able to farm or engage in trade as well. It was also easier for them to meet their familial obligations, and they were glad to be in the company of their kin and friends.

Four tailors brought their machines from the east over ten years ago, while one bought his locally seven years ago. They paid LS 20–40 for used machines; new ones were priced at about LS 60 then. In 1979, I was told that new machines cost over LS 300, and a used machine could not be found for under LS 100. This price increase was roughly in keeping with inflation. The cost of scissors and other tools raises the current value of a tailor's equipment to at least LS 110. In addition, the tailor pays for licenses, lubricants, thread, and occasionally rental of a workplace, totaling LS 40–50 per year, plus a replacement mechanism costing LS 14 every three or four years (due perhaps to the abundant sand). Thus, tailoring is a fairly costly operation in local terms.

However, the income is also quite high. In terms of returns to labor based on a ten hour day, as assumed for previous activities, tailors earn LS 3–10.00 per day, depending on their skills. As with the low-capital occupations, they do not get as many orders as they would like except in certain seasons—notably the days before the religious holidays, and the days of the groundnut harvest. In those periods, these tailors earned LS 13–25 per week. But even in the rains when people have little money, they can earn LS 2–5.00 per week, and still have plenty of time for their farming. They do spend some idle time in the market, but they try to arrange to work while they are there taking orders. Thus, minimally they can maintain an income that comfortably meets their families' cash needs, while in good times they can accumulate considerable savings. As I sat with one tailor, he pointed out his second wife, his large compound, and his livestock, saying with pleasure: "These are all from my machine." It is no wonder that tailors sometimes seem rather solicitous of their sewing machines.

SUMMARY. The high-capital occupations are not available to everyone; they require in excess of LS 100, and tailoring also requires considerable training. The returns to this outlay are substantial. Both tailors and transport workers are well paid by comparison with the low-capital craftsmen. They have a higher rate of return to labor hours expended, and they also spend little time in marketing or in processes that require idle waiting. Both produce a sufficient year-round income to comfortably provide for family consumption, while in certain seasons producing high income, which can be saved or invested.

However, most of these men are not using their investments to begin a cycle of accumulation. Even though several are small traders, the purpose of their trade is primarily to make money for consumption, and for savings in the form of livestock. They frequently say they work for "the cup of tea" (*kuba:ya ʃay*), the symbol of all imported consumer goods. They hire some labor as well but on a small scale, to reduce their workload and that of their families. Thus, as consumers, the aspirations and structural positions of most of them in the Masalit economy resemble those of low-capital craftsmen. Their incomes are higher, but they are not directly transforming the social organization of production.

Nevertheless, the jammala and tailors play essential roles in this transformation. Furthermore, in so far as their occupations are the processing or transport of exported or imported goods, and depend on the income that people get from producing export goods, their interests, like those of merchants, are in an expanded market participation by the region. Indeed, two of the tailors and several camel owners are merchants, deeply involved in the commercialization of village life. The special features of merchants are discussed next.

Trade

Trade in Dar Masalit is carried out by a wide range of people, from small traders in fruits and greens to large merchants who accumulate and export agricultural produce. These activities form a continuum with many common features, but there are important differences between small and large-scale operations. Twenty-nine males are identified as sabbabis (*sabba:bi*, 'one who gives a reason') or small traders; these include the nine jammala who also trade, mentioned in the section on transport, and several unmarried men or boys. Some Buga women work in small trade and have regular places in the center of the market, but no women in the sample villages do so. In addition to these sabbabis, sample villages include eight merchants (*ta:jir*). Two of these carry out the bulk of their trading activities in other villages where they are also married. All of these eight are considered merchants by villagers, but only five identified themselves as such; two refused to give any economic information, while the other stated that he is merely a sabbabi. His activities are such that he is more easily discussed with the merchants, but he differs from them in one important respect: he engages in trade ultimately not to increase his trading operation, but rather to raise cash to emigrate temporarily from Sudan.

History of Trade

The role of trader in the open market has been taken on by village Masalit primarily in the last thirty years, at least in the Masterei area. In the precolonial period, Dar Masalit participated in long-distance trade, but this was administered by the furshas and the Fur overlords, and later by the sultan. Rhinoceros horn, ivory and ostrich feathers had to be turned over to local authorities, while goods such as sugar, imported cloth and firearms were restricted to the elite, by sumptuary laws as well as cost (for this and the following, see Kapteijns and Spaulding 1982; Kapteijns 1985). Foreign merchants traded with local elites for these goods and for slaves, which were both locally used and exported, but commoners had little to do with the long-distance trade directly.

Local or regional trade was taxed and protected by authorities, but was not administered like the long-distance trade. Grain, livestock and dairy products, salt from Jabal Marra and the Mahamid to the northwest, spun cotton, and a few long-distance imports such as beads, incense and spices circulated among commoners, largely by barter at market places throughout the area (Nachtigal 1971:201–204, 253). Nomads also participated in these markets. At this level, exchange rates were set by local authorities for the major commodities, and a number of these performed the main functions of money. Grain, thread, salt, cloth, and livestock all served as "media of exchange, measures of value, and stores of wealth" (Kapteijns 1985:34).[20] Foreign currencies, such as Maria Theresa thalers or Spanish dollars, were used by big traders and the elite in the larger markets of Wadai and Dar Fur, but their use by commoners was extremely limited and they did not function as money in the local economy (Nachtigal 1971:125, 135, 253). Thus, the situation was that commodities were used as money, while currencies were treated like commodities.

In the typology of Paul Bohannan and George Dalton the market was peripheral; "that is, the institution of the market place is present, but the market principle does not determine acquisition of subsistence or the allocation of land and labor resources" (1962:2–3). Only the elite depended on the market, for their incomes and for goods that were prohibited to the commoners. Thus, these goods and the cash to buy them did not form a sphere for the commoners in the sense of Bohannan and Dalton; it was the population, not the goods, that was divided into two parts for marketing purposes. While the commoners were the source of the wealth of the elites, because they provided them with the goods that could be traded for money or imports, they did not participate on the basis of the market exchange principle; rather, they did what they were forced or obliged to do. Although their lives were affected by the market activities of the elite, very few Masalit had any direct contact with money or the market in precolonial time.

In George Dupre and Pierre-Philippe Rey's (1973) critique of Bohannan and Dalton, they argued that force, specifically through colonial occupation, was needed to break this sort of peripheral relationship of highly autonomous societies to the market. However, although the colonial occupation was certainly based on force, there was little change in this pattern of market activities for some time. The resident, R.B. Broadbent, wrote in the 1932 Annual Report (Darfur 1/34/175) of the commoners that they "have not yet learnt to spend money. They clothe themselves in homespun and do not purchase sugar or tea; money obtained in the Geneina market is hoarded for the tax collector." (One wonders if he would have been happier had the money not been saved for taxes!) P.J. Sandison, in the 1934 Report (Darfur 1/34/175) stated that "native life" was still firmly on a barter standard. In 1938, E.A.V. de Candole reported that the life of the Masalit was that of a self-sufficient community, depending on millet and the "meagre produce of its scantily nourished cattle, sheep and goats" (Darfur 1/34/185). In his 1939 report, he stated that "coffee, tea, sugar and factory-made cloth are still luxuries to the mass of the inhabitants.[21]

However, while the majority of the population was maintaining a local orientation, the local elite and the population of Geneina—including a garrison of Sudanese troops, West African and Sudanese traders, and employees and dependents of the government bureaucracy—were consuming sugar, imported cloth, firearms, and other luxury goods. In 1924, the resident Reginald Davies reported of Geneina (Darfur 3/3/24) "those who formerly wore homespun now call for Manchester goods. Tea, coffee, sugar and other foods are craved for by people who had barely tasted any of them a few years ago." Sandison (Darfur 3/3/24) described a divided economy in 1934; he estimated that the government enclave spent LS 8500 annually on trade goods, while the entire countryside spent a maximum of LS 1000.

Thus, a divided economy persisted at least into the first two decades of colonial rule. The reason is not hard to see. Commoners were obliged to participate in the cash economy, as elsewhere, by taxation, which was a substantial drain on local resources (Kapteijns 1985; and see next section). Because of the existence of a local market for grain and livestock, in the form of the garrison, and the availability of local wage work for building roads (albeit largely conscripted) the Masalit had local sources of cash and could meet their obligations. However, beyond supplying the government enclave there was little market for export goods, and probably little possibility of producing any additional surplus. Sandison and Candole both commented on the low level of exports in the 1930s. Thus, the amount of cash available to farmers was limited to the amount that the enclave had to spend. Most of this was then returned to the enclave as taxes.

Thus, as Kapteijns points out: "Cash remained a commodity, not money in the conventional sense of the word" (1985:233). Such resources as could be mobilized to produce cash, which had the specific purpose of paying taxes, were sold; little remained to circulate and contribute to local monetization. Some commoners bought some sugar and cloth, but the high level of taxation, low export prices and poor communications left little possibility for substantial export and import trade. Perhaps sumptuary rules also continued to operate to limit the purchase of imported goods. In addition, the government's policy of discouraging small traders who "roam about in the closed areas," only issuing licenses to "persons of good repute with a capital of not less than LE 50" maintained the gap between the common people and the world market (Darfur 3/3/23).

Annual Reports were terminated in 1940 and few local documents exist for the succeeding period, but informants indicated that this situation persisted, at least in Masterei, through the 1940s. However, during the war the stationing of American troops in Geneina, one of the chain of airports across the sub-Saharan colonies of the allies, increased the prices and demand for livestock in Geneina and may have yielded some cash surplus. (The Americans are particularly remembered for their fondness for horses.) In the postwar years there was an influx of trade goods such as coarse cotton and sugar, which had been rationed during the war by the colonial government.[22] Perhaps due to improved communications, there developed a market for various export crops, such as sesame, hibiscus, spices, and, most importantly for Masterei, groundnuts.

In the 1950s, Masalit and other traders started operations in Buga. Cash began to play a more important role in meeting consumption needs, as standards of food and clothing changed to include imported cloth, tea and sugar. Although still limited largely to the sphere of taxes, exports and imports, cash was also used locally to purchase meat and livestock from other Masalit. Over the following years, Masalit have increasingly become participants in the cash economy. It was this participation that supported the development of traders and merchants as fundamental agents in the current Masalit economy, both benefiting from and accelerating the process of monetization.

Market Structure

Currently, a well-developed private trading network permeates Dar Masalit, handling substantial amounts of imports and exports. In Geneina, the market operates every day, but in Masterei Monday and Friday are the main market days. On these days, people come from the surrounding villages and camps to buy and sell in the Buga market place, which is a large area in the center of the town. Another large market also operates in Masterei near Hajar Suleiman, by Wadi Kaja and the Chad border, on these days. A number of merchants in these markets occupy permanent shops surrounding the market place; these are open every day but do most business on market days. The Geneina-based lorries time their trips to supply these merchants and others further south in Dar Masalit before the market days and to carry out their goods afterwards. Similar trips are made in all directions from Geneina to market towns.

Approximately five secondary markets occur in outlying areas of Masterei on Wednesdays; these are smaller, do not have permanent shops, and are not contacted by lorry traffic. Some of these are particularly important to villagers two or more hours' travel from the larger markets, and also to nomads who occupy the most remote areas at some times of year. In addition to the market place activity, some traders who live in villages operate shops from their homes throughout the week. Formerly there were secondary markets on Sundays as well, but these were abolished by the Masterei rural council in an effort to enhance the Buga market.

As is explained below, there are certain trading activities that do not follow these channels. Occasionally steps are skipped, direct trade between towns takes place, or goods go from towns to a major center outside Dar Masalit. Nevertheless, in general, the market is a hierarchical one, centralized at Geneina.

Small Trade

Small traders or sabbabis occupy the lowest rung in the market hierarchy, usually dealing directly with producers and consumers in the bulking and breaking of exports and imports. Most of these trade only on market days, with a few pounds or less of working capital. Breaking requires the least money; the breaker buys one or two boxes of tomatoes, sweet potatoes, guavas, mangos, or lemons at LS 1–2.00 per box, and sells them in piles (*ko:m*) of three or four for a few piastres. They lay out a mat or cloth and display their fruits side-by-side with those farmers who choose to market their own produce in this way. Prices fluctuate quite a bit, as does the opportunity to buy these items, but the sabbabis can usually make thirty to forty piastres per box. Both children and young men may engage in this activity. There are also a few men, though none from the sample villages, who break small imported goods, such as razors, needles, incense, and cumin.

Bulking is somewhat more profitable. It is built upon the fact that agricultural exports—millet and groundnuts—are worth more in larger quantities. There are profits to be made in millet by bulking to the sack (approximately 130 kg) from the *kora* (2.5 kg in this area), and from the cup or scoop (of variable size according to price) to the kora. Since it is women who sell in the smallest measures, the sabbabis act as intermediaries between them and the town merchants, civil servants, and Arab nomads who buy millet in larger quantities. They are well paid for their efforts; the same quantity of millet is worth approximately twice as much by the sack as by the cup. However, daily profits are limited by the low quantity of millet marketed, and also by the fact that buyers quickly run out of small coins with which to buy the tiny amounts sold. (Coins and paper money in any denomination smaller than a pound are perpetually in short supply.) Thus, working with a few pounds, the sabbabi buying cups and koras alike only averages LS 1–1.50 per day.

The bulking of groundnuts is carried on at a higher volume. Groundnuts are also accumulated from the cup and kora levels, although much is sold in five to fifteen kilogram quantities. The standard unit with the higher price is the guntar (*gunta:r*, 45.5 kg). Sabbabi activity in groundnuts is greater in the harvest period, and their role is displayed in their arrangement in space. At that time, in addition to local merchants, there come agents of the Geneina oil press, and sometimes buyers from Nyala or El Fasher. At each of perhaps ten scales in the market is one man recording the purchases of the merchant, while surrounding (and also using) the scale is a ring of sabbabis. Surrounding them are the sellers, many female, each dealing with one or another sabbabi who weighs their produce. The sellers take what they are given, at a price 20 PT/guntar below the price being paid to the sabbabis, and then new sellers take their place. The sabbabis accumulate a sack or two, receive their money from the merchant, and buy more. In these hectic harvest days, a sabbabi with LS 10 can earn LS 1.50–2.50 in a market day. For most of the year, however, small trade in groundnuts is comparable to that in millet, with lower volume and lower income.

Both bulking and breaking can be considerably more profitable if combined with transport, which explains why nine of the twelve jammala who participate in long-distance transport are also sabbabis. Due to the difficulties of transport, substantial price differentials exist within the area, and a jammala who makes a practice of attending to prices and who has some working capital can increase his earnings considerably. Even locally, the prices of nuts and millet are lower in the outlying small markets; by bulking in a small market and selling in Buga, the sabbabi can increase his profit.

Price differentials seasonally exist between Masterei and the Wadi Azum villages in onions, red pepper, sugar cane and other wadi crops which are heavily grown on the alluvial soils there. Raw hides can also be purchased there and sold profitably to Masterei tanners. The trip to Azum (four days going and coming) is commonly made after the groundnut harvest, when the jammala have some money, and before onions are available from Wadi Kaja at a lower price. They can load up to LS 25 worth of goods, limited only by their cash, and frequently double their money or better selling in small quantities in the Buga market. There are also chronic price differentials between Buga and Geneina in millet, groundnuts, tanned hides, okra, red pepper, and other items; a jammala with the money to accumulate these goods can often significantly increase his income for a hauling job to Geneina by trading as well. Other price differentials often exist with the Beida-Arara area in okra, raw skins, and straw mats, while some goods may occasionally be profitably transported to or from Chad.

However, these price differentials are variable, and often information is not up to date or accurate. As often as I have heard of a man making a quick LS 20 on his return from a hauling job to Beida or Andirboro, I have heard of men who went looking for profits and found nothing. The average profit from transport and trading combined lies somewhere between these extremes—still at quite a high level compared to other activities.

Thus, the word 'sabbabi' includes a wide variety of occupations, varying greatly in terms of the capital required and the resultant income. At the lowest levels, income is comparable to that for low-capital crafts and services, while the highest level of small trade—carried out by jammala, already in a high-capital occupation—is considerably more profitable. Sabbabis have two important features in common that contrast them with merchants. First, they tend to carry out one deal at a time. Since they are usually working at the limit of their capital, they must sell whatever they have bought before moving into a new investment. This limits risks, especially for those who complete their bulking or breaking in one day at the market. Second, the vast majority of sabbabis are comfortable with a limited capital investment. They are involved in small trade as a way of producing income, just as they may be involved in a craft activity or transport; they take the occasional opportunity to make money, but most are not trying to increase their capital for larger investments in the future. However, there are always a few who are trading with the hope of eventually becoming a merchant.

Merchants

Merchants also form a continuum from small to big, and the lower rung is not clearly distinct from the small trader. As mentioned above, there is some disagreement about the classification of certain individuals. Many people consider owning a scale and trading in sugar to be the distinguishing feature of a merchant. This usage is practical and has been adopted here, since it is indicative of a certain level of capital, and a commitment to continued trade in the future. It is in part this commitment that makes the activities of merchants qualitatively different from sabbabis, as they continuously try to increase their profits and trading capital.

This aspect was illustrated in an interview with one of the first Masalit merchants of Buga, who explained the basic strategy of becoming a merchant. First, he said, one starts as a sabbabi with about LS 10, working in local crops to make one's money grow. Then one gets into cloth—coarse white cottons (*damuriyya*) and the heavy blue *azraq* worn by women, the most common cheap cloths. When one can afford it, one trades in sugar and tea. These popular commodities turn money around fast, but with low profit. Over time with increased capital, one can stock fancy cloth, flour, and other slow-moving goods with higher profit margins.

While there are other ways of proceeding, this trajectory accurately describes certain aspects of being a merchant. The goods available for trade change with one's level of capital. Merchants with a small amount of trading capital must invest in low-profit items and work hard; later, capital does more of the work for the successful big merchants. Some of the other commercial activities into which large merchants diversify are discussed below.

Large merchants sell high-priced goods, although they may also carry on the same bulking, breaking and transport activities as sabbabis and small merchants. Sugar and cheap cloth are the most important goods, and they are too costly for most sabbabis. Just one sack of sugar (50 kg) costs about LS 50; loading a full camel requires LS 200 in working capital, as well as LS 50 for a scale, weights, and license fees. They may also import and break other fast-moving, low cost items such as soap, matches, batteries, oil and salt. Merchants also bulk agricultural products, often through barter. If not pressed for working capital, they can accept millet or nuts in payment for small quantities of sugar or cloth; by accepting this produce they solve the problem of making change, and they effortlessly accumulate large quantities of crops at high profit margins.

The two largest merchants in the sample villages usually brought in at least LS 200 worth of sugar and LS 200 worth of other goods per month. They sold this at a profit of approximately 10 percent, which was doubled by receiving goods in barter, and further increased if they transported these goods back to Geneina themselves. In addition, merchants with sufficient capital profited by holding goods that they broke or bulked, to sell at times when their prices were higher. If a merchant did not need cash for his current operations, he stored the groundnuts and millet he had bought until the harvest rush was over; at that time, prices usually doubled. Similarly he accumulated large amounts of sugar and goods before the rainy season, when low supply drove the prices up.

For smaller merchants, the extent to which they can carry out these activities is limited by their capital. To continue bringing in sugar, a merchant with limited capital cannot divert much of it into bulking and holding crops. A merchant with, for example, LS 500 would probably only accumulate crops to the value of half his capital, and that only by keeping his sales merchandise limited in amount and variety. A merchant with higher capitalization can keep a variety of goods, including fancy polyesters, kerosene, and foods with higher profit margins, while accumulating millet and groundnuts for export or sale to nomads. However, there is also an upper limit on retail trade; few merchants keep more than LS 1000 in goods, due to the low demand and the limited number of different items to sell. Because other merchants supply the same items, a retail store can only do so much volume. Merchants with LS 1000 or more may increase their investment in bulking or storing by building a brick shop that is more suited to storage, buying a large scale (different from the sugar scale) to weigh groundnuts, and accumulating crops in the village for export. Two merchants have followed this course in the sample villages, and they negotiate directly with Geneina merchants to export groundnuts by the truckload.

Two activities previously discussed can enhance the profitability of trade: sewing and transport. Like the sabbabi, the small merchant can increase his profits by bringing his own sugar from Geneina and selling his bulked goods there; this requires a camel, and six of the merchants do own camels. Larger merchants use them to transport a portion of their own goods while supervising the transport of the rest by hired jammala traveling with them. Of equal importance is the use of camels in going to markets. Village trade is conducted out of one's house, but more money is to be made by going to Buga on Fridays and perhaps also on Mondays. Wednesday is the day of small markets in the outlying villages, and these are particularly profitable to village merchants with camels. Buga merchants find the distances too great, and are more oriented to the lorries that link their shops to Geneina. The village merchants, however, are quite ready to pack their scales, some sugar and other goods, and move their operation to the shade of a tree in a small rural market.

The two largest merchants in the village are also tailors, and are quite enthusiastic about the advantages of combining the two operations. Tailors who are not merchants must operate their machine in the market, where people can buy cloth and bring it to them. By selling cloth, tailors who are also merchants can keep working their machines all week, and they can do it when convenient to them. Conversely, because they sew, they attract more customers for their cloth. Thus, the two enterprises support each other and increase business.

Because of the limits on trading operations per se, and to reduce risk, merchants with enough capital diversify into other areas, primarily credit, livestock and crop production. Credit is extended in a form called 'shail' (*ʃayl*), known throughout the Sudan. Commonly extended before or during the rains when many farmers have exhausted their savings, the lender advances a low price for crops to be delivered after the harvest.

In 1979, four of the five merchants interviewed extended credit on groundnuts; the other no longer gave shail because he had problems obtaining repayment. In 1979 village merchants usually paid LS 2.00 for a guntar of groundnuts to be delivered; at harvest, groundnuts were worth LS 3.50–4.00. Some gave one sack of groundnuts in the planting season to be repaid by two sacks later. These four merchants accumulated one hundred forty-six guntars of groundnuts through these contracts.

Shail is a rather complex issue in the Sudan; due to the high profitability, it seems to some morally wrong and a particularly exploitative type of transaction. Thus, it is sometimes illegal (O'Brien 1980:189), and has been condemned by several writers (for example, Adam and Apaya 1973; Karrar 1966; Shaw 1966). Shail seems to vary in the levels of interest charged in various parts of Sudan; while profits of up to 200 percent are reported by these writers, I have not found this in Dar Masalit. The rate of profit observed is not exceptional from the merchant's point of view. If he invested the same LS 2.00 in sugar, he would hope to double his money in six months. Those who extended nuts on a two for one basis made less money than it seems, since nuts were worth LS 5.00 or more at planting time.

For these merchants, shail appears to be worth carrying on, in part because it eases the job of accumulating groundnuts at the harvest season, and also because it provides people money to buy things from them.[23] In support of the latter point, it is worth noting that two of the merchants also extend consumer credit, in millet or cash, to regular customers without interest.

Edward B. Reeves (1983) found a similar situation in Kordofan, where shail was extended as credit on consumer goods with a 0–10 percent markup; as in the Masalit case, the primary benefit to the merchant was in accumulating export crops at the harvest season. Reeves also suggested that the kinship of merchants with villagers placed limits on unfair business practices, which may also be the case in Masalit villages.

While not, perhaps, living up to its reputation as an extortionate practice, shail can nevertheless play a significant role in transforming an economy and extending the control of merchants over it. Tony Barnett (1975:196–197) argues that credit in the Gezira plays an essential part in the maintenance of class divisions by making it possible for laborers to survive while maintaining their dependence on shopkeepers. In the Masalit case this aspect is compounded by shail's effect on crop choice. Because shail is available almost exclusively for groundnuts, people who run short of money are obliged to grow more groundnuts, even though they also may be short of food. Currently, profits in bulking groundnuts are limited by the volume marketed; thus, merchants may attempt to expand their shail operations in the future as they compete to accumulate greater quantities of groundnuts. (Compare O'Fahey and Spaulding 1974 on the role of shail in the history of the eastern Sudan.)

Merchants also invest in livestock, as do other Masalit with money to save. Their operations resemble those described above in the section on livestock, but there is one major difference. Merchants are more likely to own bulls rather than the milk-producers favored by people with few animals. Bulls are more important as exports than cows, because they can travel better with less weight loss. Thus, they are in regular demand, and their price is subject to considerable fluctuation. Traders' herds have high proportions of males for three reasons. First, they speculate on price fluctuations; second, they do not need the income and food from more than a few milk cows, and third, they can afford these more expensive animals.

The other major operation engaged in by merchants, like all other villagers, is farming. There is not a village merchant who does not cultivate millet, along with his family. However, their commercial orientation again makes their activities somewhat different. Merchants cultivate more groundnuts than other villagers, and hire more farm laborers. (The five merchants interviewed planted over twelve hectares of groundnuts between them, and spent LS 123 for hired labor in weeding alone—far more than any non-merchants.) They are limited in their agriculture, however, by the availability of land. They have holdings comparable to others, although those who are polygynous (seven of eight) can often get access to more land through their wives. They also borrow land in small plots here or there, but the amount of land available for borrowing is limited. At present there is no rental or sale of any but orchard land, so merchants cannot expand their land holdings very much. However if customs change or land registration is carried out, it is likely that they will accumulate land from the impoverished or from emigrants.

With all of these intertwined activities, it would be difficult to accurately determine the return to labor of merchants for comparison with other occupations. While it is clear that some activities of village merchants require quite a bit of work, the returns to that labor are in a class by themselves. As the capital of a merchant increases, his potential income increases more than proportionately, at least to a point, because of his ability to carry on several kinds of activities at once. The quantities of money involved are perhaps best illustrated by some cases.

Let us first consider the largest merchant in the sample villages. In 1969, he returned from the Nile valley with his sewing machine and LS 15 in 'old' notes. The Sudanese currency was changed and he had missed the deadline to exchange his money, but he found a merchant who would accept old notes for sugar. Seeing this as his only chance to use his money, he borrowed an additional LS 2.00 and bought a sack for LS 17, then he sewed to earn LS 5.00 for a box of tea. Having found it profitable, he continued to trade in sugar and cloth, and he eventually earned enough to buy a camel and the necessities of being a merchant. By living much of the year in a bush camp, he carried on a profitable trade with Arab nomads and with people of remote villages. He regularly went to the Buga markets, where he built a straw shop, and to an outlying Wednesday market. In 1979, he built a brick shop in the village, where he had married a second wife, leaving his fifteen year old son to oversee the bush camp operation much of the time.

This man's current working capital in 1979 was about LS 1400, plus a shop and equipment worth LS 500, livestock worth perhaps LS 2500, and smaller amounts in credit and wages expended on crops not yet received. Roughly, he has increased his capital by 80 percent per year. If we estimate very conservatively that he was earning a 50 percent annual return, his income in 1979 was over LS 100 per month. He continued to sew and go to the markets, and he was the largest lender and employer in the village. He was making contact with Geneina merchants, brought trucks to the village to ship out groundnuts, and was likely to continue as a major bulker and exporter.

Profits and rates of increase of capital are variable. Two other merchants had only been trading for three years; one started with a sewing machine and LS 80 earned by sewing, while the other started with a camel, which he used to bulk grain and transport it to Beida until he had LS 75 in cash. Both began trading sugar and goods at that point, and both increased their capital to approximately LS 2000 in 1979 (a 300 percent annual rate of return.) The tailor continued to trade and sew, and built a brick shop, while the other invested in livestock and shail, and continues to work about LS 500 in retail trade. Two other merchants interviewed did not trade constantly over their careers, which made rates of return difficult to estimate. It is worth noting that retail cooperatives in the area, presumably working on lower margins, often showed annual profits in the 50–100 percent range.

However, profits are not automatic. Price fluctuations in sugar and crops are often dramatic, and bad luck or poor judgment can lead to low profits or losses. One former merchant went out of business and fled to the east when he could not repay a large loan, and another gave up trade because it was not profitable for him. There are numerous sabbabis who never accumulated enough money to move into sugar. Returns to capital are quite high in the villages, but this does not eliminate a substantial element of risk, and the need for hard work, an ability to use one's money cleverly, and good luck.

Masalit village merchants are of course relatively well-off within the villages, but their position in the hierarchy of Sudanese and global trade is rather low. The traders of Buga, some of whom are Masalit and some not, operate with a range of capital about double that of village merchants, from LS 1000 to LS 10,000. Many of them have substantial livestock and credit operations, but their range of goods is not much larger than that of the village merchants, and it is possible that some of their positions will be usurped by the hard-driving villagers. Both Buga and village merchants are strongly oriented to Geneina; only sabbabis find intra-rural trade enough to occupy their capital.

Geneina merchants are overwhelmingly non-Masalit, as they have been since the British began licensing Geneina shops in the 1920s. Most are in turn oriented, by Nyala or El Fasher, to Khartoum and Port Sudan, through a network of personal and economic relationships. At each level, the capitalization of the merchants and the volume of trade increases. Merchants in Geneina, operating at levels unreachable by village merchants, nevertheless consider themselves to be conducting a small frontier operation; as one of Fatima Mahmoud's informants stated: "In western Sudan, one can make a fortune of thousands but not millions" (1984:88). In spite of the fact that the operations and incomes of village-level Masalit merchants appear trivial from the viewpoint of the global economy, they play an important role in that market, and have a very significant local effect. They are the local vanguard of the world market.

Conclusion

It is clear that the dominant pattern of trade in Dar Masalit today is directed to the world market. In this respect it has some similarity to the long-distance trade of the past, which produced goods with no local use-value, in exchange for goods for elite consumption that could not be locally produced. The major difference between the trade under the Ancien Regime and the current pattern is the nature of the involvement of the common people. From an administered trade, restricted to the political elite, commerce has now come to the village level. Imported cloth, formerly a sign of high status, has now replaced local cloth. Tea, sugar, chili peppers and imported spices now add variety to a diet depleted by the loss of the forest. Glasses and aluminum utensils have partly replaced gourds and clay pots. In these and other ways, trade in imported goods has substituted for many locally made products.

In the process of this trade's expansion, village merchants have come to exist; they profit by bringing the trade network virtually to the doorstep of their fellow villagers. These merchants have placed themselves on the lowest rung of a hierarchical structure of traders, sending exports into Geneina, thence to Khartoum and global markets beyond, and selling imports. As shown, village trade can be a profitable enterprise, with an income well above other occupations for those who are successful. A merchant at least hopes to accumulate capital to the point where he secures a high level of consumption by local standards through profits in retail trade. By increasing the scale of retail trade and other investments, he can further increase his income and capital. As is argued in the next chapter, the possibility of accumulating capital has important socioeconomic effects at the village level.

As externally oriented trade has increased in volume, regional trade has dwindled. Kapteijns (1985) has pointed out that regional trade was of considerable importance in Dar Masalit under the Ancien Regime; salt, cotton, millet and livestock were bartered throughout the area. Regional trade still exists, but price relations are dominated by market forces, such that export goods cost more in markets closer to Geneina, while imported goods cost less. Only a few small traders—certainly no merchants—trade across the lorry routes, taking advantage of east-west price differentials in the southern Dar. The amount of goods currently traded within the Dar for local use is very small compared to the amount exported. Even the sale of millet to Arab nomads, which predates colonial occupation, is now essentially underwritten by the nomads' sales of animals to townspeople and exporters. The loss of regional trade contributes to reduced local autonomy and increased dependence on world market conditions.

Migration

In discussing the village economy and the economic activities that are available to or incumbent upon the residents, one must include a very different kind of activity: leaving, either temporarily or permanently. Migration is an alternative that individuals compare with farming and other opportunities that are locally available. However, it involves more than a comparison of incomes in a number of occupations; it is an option that changes the migrant's whole life, and this must be taken into account in understanding the decision. The absence of current migrants and the experiences of the returners also indirectly affect Masalit economy, society and culture, sometimes in subtle and often in dramatic ways.

The phenomenon of migration is no more reducible to the level of the individual decision than are patterns of trade, sewing, or gathering. Once the rationality of a decision is clear, there remains the problem of understanding the context of that decision. In the case of Dar Masalit, an individual's choice of migration may be motivated by an insufficiency of resources for survival in Dar Masalit, or by the hope of accumulating enough money to enter a high capital trade. In both cases, the individual motive exists because of the impoverishment of the Dar and the relative wealth of the Nile Valley, which are results of past and current government policy (Lipton 1982). It is argued that migration contributes to the maintenance of this structure, and therefore perpetuates itself. While providing cheap labor to the Nile Valley, migration allows divided families to continue to exist on inadequate lands in the Dar, contributes to local inequality, and increases demand for consumer goods, all of which stimulate more migration (compare Wiest, in press).

A number of types of data pertinent to understanding migration were collected at the village level, in addition to the district and province level data discussed in chapter 3. A comprehensive list was compiled of absentees who had actually departed from the sample villages to areas outside Dar Masalit, or to Geneina, Buga, or other Dar Masalit towns.[24] Emigrants who departed from the sample villages would not necessarily be living in these same villages if they had stayed or returned to rural Dar Masalit, but they represented a well-defined sampling universe of rural absentees matched to the sample villages. A list of one hundred ninety-one known emigrants was developed primarily in the process of gathering kinship and household information, in which the locations of relatives were collected; other absentees were discovered in mapping the village and through interviews. Information about each migrant was collected from his or her *'ami:n* (authorized representative) if someone had been so entrusted with their affairs; otherwise I interviewed a near relative, or the migrant if he or she was located in Buga.

Of these one hundred ninety-one absentees, thirty-nine were current members of twenty-nine large sample families from whom complete family level information was also available; current members were considered to include spouses or children from resident households who were absent less than five years and had not married in the receiving area. In addition, migration (and marital) histories were obtained from an age-stratified 25 percent sample of men currently present in the sample villages, and briefer information on current and previous migrations was solicited from the entire large sample.

These three categories of data—absentee characteristics, migrant household characteristics, and migration histories—provide information on different aspects of the issue. They are supplemented by key informant interviews with older men, data from colonial records and Kapteijns (1985) concerning the history of migration, and visits in 1980 to migrants in Southern Darfur, Khartoum, and the Gedaref area. Interview information about the nature of the economy and labor market in the receiving areas at various times is interpreted with the benefit of recent studies by Mark R. Duffield (1981), Mohammed El Awad Galal-el Din (1978) and John James O'Brien (1980) which provide valuable contextual information.

As has been discussed in the previous chapter, Dar Masalit and Darfur in general contain fewer males than females, especially in certain age groups, as a result of emigration. The sample villages reflect this pattern. As shown in figure 4.3, the population pyramid of the sample villages for residents shows a marked deficit of males, especially in the 11–50 age group. The addition to this pyramid of the one hundred ninety-one migrants largely corrects this imbalance, because of the high proportion of males in the migrant population. (The composit pyramid is not a true total population, since absentee children of emigrants are not included.) Clearly migration has a substantial effect on the composition of the village population.

Early Migration

Mobility is not strange to the Masalit. For hundreds of years they have been moving and expanding in the general area of Dar Masalit (Haaland 1980; Tully 1985), with a form of frontier adaptation. Villages were constantly being founded, and founders would clear land and invite people from other villages to join them. As soil fertility was exhausted, fields were abandoned and new ones were cut. Localized droughts and locust plagues, crop failures, epidemics and warfare also caused precolonial mobility to be high, and in some areas the policies of the Sahelian empires of Dar Fur and Wadai encouraged or forced migration as well. The current sporadic distribution of lineage segments throughout and beyond Dar Masalit indicated frequent resettlement by groups of people in the precolonial period.

This mobility has also included migrations of large numbers of people over hundreds of miles, to settle or conquer new lands which were not contiguous with those occupied by the original population; thousands of Masalit have lived in Wadi Batha, which is southwest of Abesher in Chad, and in the vicinity of Gereida, Southern Darfur, for hundreds of years at least (Tully 1984). Daju, Zaghawa, Gimr, and other ethnic groups of this area similarly are found in geographically separate areas, with varying degrees of contact; these settlements may be the result of emigrations due to political disputes, environmental

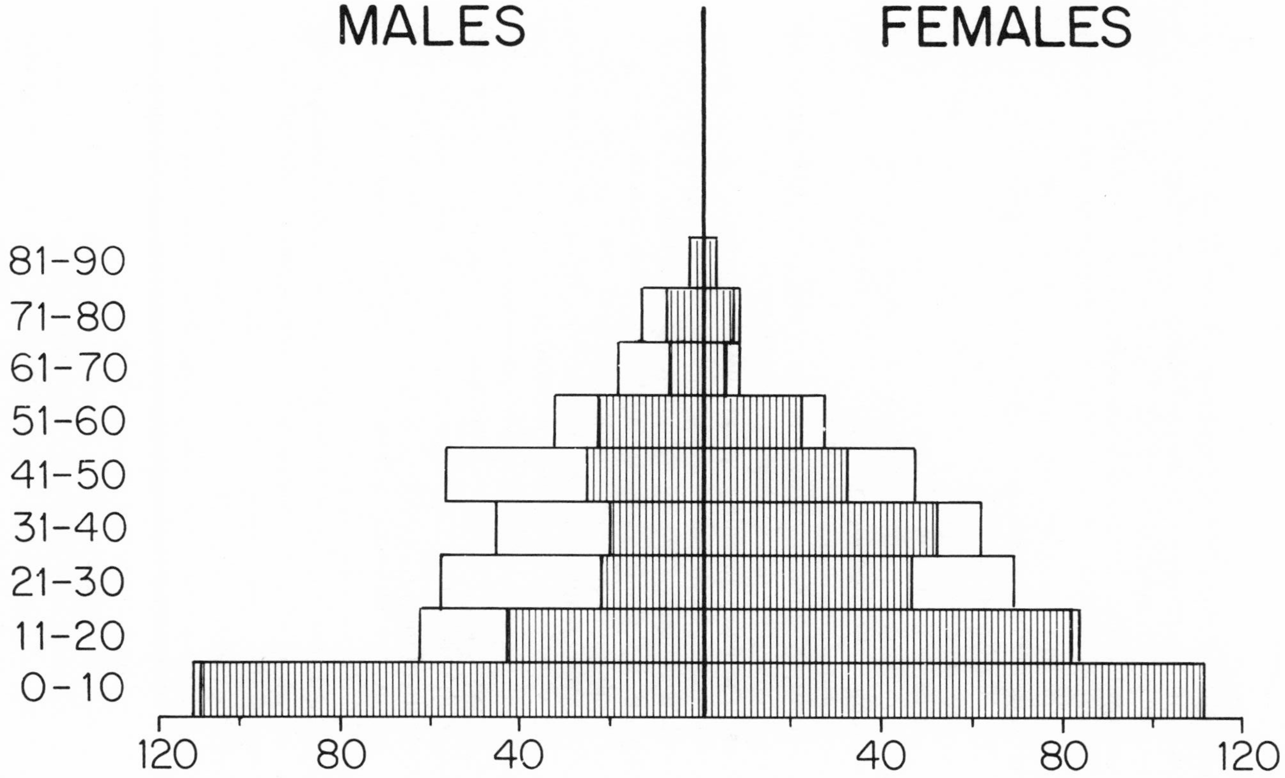

Figure 4.3. Age and sex pyramid of the sample villages. Shaded areas represent current residents; unshaded areas represent emigrants from the sample villages. Polygynous males with non-village wives are proportionately weighted. Cases not shown, of unknown age: one male, fourteen females.

pressures, disease, or the direct orders of precolonial sultanates (Tully 1985).

As Mather states: "Where migration is a natural feature of life, it becomes the automatic outlet and solution to conflict and difficulty arising from . . . human problems" (1956:121). The option of resettlement may reduce the likelihood of enduring interpersonal ties, shared values, local dispute settlement and close supernatural or emotional bonds with particular geographical features. Through whatever mechanisms, the result is a people "lacking hostility to the tearing up of one's roots" (Caldwell 1975:13), at least relatively. It may be argued that the existence of such precolonial migration justifies policies that encourage labor migration, on the grounds that this result is only a modification of an autochthonous pattern. Keith Hart (1982:123) is a recent example; he mentions precolonial mobility as an "antidote" to criticisms of migration as induced by colonialism.

However, it would be more accurate to say that colonial policies have interacted with precolonial patterns in ways that have given individuals in a highly mobile population new incentives to emigrate. The migration has been of a different type, however, and the effects of the individual choices on society are not the same in the case of labor migration as in the case of precolonial resettlement. Rather than the expansion and reproduction of independent Masalit society, composed of farming families, labor migration contributes to a transformation of the Masalit into a people dependent on economic and political constraints that are external to their society, beyond their control, and often disadvantageous. The individuals who migrate do not choose this result; they merely decide to go and work for a time, and they can not be aware of the social effects of a pattern of such decisions. In the present context, even if one disapproves of the effects of migration it may still be impossible to stay in Dar Masalit.

To understand the development of migration as a pillar of the Masalit economy, one must consider its origins and the changes it has undergone. After the British and French ratified a border treaty that left one-third of Masalit territory in French hands, the current Dar Masalit was occupied by the Anglo-Egyptian Sudan in 1922. As previously discussed, the first two decades of colonial rule saw substantial immigration from French territory. With incorporation into the Sudan, Dar Masalit at this time also witnessed the beginning of certain patterns of emigration, both permanent and temporary, which came to play a powerful role in binding this area to the global economy. Improved communications and political unification with the east facilitated movements, which were encouraged by new pressures and new opportunities.

According to Kapteijns (1985:237–243), colonial taxes in the 1920s stimulated migration, either to earn money or to escape the obligation. Taxes were imposed in cash at an early stage, and money was scarce. From the late 1920s through the 1930s, LS 3000–4000 per year was collected in poll and animal taxes, or approximately 15 PT per adult male. This was exacted in spite of the effects of the depression, epidemics and crop failures. Resident Sandison, analyzing a "taxpayers strike," in 1934, notes that the tax assessment represented "24 percent of the market value of all the listed animals of Dar Masalit" (cited in Kapteijns 1985: 236).

I was told that people also fled from compulsory labor on roads; it was clear in a 1922 report from the Dar Masalit field force that labor was being forcibly extracted through the "arrest" of large numbers of "malcontents," who always happened to be "able-bodied men" (Intel 2/51/430). Road building by forced labor only ceased at independence, according to my informants. While conditions were being made more difficult in Dar Masalit, there were new economic opportunities in the eastern Sudan, to be described below.

Concomitant with the economic pushes and pulls was a religious incentive—the attraction of Sayyid Abd al-Rahman al-Mahdi, son of the Mahdi, who was receiving pilgrims at Aba Island in the White Nile. Pilgrims were put to work on the Sayyid's cotton plantation. Both the sultan and the British were alarmed by emigration to Aba, and the British attempted to restrict emigration and repress Mahdist sentiments locally. According to Kapteijns, "most Masalit believed in the Sayyid and . . . many took the trouble to go to Aba and see for themselves" (1985:242).

It is difficult to quantify the movement to Aba, because of the subjective nature of the records. The sultan himself, although disturbed by the emigration of his subjects, pointed out that: "It was really impossible to tell who were going on pilgrimage and who in search of work" (Kapteijns 1985:242, quoting Arkell in Darfur 1/24/134). The British were alarmed by any Islamic activity in the wake of the Mahdiyya and, more recently, the Nyala uprising of 1921, in which thousands of rebels under the leadership of a feki attacked British forces in southern Darfur (MacMichael 1934; Davies 1926). During this attack, the border post in Dar Masalit "was virtually in a state of siege," as the Masalit waited to see if it would be successful (Kapteijns 1985:212).

Sir Harold MacMichael, a long-time intelligence officer and administrator in the Anglo-Egyptian Sudan, dismissed the event as fanaticism, while in the next breath he made clear its basic economic motivation: "Its proximate cause was no more nor less than one of the periodic waves of fanaticism which excite the ignorant upon comparatively trivial occasions. The occasion in this instance was the introduction of a regular system of taxation" (1934:136). By considering the religious articulation of protest as its cause, the British precluded any understanding of such events while increasing their own fear of Islam. However, they were thus able to maintain their self-concept as benevolent rulers; witness the governor of Dar Fur, Seville, asserting that he "was at a loss to explain this outbreak as the people were prosperous and contented . . . the rebels must be composed of Baggara Arabs who are liable to outbursts of religious excitement" (Daly 1980:81).

In this environment, statements that the Masalit were migrating heavily to Aba are suspect, especially when reports of two men visiting the Sayyid in one instance, or six families requesting permission to do so in another were sufficient to attract government attention (Darfur 3/3/20). Reginald Davies in 1921 drew a distinction between the "masses" and "Mahdist fekis," which may mean that they were a very visible minority. In the sample villages, my older informants minimized the size of the pilgrimage movement, but allowed that there were certain areas from which groups of migrants did go to Aba.

Of greater importance at this time was probably simple resettlement in the Nile Valley; Kapteijns states that this was particularly heavy in the 1925–35 period. It appeared that this movement included large numbers of Masalit slaves taking advantage of the British prohibition of slavery (Kapteijns 1985:238–239; and personal communication). Similar desertions of slaves under British rule were reported from Kordofan (O'Brien 1980:165) and Blue Nile settlements (Duffield 1981:39).

We do not know the extent to which slaves were owned by commoners in Dar Masalit, but undoubtedly the political elite dominated in this. Slaves would have been concentrated in the Goz, the political center of the Dar. It may be for this reason that my key informants in Masterei did not report substantial emigration at that time; there were fewer slaves in Masterei, and furthermore my informants were commoners and less likely to be aware of slave emigration. Several informants said that a few young men emigrated; they left alone carrying water, and have not returned. Others denied that emigration in this period was of any significance.

The emigrant list also supports the view of a low level of emigration from Masterei before 1940; only three of the one hundred ninety-one absentees have been gone since that time. However, this listing would be least accurate for long-time emigrants, since people may be forgotten, their kin may have left the village, and many early migrants must have died by now. It is also likely that slaves would have been undercounted by my procedures for producing an emigrant list, since the compilation relies heavily upon kinship between emigrants and residents.

Most notably absent from the migration pattern in this period, considering the British demand for labor in the Gezira scheme, was any significant temporary migration to cultivate or pick cotton. There were several factors militating against this type of activity. First, seven hundred miles was a long way to go on foot, especially through unknown lands to an unknown destination. Rural Masalit knew little Arabic and did not have much idea of the opportunities to travel or work in the east, until the first few migrants who returned brought more information. Elsewhere in the Sudan, recruitment through advertisement, underwritten transport and conscription was carried out by colonial authorities (O'Brien 1980:168–172), but I found no evidence of this in Dar Masalit at this time; on the contrary, emigration was restricted for fear of supporting Abd al-Rahman at Aba (Kapteijns 1985:24). As mentioned in the last chapter, the government also believed that Dar Masalit was underpopulated, and it would therefore not be likely to promote emigration.

In addition, since most labor was only needed during the dry season cotton harvest in Gezira, the Masalit were not ideal from the government's point of view; a labor supply was needed that was close enough to keep transport costs low, composed of families so that children's labor contributed to lower wages, and preferably organized into groups that regulated their own affairs and therefore minimized problems for the employers. Most importantly, since they were not paid enough to live on for a year, and in some years fewer laborers might be wanted, they had to return home after the harvest to grow food (Galal-el-Din 1978:76–81; O'Brien 1980:156–237). Dar Masalit was too far away for trips of only a few months, especially by families. Thus, the establishment of a cheap labor force for the Gezira drew upon existing villages closer to the scheme, and beyond that on encouraging and exploiting the settlement of Central and West Africans near enough to the Gezira for the desired seasonal migration. (Galal-el-Din and El Mustafa 1979; Duffield 1981:32–43; O'Brien 1980:150–161, 217–218). Early migration from Dar Masalit took place without assistance and with little information, and therefore was limited in volume. (However, it is likely that more emigration was occurring from the towns than was indicated by the sample villages).

A number of men did migrate in the 1940s and a few in the 1930s; in the migration history sample, eight men were interviewed who had migrated to the eastern Sudan before 1950. All but one went entirely on foot; when asked what they took, "a *jara:ya*" (hoe) was the usual answer. They walked for a few days, then stopped to weed in someone's fields for a few days, in exchange for food, shelter and enough to eat on the road for a while. When that ran out they stopped and worked again. In some ways this was patterned after precolonial labor practices, in which people in need migrated about and weeded for food (see chapter 5). These men left in the early rainy season and weeded their way across the Sudan, arriving in the Gezira and sometimes Gedaref at the time of the grain harvest, when work could be found in these areas. In the dry season, all but one worked in the Gezira cotton harvest at some point.

For the remainder of their stays in the east, ranging from one to five years, these men engaged in a variety of activities, at different times. One worked in a factory, one worked as the agent of a merchant, and one joined the army, but agriculture was their most common occupation. Six of these men made fields of their own at some point, most frequently sesame fields in Gedaref, and most continued to pick cotton in the dry season or engage in other agricultural labor. Land seemed to be fairly abundant in the rural areas of Gedaref, and local sheikhs allotted fields to newcomers, perhaps hoping that they would stay on. Many did; Masalit villages (and villages of other westerners) grew up in the Gedaref area at this time, and still exist. Migrants were also resettling around En Nahud, Kordofan, which was well-connected by road to Khartoum.

There seemed to be a good market for crops at this time, because the men who made fields in Gedaref considered it to be quite profitable; government purchases during the war years were partly responsible. The government also undertook rainfed sorghum cultivation for the war effort, which provided relatively well-paid employment in Gedaref (O'Brien 1980:178). In the postwar period there was a pressing need for oil-seeds in Europe, and Sudanese production of sesame was rapidly increased (Karrar 1966). As a result, these early migrants were pleased with their acquisitions; all brought back abundant clothing for themselves and their kin, often thirty pieces or more. This was at a time, as stated above, when imported clothing was replacing locally made fabrics, and former sumptuary laws against the wearing of imported fabrics by ordinary farmers gave way. However, clothing was expensive locally and cash was rare. The migrants brought back cash, from LS 5–40, at a time when LS 2.00 would buy a cow. A few animals were purchased, but most stated that the money was used for *maSa:ri:f* (expenses); that is, purchase of consumer goods. Into a context where the use of sugar, tea and other imported goods was minimal, these early migrants brought new standards of clothing and consumption, which had only been relevant to the elites up to that time.

Increasing Numbers of Migrants

As one of these men ruefully noted, the clothing did not last; however, the example and the information that men such as these brought back did last, and paved the way for a surge of emigration from Dar Masalit in the 1950s. It is argued below that the development of land scarcity was an important stimulus to Masalit emigration, but the increasing standards of consumption, and the impossibility of making enough money locally to meet those standards, were also important.

As John James O'Brien pointed out, this was not accidental; the government Labour Board continually lobbied other branches of government to suppress indigenous production of textiles, undermine rural agriculture and crop markets, increase taxes to eliminate any rural prosperity caused by rising prices, and aggressively market cloth, sugar, tea and coffee. Moreover, the distribution of these goods was skewed to make them more scarce outside the "producing areas" of government agricultural schemes (1980:165–176), which explained the migrants' inclination to carry back large amounts of clothing. In order to create a supply of cheap labor, the government worked to create a demand for market goods, and to ensure that people migrated in order to get them. These early migrants unwittingly catalyzed that process in Dar Masalit, even though the Dar was not specifically cultivated as a source of labor at that time.

In the sample villages, migration rates increased dramatically in the 1950s; by the time of the 1955–56 census, Masterei had a masculinity ratio of 0.81 as a result of male emigration. This cannot be attributed to drought; as pointed out in chapter 2, the 1950s were a time of high rainfall. Nevertheless almost everyone who was not too old or did not have large numbers of animals was going to the east. The suddenness of the shift can be seen in table 4.25. Seventy percent of sample village men who were in their thirties in 1950 have emigrated at least once, compared to only 20 percent of men who were over forty. In the following years, as this table shows, migration became nearly universal for men. Resettlement also continued throughout this period.

Table 4.25
Rates of Past Emigration by Currently Resident Males of the Sample Villages according to Age

Age in 1980	Age in 1950	Percentage who ever Left Dar Masalit
Over 70	Over 40	20
61–70	31–40	70
51–60	21–30	78
41–50	11–20	89
31–40	1–10	100
21–30	–	95

The explanation of this phenomenon was the conjunction of new consumer demands with opportunities for wage employment in the Nile Valley. The increase in commercial agriculture in Sudan since 1950, including exploitation of rainfed areas, created a regular labor demand in Gedaref (O'Brien 1980:231; compare Mahmoud 1984: 48,92 ff.). This occurred at a time when there was a substantial decrease in the rate of West African immigration, which had been the main source of labor in commercial agriculture since the beginning of the Gezira scheme (Duffield 1979). Thus, agricultural laborers from Dar Masalit were welcome in the Nile Valley, and were probably encouraged to migrate by the policies of the Labour Board mentioned above (the absence of annual reports after 1939 makes it impossible to date the local government's change of policy with respect to migration). Migration and resettlement have continued to increase. According to Mohammed El-Awad Galal-el-Din, net migration from Darfur in 1973–74 was almost four times as great as in 1955–56 (1978:116).

The data do not permit quantification of emigration from Dar Masalit as a unit, but local accounts and migration histories make it clear that it has been rapidly increasing. For the sample villages, table

4.26 shows the number of emigrants of each sex according to their decade of departure. As stated above, older cohorts may be undercounted, and are certainly depleted by natural mortality, but these effects are insufficient to account for the accelerating trend.

Table 4.26
Dates of Emigration of Absentees by Sex and Location (large sample)

	Pre-1950	1950s	1960s	1970s	Total
		Out of Dar Masalit			
Males	3	11	21	81	116
Females	0	2	3	37	42
		Within Dar Masalit			
Males	3	2	5	10	20
Females	0	2	2	5	9

While rates of absentees departing in the 1970s are far above preceding decades, these include larger numbers of temporary migrants. To estimate resettlement as a proportion of emigration, other factors must be considered. Migrants absent prior to 1970 are very unlikely to return, since they have lost access to land in the rural areas. Even if we assume that two-thirds of recent emigrants return, the trend of resettlement out of Dar Masalit would still be strongly upward for the last three decades. However, it is unlikely that so many will return. Within Dar Masalit, most movement to towns has taken place in the last ten years, and very few of these internal migrants say they expect to return to the villages. More significantly, the 1970s are distinguished by a sudden increase in the proportion of female migrants out of Dar Masalit. Female migration has almost always been permanent; only six women resident in the sample villages have ever been out of Dar Masalit. It is possible that this high rate of emigration in the 1970s represents a new pattern of female temporary migration, but this is not likely; the vast majority of these women have joined or gone with their husbands, and as is explained in the next chapter, it is very difficult to maintain land ownership if a family member is not present to cultivate.

In view of this information, it is relevant to recall the data presented in the last chapter concerning the masculinity ratio of Dar

Masalit in the two censuses. The ratio of 0.84 in 1973 compared to 0.83 in 1955–56 may be misleading; because of female emigration, the same masculinity ratio is the result of higher overall emigration in 1973 than in 1955–56, and a higher proportion of females among the emigrants. This is consistent with the provincial data cited above and local interviews.

Pushes and Pulls

As migration has increased, the context of migration has not stayed the same. While migration before 1950 appears to have been relatively profitable, between 1950 and the 1970s the situation has reversed. The economic returns to migration appear to have been rather poor of late. Recent migrants complain of the low wages and lack of opportunity in the eastern Sudan. While there is a certain element of comparison with an idealized past, the complaints are borne out by the experiences I have recorded of nineteen trips (by sixteen men) undertaken in the 1970s. The amounts of cash they brought back are listed in table 4.27; the mean is LS 41.92. Excluding the four most successful trips, the mean cash saved was LS 27.10. These levels of cash savings are comparable in absolute terms to those of pre-1950s migrants discussed above, but there is one great difference: the currency is worth one-tenth or less of what it was in those early days.

Table 4.27
Cash saved by 16 Migrants on 19 Trips in the 1970s

Cash (LS)	Number of Trips
0–10	4
11–20	3
21–30	2
31–40	2
41–50	4
Over 50[a]	4

a Actual cash saved by these migrants was LS 70, 80, 80 and 160.

Recent migrants also brought clothing, but most brought fewer than ten pieces. Those who brought LS 50 or more considered themselves fortunate, and some of these bought a cow or other stock to form a part of their bridewealth. Those who brought LS 10 or less barely covered the amount it cost them for transport in the first place. From another point of view, one may consider savings per year. These migrants were absent a total of approximately thirty-seven years, and their savings average a mere LS 21.50 per year of absence, with a range from LS 0–80. In addition, migrants frequently have to buy food for themselves or their families upon their return. Thus, temporary migration is a poor source of cash in most cases.

The reason for the low rate of cash brought back is not that savings are sent in the form of remittances. Migrants send very little cash or clothing (table 4.28). This is due to the poor communications as well as the fact that migrants have little to send. Michael Lipton (1982:209–213) points out that remittances are generally quite low in cases of rural-rural migration.

Table 4.28
Remittances to Families or Relatives by Dar Masalit Emigrants

Remittance	Number of Migrants	Migrants in 1970s Only
Nothing	151	110
LS 1–5	5	2
LS 6–10	2	2
LS 21–30	1	0
LS 31–50	2	2
Money, Amount Unknown	4	3
Clothing, Value Unknown	10	7
Money and Clothing	4	3

Thus, as an economic option temporary migration hardly seems to be appealing. The question arises, then, of why people are emigrating in higher numbers than ever when the returns to migration are much poorer than they used to be. In some cases, it may be that the 'pulls' of high income possibilities are still effective; migration is attractive to those who have or would like to learn a profitable skill, such as tailoring, and for those who hope to get a high-paying urban job or work in Saudi Arabia. Opportunities for these situations are limited, but many are willing to take the chance, and some have knowledge or contacts that improve their chances.

However, most migrants are aware that their incomes will be low, their living situation difficult, and their chances of saving enough money to make a substantial difference in their lives small. They go anyway, because of 'push' factors. The main problem is the impoverishment of Dar Masalit; aside from trade, the high-capital occupations, and agriculture there are not many chances to make money at home. Few people have the resources to undertake the first two. As for agriculture, land has become so scarce and unproductive that it is not sufficient for the cash needs, and in many cases the food needs, of the population.

Many migrants explained their actions to me in terms of land shortage. This was supported by the fact that the majority of the one hundred ninety-one absent migrants owned little or no land when they left. More solid support based on direct evidence was provided by analysis of the land areas held by families of the large sample. Twenty-nine families have thirty-nine members who were absent temporary migrants. The individuals so defined were still considered part of the family—spouses and unmarried children—and they were absent less than five years. These restrictions delimited a population for whom one can know each family's land situation precisely.

Comparison showed that families of migrants on the average cultivated twenty-eight percent less land per capita, counting migrants, than families with no current migrants (table 4.29). If the migrants were subtracted from the family size, families of migrants actually cultivated slightly more land per capita than families without migrants. Thus, on the average, emigration raised the families of migrants from a position of severe land shortage to one of land holdings comparable to other villagers.[25]

Table 4.29
Field Area Per Capita of Large Sample Families with and without Migrant Members

	Mean Hectares Per Capita[a]
Families without Migrants (N = 140)	1.31
Families with Migrants (N = 29)	0.95
Families with Migrants, per Current Resident[b]	1.44

a Significance of difference of means: $t = 1.25$, $p = 0.03$
b That is, excluding the migrants

In a family which is short of land, the limited holdings must be devoted to millet cultivation for food. Growing millet requires less labor than groundnuts, and added to small fields it results in a relative abundance of labor in land-poor families. Men in a few such families have the capital to work in transport or trade, which are good sources of cash; however, most men are restricted to earning money as agricultural laborers or low-capital craftsmen. These activities, as described above, are not nearly as remunerative as groundnut cultivation. Thus, even if land-poor families can feed themselves, they find it hard to meet the limited local standards for consumption of meat, sugar and other foods as well as clothing.

The situation is particularly difficult for husbands and fathers, who are in principle responsible for the cash needs of their wives and children. As a resident, the husband in a land-poor family is at fault before his family as a poor provider, eats from the same food that his family needs, and is somewhat underemployed on the farm. He is faced with the humiliating fact that his absence is better than his presence for the purposes of his family's subsistence. If he leaves, he can at least maintain himself, and his family can grow more food per capita while devoting some land to groundnuts.

Thus, as in Lourdes Arizpe's study of some Mexican communities, migration by one member of the household can be a strategy to maintain a rural household with a degree of autonomy (1982:43–45; compare Tully 1981b). This is not to say the rural household becomes well-off with the departure of the husband. A woman alone cannot hope to attain the cash income of a couple with sufficient land, and she may still experience low consumption possibilities. That fact, furthermore, must now be borne alone by the woman. She cannot effectively demand remittances from her husband several hundred miles away.

Young men in land-poor families are also likely to emigrate. In addition to the fact that they may have a good deal of optimism about their prospects in the east, they have good reason for pessimism about their prospects in Dar Masalit. If their parents cannot afford to turn over land to them, and their fathers cannot give them money, they have few opportunities for income and much time on their hands. Frequently sons of migrants join their fathers in the east.

Land scarcity at the family level is the symptom of land scarcity at the population level. It has developed in Masterei at about the same time as the migration phenomenon, that is, the 1940s–1960s (chapter 5). With the reduced rains of the 1970s, it is probably the case that families with marginally sufficient land in better years were forced into migration, which would explain the high emigration rate of the last decade.

Although land scarcity is a major factor pushing migrants out of Dar Masalit, not all migrants leave primarily or even partially because of a lack of land. Even for a person with land, the lack of money in Dar Masalit is acute, and many hope to do better, or to find out if they can do better, in the east. Some people, who already have resources, may use a trip to the east to increase those resources, perhaps with a strategy of emigration from Sudan. Thus, migration can be many things to many people. To understand migration as an option, I will discuss each of the major receiving areas in terms of the opportunities available to migrants there, and the economic position of Masalit in these areas.

Migrant Destinations and Occupations

Of the one hundred ninety-one absentees, the overwhelming majority are now located in the eastern Sudan, with one hundred one in Gedaref, five in the Medani-Sinja area, fifteen in Khartoum and four in Port Sudan (table 4.30). The next most common destination is the southern Darfur-Kordofan area, with thirty-three migrants. There is one migrant each in southern Sudan, Chad, Libya and Saudi Arabia. Finally, within Dar Masalit there are twenty-nine rural-urban migrants.

Table 4.30
Current Locations of Village Emigrants

Eastern Sudan	
Gedaref Area	101
Medani-Sinja Area	5
Khartoum	15
Port Sudan	4
Western Sudan	
Nyala and Area	4
Gereida Area	6
Wad Hajam Area	15
Ed Da'ein Area	3
Kordofan	5
Out of Northern Sudan	4
Within Dar Masalit	29
Total	191

DAR MASALIT INTERNAL MIGRATION. Within Dar Masalit, emigrants to other rural villages were not counted, as this sort of movement is a normal part of Masalit rural life. Through marriage or other processes, people find themselves changing their village of residence. However, migration to the towns is in large part a function of their roles in the market economy and the political structure, which present opportunities for those who are situated to exploit them.

Geneina, the capital of Dar Masalit, tripled in population from 1955–56 to 1973, according to the censuses cited earlier. However, Geneina is primarily a non-Masalit town, and is not a major destination for Masalit of Masterei; only five sample village men were there. From the Masterei rural areas, most internal migrants moved to Buga, including twenty-two from the sample villages. Census data did not reveal the rate of growth of such small towns, but by local accounts they have expanded rapidly over the last twenty years as commercial activity increased.

Marriage played a role in this process, as in inter-village migration; eight of the twenty-nine internal migrants married into a town and stayed, while two other people divorced village spouses and returned to families in town. However, half of the migrants moved as married couples. Since that time, three of the marriages dissolved and only one person returned to the village. Twenty-one new marriages (four now ended) occurred in the towns. Thus, many migrants within Dar Masalit explained their current location in terms of their marital history. Nevertheless, the net movement of spouses was towards the towns, and it was clear that the opportunities for making money, as well as the choice of a more nationally oriented cultural milieu, played a role in this. Five of the migrants were involved in trade, while nine had some sort of profitable occupation, such as sewing, making shoes, or working at the school.

In most cases of internal migration, one's animals can be taken along and fields are continued in cultivation. This reduces the opportunity cost of this form of migration for older, more established farmers who may have gone east in their younger days (eighteen internal migrants have done so; this appears to be the reverse of 'stepwise' migration observed elsewhere). Eighty-six percent of internal migrants are over thirty, compared to 59 percent of Dar Masalit emigrants. The fact that only four of the seventy-one village emigrants in the 11–30 age group have gone to Dar Masalit locations is a good indication of the limited extent of local economic opportunity currently. Those who have moved to local towns are those with agriculture to support them; except for two Geneina residents with good jobs, the migrants continue to farm. Living in town increases their ability to earn money from a craft or job, but does not eliminate their rural orientation.

MIGRATION TO THE NILE VALLEY. The Nile Valley, called *da:r aS Saba:H* (home of the morning) by the Masalit, has been the focus of economic development efforts in Sudan at least since the opening of the Gezira Scheme in 1925. Government and private investments in Blue Nile and Kassala provinces have exploited the Nile and its tributaries for irrigated plantations, and the rainfed plains for mechanized agriculture. Industrial development has been centered on 'the three towns' (Khartoum, Khartoum North, Omdurman) at the Nile confluence. The development of roads, markets and government services has also been much greater in this area than in the rest of Sudan. Thus, it is hardly surprising that this area is the major receiving zone for emigrants from the sample villages, as for other westerners.

Within the Nile Valley, however, various populations of immigrants are differently situated. The Gezira cotton plantations and the three towns receive many western migrants but are not major destinations for the Masalit. A few go to the Medani-Sinja area, but rarely to pick cotton for any substantial period of time. This is because Masalit migration is primarily undertaken by men, with women and children usually brought only if the migrant becomes somewhat established. Cotton picking in the Gezira, on the other hand, is primarily attractive to transient families. As O'Brien pointed out: "The wage rate in cotton picking has long been based on the predominance in the picking labor force of family groups" (1980:240). Wages can be kept low on a piece basis because children can contribute to the overall income of the family.

Instead of picking cotton, Masalit solo male migrants tend to work as much as possible in sorghum cultivation on rainfed schemes in Gedaref, where wages are higher. Gedaref and its vicinity is the most important receiving area for the sample villages (table 4.30), and from my observations, for Masalit in general.

According to informants in Dar Masalit, at least twenty-two of the seventy-seven listed male migrants to the Gedaref area or the Medani-Sinja area are known to be employed as laborers. An uncertain number of the others also work as agricultural laborers for much of their time to supplement other activities. Young and first-time migrants are strongly represented in this occupation, because it is an entry-level job requiring skills that they already possess, and no Arabic.

Agricultural labor is usually undertaken on a contract basis by small groups of men. An agent of a scheme or plantation negotiates a fixed price for a certain piece of work, which usually requires a month or two to complete. Most commonly they harvest or thresh, or both, a given area of sorghum. Weeding sorghum is still done by hand in some locations, and sesame growers also hire labor for various operations. While they work, the plantation or scheme provides minimal food and shelter, while advancing credit for sugar, tea and other optional goods. It is possible to net LS 10–20 per month in steady work. In spite of this, temporary migrants do not remit or accumulate large amounts of cash. There are a number of inhibiting factors.

Agricultural labor of this sort is very arduous, being more continuous and faster in pace than similar labors in Dar Masalit. Galal-el-Din points out that migrants are not well nourished and get an unbalanced diet, low in calories, in spite of the fact that their caloric need "exceeds the average need of an ordinary worker by ⅓" (1978:110–112). Concerning laborers returning to Kordofan, he notes: "Almost half of the migrants at their return were very exhausted and sick and needed a long period of time to recover their health and strength" (Galal-el-Din 1978:111). Migrants are also exposed to illnesses and accidents, and "in most cases the workers found no help from the scheme owner or the Gezira Board with reference to financial aid, treatment, or assistance to return home" (Galal-el-Din 1978:111). We may assume that exhaustion is partially responsible for the frequently reported intervals between contracts, in which the men live in crowded quarters in the towns; in these circumstances, money is rapidly spent on food and shelter as well as diversions while the worker rests.

Another factor inhibiting savings is the seasonality of labor. In the harvest season there is much work available, but later in the dry season there is hardly any work outside the Gezira, and in the rains there is little weeding work available due to mechanization. At the end of the harvest season, a worker may spend his savings on food and lodging while hoping for another job which may not come. Migrants' fortunes wax and wane, and this interacts with other factors to result in low savings at the time of return. A migrant may have to return suddenly because he gets sick, receives news of a death or food shortage, or runs out of funds.

Although typical savings are very small compared to the 1950s, they are still sometimes preferable to Dar Masalit, especially for landless young people. Even with LS 10 and a new set of clothing, a young returning migrant can make an impression on his friends, while an adult can buy enough millet for a month or two, so the trip is not a total loss. Thus, from the point of view of the laborers, there is at least a little money in the east; for young migrants especially, these small sums may be more than they have ever seen.

Not all agricultural laborers are temporary; some stay on and lose touch with their families. In Gedaref town there are communities of Masalit bachelors, living in barracks type arrangements, who take odd jobs and work seasonally in agriculture. Rates of alcohol consumption appear high and morale low, but further study is required to determine how general this pattern is. There are very few women in these communities, and they do not appear to engage in agricultural labor, in spite of the fact that women harvest and thresh in the west. Women in these communities can make a living by brewing, making food, and other odd jobs.

Men are unable to call upon family women for customary female services, and so must depend on unrelated women. One woman I met was a sort of house mother. A man visited by my assistant and I made special arrangements with a woman to receive us at her house and make tea, since he had no house or kitchen. With increasing female migration in recent years, there will undoubtedly be more independent town women in the future.

The occupation most commonly reported in the Gedaref-Medani area is that of farmer; 47 percent of those with known occupations farm. Many of these are also laborers, but the designation farmer means here that they have at least some access to land. These people usually live in large villages south and southwest of Gedaref, some of which are Masalit and some of which are composed of several ethnic groups. Other westerners also have villages there. These villages have grown up as sheikhs have invited migrants to settle and cultivate. As mentioned above, independent farming was a profitable temporary occupation in the 1940s and 1950s, and continues to be practiced by temporary migrants who can get access to land.

However, these villages are now rather large, and permanent residents predominate; many settlers have been able to marry in Gedaref or bring their families from the west. Thus, the ratio of females to males is not as low as in other receiving areas, and families with typical Masalit housing arrangements are common. Some degree of stratification has developed within the villages, as certain villagers have become involved in trade, transport and oil pressing.

Most villagers I talked to considered the economic situation better than in Dar Masalit; they pointed out that crop prices were higher and the prices of consumer goods were lower. However, there was some feeling that land was declining in quality and availability, in part due to the expansion of mechanized schemes. Thus, resettlement as a farmer in these villages appeared to be less possible and less attractive as time went on. Nevertheless for existing residents it represented a way of maintaining some degree of Masalit identity and lifestyle, while participating substantially in the Sudanese national culture and economy.

In addition to the agricultural laborers and small farmers of the Gedaref-Medani area, there are a number of migrants who engage in some nonagricultural activity as their primary occupation. The most important of these is sewing, while people with small jobs or handicraft skills include a builder, a watchman, a gas-station attendant, an ironer, and others. There are a few traders and lorry drivers among the migrants as well and these are well-paid, high status occupations. Because many of these are located in urban areas of the eastern countryside, I consider them in conjunction with similarly employed migrants in Khartoum and Port Sudan (table 4.31). Laborers in Gedaref may also occasionally engage in nonagricultural labor, and the four Khartoum laborers in table 4.31 are presumably 100 percent nonagricultural.

Table 4.31
Primary Occupations of Emigrants in the Eastern Sudan

	Gedaref-Medani		Khartoum-Port Sudan	
	Male	Female	Male	Female
Laborer	22	1	4	0
Farmer	27	16	0	0
Small Job or Craft	7	0	1	0
Tailor	8	0	3	0
Transport	2	0	4	0
Trade or Shop	2	0	0	0
Brewing	0	3	0	0
No Job	1	3	0	4
Unknown	8	6	3	0
Total	77	29	15	4

Work in service jobs and survival in urban locations require social skills and a knowledge of Arabic that are not needed in farming. Sewing, driving and some other jobs also require substantial training. Getting access to a job as watchman or getting started in training as a tailor may depend on one's luck in meeting and impressing people, but they also frequently result from the contacts of friends and relatives. This is especially true of sewing, which is something of a Masalit specialty.

In eastern Sudanese towns, tailors usually operate in conjunction with merchants who sell cloth; several tailors usually work in a shop. The merchant may own the machines and allow a tailor to work on a 50–50 or other basis with him, or he may rent a working place to a tailor with his own machine. One who wishes to be a tailor must first carry out an apprenticeship of several months, for which the apprentice generally pays. He must then seek out a merchant who hires him to use his machine. Over years, he may try to accumulate enough money to buy a machine; if he does so, he may stay in the east and sew with a higher income, or he may take his machine to Dar Masalit, as described earlier. At several stages in this process, well-connected friends or kin can help, for example, in arranging or providing the apprenticeship, supporting the apprentice, and finding a place for the trained tailor.

Sewing, which demands long hours all year long, is considered difficult work in the east, but it often pays well (although it is a highly variable and competitive business). A number of tailors have been able to bring their families to live with them in the east or marry there, in spite of the high costs of urban living for a family. Women in cities are generally unable to contribute to the family income (table 4.32). These tailors, as well as other relatively highly-paid Masalit from the villages, are models of success for many of the other migrants who aspire to an urban life.

Table 4.32
Marital Status of Male Emigrants in Eastern Sudan according to their Primary Occupation

	Spouse with Migrant	Spouse only in Dar Masalit	Unmarried
Laborer	1	5	19
Farmer	13	3	9
Small Job	4	2	2
Tailor	6	3	2
Transport	3	0	3
Trader	2	0	0

These types of jobs, as well as homesteading in an eastern village, make relatively permanent settlement feasible for emigrants; whether it is attractive or not depends on their circumstances at home. Wage labor, on the other hand, does not provide enough income to support a family. Thus, laborers may either return home after a period of time, or resign themselves to a single life. Labor is also used by migrants to sustain themselves while looking for other work and acquiring Arabic or other skills.

Because of this flexibility, it is not possible to clearly distinguish temporary and permanent migrants; if a migrant finds a good farm or other opportunity, he may well decide to stay, marrying locally or bringing a family from home, even if his original intention had been to return with cash; alternatively, if he has no luck or gets sick, he may be forced to return even if his intention had been to resettle. An initial trip, even if unprofitable, increases one's knowledge of opportunities and procedures in the receiving area, and increases the likelihood of later success; most men who have secured good jobs or farms have not done so on their first trip.

However, over time a man's family also grows, increasing the costs of resettlement; meanwhile, it is possible that he may inherit some land or develop other economic ties to Dar Masalit. If one has not found a suitable opportunity to resettle by the time he is forty, his future is probably going to be based in Dar Masalit, possibly with additional trips until he is too old to migrate.

Thus, the choice of migration by an individual, and possibly of resettlement at a later time, depends on the circumstances of the migrant and his family in Dar Masalit, including their economic and social position and their values and aspirations. It also depends upon their experiences and perceptions of possibilities in the east. The variety and complexity of the individual decisions can be baffling. By contrast, the overall pattern is fairly simple. These decisions are being made in the context of an impoverished Dar Masalit, and a concentration of investment in the Nile Valley. Through a diversity of strategies, migrants try to get some individual benefit out of that investment.

MIGRATION WITHIN WESTERN SUDAN. A smaller number of emigrants from the sample villages (thirty-three) have left Dar Masalit for southern Darfur or Kordofan locations. These include a driver, a horse-cart owner, and a *mu'azzin* (one who calls the faithful to prayer) in Nyala, and four laborers in various locations. The remainder are farmers. Because they are close to the railroad, these areas offer some of the advantages of the Gedaref area; prices for farm products are higher than in Dar Masalit, while prices for consumer goods are lower. They are also close enough to the Nile Valley for seasonal migration, and they receive more government services than Dar Masalit. Although many migrants passed through this area in working their way to the east in the past, western Sudan has only become a major destination in the last fifteen years. In particular, areas south and southwest of Nyala may be expanding Masalit areas in the future.

Masalit have had a long history of residence in the Gereida area, and a respected elder there told me that the sultanate of this area predates the sultanate of Dar Masalit. Sultan Andoka told the resident in 1921 that the Masalit of that area had been separated from those of Dar Masalit for approximately two hundred years (Intel 2/51/429). However, there appears to have been a certain amount of continuing communication between the two areas.

The soil here is goz, and millet and groundnuts are grown as in Dar Masalit. There is still fallow land here for rotation and there is more rain. With the rainfall decline in Dar Masalit in recent years, especially at the peak of the drought in 1972–73, many Masalit came to this area, particularly from the northern Dar. A few migrants from the sample villages still live in various parts of the Gereida area. However, according to the local informants, most only stayed for a year and then went to Wad Hajjam. With fifteen emigrants from the sample villages, Wad Hajjam is the most important receiving area in the west.

Wad Hajjam is a market town south of Tullus, and is also the site of a borehole. It is inhabited by nomadic Habbaniyya as well as various settled populations, and relations between Habbaniyya and Masalit appear to be relatively good. Villages have been founded around Wad Hajjam on the extensive goz soils, where millet and groundnuts are cultivated. Land is available for the taking, but limited water keeps the population density low. Migrants in Wad Hajjam have tended to come as families, joining relatives or friends in Masalit villages of balanced sex ratio.

As some settlers pointed out, there is not a great deal of money in this area; for those who aspire to a well-paid job or occupation, Wad Hajjam is disappointing. However, others are very happy with life there; the rains are good and there is a ready market for both crops and 'low-capital' crafts. It is clear from the amounts and types of clothing, food and household goods used that there is more market participation here than in Dar Masalit, and greater adoption of Sudanese norms. Arabic is spoken by many Masalit among themselves, and marriage by cash instead of livestock is general. However, in many ways these homesteaders, like those in Gedaref, are recreating Masalit rural life in a way that is integrated with the market while preserving a certain measure of autonomy. For those who aspire to the rural life, but either lack land in Dar Masalit or desire higher levels of market consumption, this area may prove attractive in the future.

This is particularly significant in view of a recent suggestion that settlement in Goz Dango, the sparsely populated area immediately west of Wad Hajjam, be encouraged to ease the pressure on overcultivated areas subject to desertification (Bakhit 1983:8). This requires the development of water resources in the area and a thorough understanding of current land use by pastoralists (Tully 1985), which may have been underestimated; nevertheless it seems quite possible that if the government wishes to promote small farms in the west rather than migration to the east, it has a good opportunity to do so here.

DESTINATIONS OUTSIDE OF NORTHERN SUDAN. There are four men in this category—one each in southern Sudan, Chad, Libya and Saudi Arabia. As such, each could be considered a special case hardly worth mentioning; however, it is necessary to discuss emigration of this sort in terms of its possible future importance. The wealth to be had in Libya and Saudi Arabia is a recurring topic of conversation among a handful of men with experience in the east. A few villagers of the Masterei area are employed in Saudi Arabia, and have come back on leave with trunks of elite goods—radios, tape recorders, fancy fabrics, perfumes—as well as ample quantities of cash to buy livestock, get married, or help relatives and friends. The effect may be like the effect forty or fifty years ago of the first emigrants to return from the east with imported clothing, tea and sugar; expectations are changed as people compare themselves to a new standard by which their position is very low.

However, it remains to be seen whether external migration can become as general as migration to the east. There are many obstacles, for instance, getting proof of one's Sudanese nationality requires persistence, then getting a passport requires even more persistence and money. Also, there is the problem of getting employment, when there are thousands of Sudanese with relatives and contacts closer to the employer's agents than any Masalit. All of this requires time, as well as money to survive in Khartoum during that time. It may be possible for more Masalit to engage in emigration to Saudi Arabia in the future, in spite of reduced hiring levels in the wake of the drop in oil prices. (Indeed one of my field assistants went there after my departure.) Because success in emigration to a wealthy country will probably be restricted to a few, it is more likely to become part of a cycle of accumulation leading to local differentiation in productive activities. On the other hand, previous emigrants abroad have not been anxious to return permanently to rural areas of Dar Masalit, and this may play a role in insulating the Dar from foreign emigration in the future.

Migration and Market Incorporation

Migration is an activity which takes a variety of forms according to the resources, purposes and luck of migrants, and it has changed in nature over time. The nineteenth century migration pattern was one of regional movement, involving the founding of new villages and colonization or recolonization of bush lands. This pattern barely continues to exist at present. With the development of major capital investment and export markets based in the Nile Valley, a new pattern has become predominant—migration towards areas of high capital investment. For some this has presented a new type of resettlement opportunity, while for others it has been a means of acquiring cash for taxes, consumption and other needs. More recently, this pattern has degenerated to one whereby the majority of migrants merely maintain themselves outside of the Dar in order to reduce the number of family members subsisting on their limited land.

On the other hand, for some Masalit, migration to the east has been a source of cash or other assets that are now employed as capital in Dar Masalit. As mentioned in preceding sections, migration has played an important role in the histories of most tailors and traders who are currently operating in the villages; almost all brought their machines or their trading capital back from the east. Many camels have also been bought with cash from migration. Currently, some villagers discuss the possibility of raising trading capital in other countries and settling with it in the village, although this has not yet occurred.

In this section emigration has been described as an economic activity for comparison with other activities. The purpose is to make it possible to discuss decisions to migrate, as opposed to engaging in local agriculture, trade or handicrafts. However, to a large extent these activities are not comparable nor are they in the same category as options. It has been impossible to be as quantitative with migration as with the other activities, simply because there is so much uncertainty over the effects of and returns to a given migration decision.

Furthermore, migration changes many things in addition to one's income; for example, one's family ties, attitudes about money, rights to land, valuation of Masalit identity—some of which may be known by the migrant beforehand, and some not. Therefore, instead of reducing the "returns to migration" to a number based on urban incomes and the likelihood of obtaining a job (Todaro 1976), I have attempted to describe something about the lifestyles and communities that present themselves to the potential migrant. Some migrants may just want cash, or a farm, or an urban job, but I believe that most do not know enough about the east to understand what these goals entail until they have migrated at least once. In that process they change, develop new skills, hopes, and plans, and luck and coincidence affect their decisions as well.

The young in Dar Masalit grow up knowing that there is another world, which stands as an alternative to their direct experience. They know that most of their parents, kin and neighbors consider themselves poor, and that there is wealth in the east; thus, migration presents itself as a strong attraction. Whether they migrate, how long they are absent, and whether they resettle depends very much on their alternatives in Dar Masalit. These are, in part, the context of their decisions.

As I have argued above, both agricultural and nonagricultural activities in the Dar have been weakened to the point that many people cannot maintain a minimal standard of living. Thus, migration has become inevitable for them. This is obviously not a case where migration absorbs surplus labor from an unchanged traditional sector; rather it is an outcome of the underdevelopment of the local economy, and the concentration of national economic development in the eastern Sudan (compare Lipton 1982; Mahmoud 1984:29). Labor as a commodity takes its place alongside the crops, livestock and forest resources that flow toward the Nile Valley from rural Dar Masalit.

Migration also contributes to local processes of market integration. First, migrants populate the towns and cities which mediate the flows of commodities between the villages and the urban centers. They move, sell and process the goods that are imported and exported, with varying degrees of specialization. Second, migration contributes to the transformation of social relations within the villages. Successful migrants can invest their earnings, while the absence of men in many families increases the control of production by village-level merchants. The mechanisms and effects of this process of differentiation are discussed in the next chapter. Third, from the very beginning, migration has introduced new tastes and consumption standards. This has reduced the demand for local manufactures and has increased demands for imports. These processes cannot precisely be considered to be results of migration, since they are part and parcel of the same larger dynamic. Urbanization, rural differentiation and labor migration are simultaneous, mutually reinforcing processes that further incorporate Dar Masalit into the world economy.

Conclusion

This chapter has analyzed the major activities that the Masalit carry out in order to produce use values and commodities, and also to obtain income through commerce, employment, or migration. I have discussed the values that people place upon these activities, their place in Masalit life, and changes in importance they have undergone in the process of market integration. To make comparison possible, the labor and capital requirements of the various activities have been stressed, as well as the incomes they produce. Across a broad range of activities I have demonstrated that labor requirements to meet subsistence have increased for the poor, who comprise the majority of the population, and that new income sources have been much less rewarding for the poor than for those with money to invest. I have also shown that market forces have affected every major category of Masalit economic life, often profoundly. There follows a review of some of these points.

In the domestic sphere, subsistence labor requirements have increased, primarily as a result of the effects of urbanization and agricultural intensification upon forest resources. Essentials for food preparation and shelter require a greater expenditure of labor or money than has formerly been the case; only the well-off can maintain a quality of housing and a variety of diet that have formerly been the norm. The increased labor requirements present particular difficulties to women, because female domestic activities conflict with peak-season agricultural activities.

In agriculture, production has been intensified in order to obtain money by supplying market demand; this has led to higher labor requirements, and possibly reduced yields and increased erosion. One-fifth of the agricultural land, most of it of the best quality, is devoted to groundnuts, and their cultivation requires approximately one-third of peak season labor. Millet sales to town populations and nomads are also substantial. For those with land and enough money to hire labor, crop sales can be profitable, but for those who must sell their labor, agricultural work is a very limited source of income.

Changes in domestic and agricultural activities are mirrored in and reinforced by changes in nonagricultural activities. Production for local exchange is poorly paid and declining. The profitable new activities are transport and sewing, which require substantial capital investment. Camel owners derive income from the increased flow of crops and forest resources onto the market, and the return flow of imports. Tailors are hired to sew imported cloth with the income generated by exports. At a higher level, merchants are profiting from both sides of world market participation, being exporters of the produce of the land and importers of consumer goods. Finally, the most extreme example of participation in the world market at the expense of the local economy is found in migration, where people actually remove themselves as producers and consumers for varying lengths of time. This increases rural inequality, while the changed tastes of returned migrants undermine the demand for rural goods.

Thus, the local orientation of production and exchange has already been reduced in a variety of ways, and local autonomy diminished. Production for local exchange, with the exception of food production for towns, is of little consequence compared to the export and import of commodities. Indeed, regional trade is too limited in volume to occupy the capital of village merchants, and is left in the hands of sabbabis with less money. The undermining of local exchange is not an inevitable part of market incorporation. Carol Smith (1978) reported the case of western Guatemala, where market participation provided the basis of an expanded regional economy with much intra-rural exchange. Similarly, data from Kenya (Mbithi and Chege 1973; Mureithi 1973) and Africa generally (Byerlee et al. 1977) point to substantial rural diversification into small manufacturing enterprises. Dar Masalit, on the other hand, maintains what Smith calls a hierarchical structure of markets; exports flow outward and upward to ever-larger centers, while imports flow down the same structure. We need to consider the circumstances under which production for local or regional use is either supported or eliminated by market integration.

In the case of Dar Masalit, there are a number of factors that militate against regional autonomy. First, the orientation of export and import to Port Sudan, as opposed to the precolonial orientation across the Sahara, leaves the Masalit badly situated with respect to communications. All of Sudan lies between them and the world market. As a result they are in a weak bargaining position. As producers and consumers of the same goods as many other Sudanese, Masalit farmers have been unable to get much money for their crop exports, but they pay high prices for imports. This limits rural purchasing power, and therefore the money income available from manufacturing for the rural market.

If local manufacturers could produce adequate substitutes for imported goods, the distance factor would favor local exchange. However, this is not the case. The second factor is that the nature of the most important imports—fabric, sugar, spices, and others—makes the production of local substitutes technically infeasible. Indeed, competition with imported fabric has destroyed the local manufacture of cloth, which was a major nonagricultural activity, while demand for sugar and spices has probably been increased by the destruction of forest resources, and the consequent reduction in dietary diversity.

Third, inhibition of local manufactures goes beyond direct competition in consumption to competition in production. Incomes are higher in production activities oriented to export than they are in comparable manufactures oriented to the local market. As shown, in the rainy season, agricultural laborers, usually hired for groundnut production, are paid more than they can obtain in almost all low-capital crafts. The exception is tanning of hides for export, which has the highest income of all nonagricultural manufactures in all seasons. External buyers and sellers can afford to compete in this way with locally oriented production because of the local scarcity of money, and presumably, because high profits are available in the bulking and resale of goods produced in rural areas. Furthermore, for those with money to invest, high and secure incomes are available in occupations directly linked to the world market; as a result merchants, tailors and jammala rarely engage in crafts oriented to local exchange.

On another level of analysis, the issue of relative autonomy involves more than the orientation of productive activities. In many respects this is a result of the structure of control of productive assets, which determine how assets and resources are deployed to one or another activity. Consequently the next step is to go beyond the study of economic behavior to analyze some conditions of that behavior, or the distribution and control of assets and resources.

5. *Assets and Resources*

To comprehend the actual working of a socioeconomic system and to relate the system to the individuals in it, a description of economic activities alone is not sufficient. Based on the incomes available in the activities just described, anyone might wish to be a merchant or tailor, or to hire labor to cultivate large areas of groundnuts. These activities require certain kinds of assets, such as land and money, which are not evenly distributed. Certain activities are restricted by gender in local practice, and as previously described, the assets required for some activities are also differentially distributed by gender. In addition knowledge, training and contacts are required for many activities. To explain the adaptations of individuals, it is necessary to know what their options are in terms of assets, resources, and cultural factors.

Therefore to complete the task begun in the last chapter, information is presented on the distribution of the main productive assets, restrictions on their use, and patterns of access to them. Next, the effect of market integration on the value and control of these assets is analyzed. Finally, I discuss the extent to which current patterns of control of assets make a class analysis relevant, and the predictions suggested by such analysis.

In the preceding chapters I have described various changes in the local economy that have taken place in the colonial and postcolonial period. With integration into the world market there have been increases in export crop and hide production, and largely as a result, in transport and marketing activities. Labor migration has also increased. In contrast, some local economic activities have declined, and forest resources have diminished.

These changes are fairly easy to see, but associated with them have been changes that are somewhat more subtle in the realm of productive assets. Not only has the distribution of assets changed; their relationships, meanings and values have become fundamentally different. Land has become a scarce resource relative to labor rather than vice-versa. Moreover, the socioeconomic system is now more oriented to cash, which is increasingly dominant over both land and labor. Communal resources, such as forest goods and water, and intangibles such as training have come to be more easily available to those with money than to those without. These transformations of relationships among productive assets are associated with profound changes in the relationships of human beings, including the basis of wealth and power in Masalit society. Formerly political organization was focused on the control of people, and through their labor, the control of land; now money is the greater determinant of power.

This sort of monetization of economic and social relationships, which entails the creation of new bases of inequality, is one of the most general features of the incorporation of small-scale societies into the world market, and it is crucial to understand the processes by which these changes occur. Therefore each of the major categories of productive assets is discussed in turn, with consideration of their distribution, patterns of access to them, their roles in the local and global economy, and the ways in which these things have changed over time. Having done so it is possible to examine the current nature of wealth and power in more detail, and whether or not a process of class formation can be discerned. We are also able to consider what this portends concerning future socioeconomic processes in Dar Masalit.

Land: The Development of Scarcity and its Effect on Rights

As Dar Masalit has entered the cash economy, the people have continued to farm even as they trade, sell beer, and buy tea. To a large extent the technology used in agriculture appears to have changed little in hundreds of years, and the principle crop continues to be millet. Yet the land on which people obtain their livelihood has acquired a very different meaning in the Masalit world. From an asset that was relatively abundant, land has become a scarce possession, rights to which are carefully protected. Although its productivity has declined and its central place in Masalit economic life is now shared with new sources of income, access to a reasonable amount of productive land is still a prerequisite for residence in rural Dar Masalit.

Customary rights of access from precolonial Masalit culture have been carried into the present, but they have been supplemented by new patterns which are related to the market economy. In the context of land scarcity, these patterns have led to inequalities in land ownership and changes in the ownership of land by sex. Land has still not become a monetized asset, subject to purchase and sale, although it is possible that this can happen in the future; such a change would imply a very deep transformation of Masalit socioeconomic structures.

The following description of land use and access in the past draws primarily on interviews with older men concerning the early colonial period. Their testimony is confirmed and supplemented by settlement histories of a number of villages, camps and agricultural areas in the Masterei area, and histories of several families long resident in the area. The pattern of land use described is predicated upon an abundance of land relative to the population and its needs. As stated earlier, there was a good deal of immigration and emigration in the period of Masalit independence; therefore one does not know the demographics of nineteenth century Dar Masalit and the ratio of people to land. However, the data I have collected concerning the expansion of particular clans, as well as other aspects of social organization, are consistent with the pattern described and suggest that it was characteristic of Masalit society over an extended period of time, and not just the early colonial period. This pattern continues to be the basis of ideal explanations of land access which have been put forward to me on a number of occasions, but which are in fact observed only in the breach.

Before the development of land scarcity, Masalit practiced a form of shifting cultivation, as did many peoples of the Sahelian zone. There are in general two ways by which a population may distribute itself in shifting cultivation. On the one hand, farmers may maintain stable residences and several nearby fields, which they cultivate and fallow in some form of rotation. On the other hand, entire villages may cultivate all nearby arable land, and then move when it is desirable to cultivate fresh land. The latter case actually comprises two possibilities: villagers may move periodically as a group, or alternatively, old villages may gradually dissolve while new villages grow up, absorbing those people who choose to move.

All three of these patterns existed simultaneously in precolonial Masalit society, but the last was dominant. Villages appear to have gone through a developmental cycle. One or several men identified a promising agricultural area, marked it with their axes and began to clear land. The good yields of new land were offset by the extra work involved, the depredations of birds and wild animals, the insecurity of small numbers in the face of raids, and the lack of the pleasures of village social life. However over time the founders persuaded new settlers from among their friends and kin, and they also tried to keep their children with them after they married. To do this they helped their children and the newcomers to cut their fields and build their houses (compare Gulliver 1971 for a similar pattern in southern Tanzania).

As a village grew, social life improved, cooperative work, hunts and other ventures were more successful, and the village was secure, which attracted more people to settle. Due to weed problems and declining yields, fields were usually abandoned after six to ten years, and a local rotation took place. Sooner or later, depending on the amount of arable land and the rate of village growth, local virgin land was exhausted and fields became insufficient for long enough fallows to take place. Some villagers then moved as a group, while others began new villages or joined existing villages at some later stage in the development cycle, according to their tastes and circumstances. The site reverted to forest until it was reopened in another cycle.

It is important to the interpretation of current patterns of land rights that one understands their basis in this former mode of adaptation. Most of this movement took place within clan territories, or *haku:ra*s. In each hakura, a malik represented the clan to the outside, and also represented the clan's rights to land within the territory. A malik led the clan in defending its boundaries or in conquering new territory. A man or several men, who wanted to open a new agricultural area, would get the permission of the malik to do so; he then could establish rights as sid al-fas (*si:d al fa:s*, lord of the axe), by marking and clearing territory as described earlier.

Village founders sometimes established contiguous but distinct fas territories around the same village; for example, in the village in which I lived three village founders of different clans established fas territories. Many of their grandchildren are village men and women in their 40s to 60s today, and these people sometimes spoke of these areas as clan territories; however, they were in fact held by groups of kin who, while sharing membership in particular clans, did not necessarily make up a distinct clan segment. One of the descendants is sometimes recognized as the current sid al-fas, but all older descendants speak of having fas rights, or land 'from the ancestors.' (Compare Saul 1983:78–79 for a similar pattern of land rights in Upper Volta, and Berry 1975:90ff. for a number of similar features in western Nigeria.)

If a holder of fas rights attracted individuals to join him, he became a village founder. By allocating land to settlers he became their benefactor; they acknowledged this each year by delivering a small portion of the harvest to him. In the future he helped settlers to find new fields for themselves or their children, and he protected their land from encroachment by other settlers when they allowed it to lay fallow. It also seems consistent with my information and with current practice, that the position of sid al-fas and village founder was a good basis for a person to become a central figure not unlike a "big man" (Sahlins 1963). That is, as a village founder grew older, with his children, kin and friends around him and indebted to him, his reputation grew; he was able to do favors for those who settled with him concerning matters other than land itself, such as resolving disputes, interceding with the malik, and arranging a good marriage.[2] However the weakness of the sid's position was the temporary nature of agricultural settlements. As land became less abundant, consituents sought to settle elsewhere. For this reason some men founded settlements two or three times in their lifetimes; they always needed new land to allocate in order to maintain their influence.

The sid al-fas maintained residual rights in the land he allocated, and when the land was left fallow he could reallocate it or use it himself if he so desired. Similarly the malik had residual rights to fas territories. Fas rights were meaningless in the case of a military defeat in which a malik lost a territory to another malik; the area was then open for reallocation by the new malik.

Marshall D. Sahlins (1961) pointed out that a segmentary lineage organization such as that of the Masalit, especially in conjunction with a war organization and opportunities for incorporation of conquered neighbors, was well-suited to territorial expansion. I suggest that a pattern of land rights such as that of the Masalit is also eminently suitable and conducive to such expansion. The wide distribution of maliks and clan territories, and the oral histories of certain clans suggest that some had been moving and growing over a substantial period of time before the founding of the Masalit sultanate, at the expense of each other and of neighboring non-Masalit. With the advent of furshas and sultans, malik territories were enforced, created, or abolished from above rather than by local contests, and a new level of residual rights over land was established. Nevertheless, as described in chapter 2, expansion by maliks was allowed to continue by the sultans because it was in their interests as well.

In spite of the existence of superiors with some rights over the land under cultivation, from the farmer's point of view possession was nine points of the law. By cultivating a piece of land a farmer acquired and maintained rights to cultivate it in the future, to give it away, lend it, or specify an heir for it. On the other hand by letting it fallow for a few years, he or she gradually lost rights over it. If someone asked the sid for permission to cultivate fallow land, he could give it away without asking approval from the previous cultivator. If a new farmer simply cut the fallow and began to cultivate, rights to the land became ambiguous, and the new farmer stood a good chance of keeping the land.[3] However, as long as land was abundant, there was little reason to contest a given piece, and rights to resume usage after fallow were usually respected if the farmer wanted to maintain them.

This dependence of land rights on use strengthened the position of the farmers in relation to the sid al-fas. It was unlikely that fas rights were maintained if no one settled with the sid and cultivated the land, since effective possession never occurred; besides, there was little point in being sid al-fas alone in the bush. The sid needed settlers who would agree to accept land from him. Although it appeared as if land were the basis of social relationships, in fact land was abundant and settlers could choose among many villages or start their own. Land was merely the idiom of social relationships, which were also based on a variety of personal relationships between founders and settlers. The founder needed the settlers to use the land in order to maintain his residual rights over it, just as they had to use it to maintain their own rights.

The above description is essentially in agreement with Jack Goody's (1971) model of African societies, in which land is not seen as an effective means of control over people. G. Michael La Rue contests this view, using evidence from land charters issued under the Fur sultanate. He rightly argues that land has differing value due to variation in quality and location. The latter would be especially important in the vicinity of administrative centers. He also notes the importance of improvements, which would be of great importance in terraced areas of the Fur heartland. These points are practical and should be kept in mind when considering the abundance of 'land' as a resource.

However most of the Sahelian zone was probably more similar to Dar Masalit than to the immediate vicinity of the sultan of the Fur. In the hinterlands, good land is likely to have been relatively abundant in the nineteenth century. Further, as argued in chapter 4, rotation of village sites was a feature of the cultural ecology, and played an important role in weed control and in the maintenance of soil fertility. With reason, La Rue points out the difficulties of moving, and yet movement was frequent, due to marriage, remarriage, divorce, and the developmental cycle of extended families. These demographic events are now the precipitators of most moves, and they probably also were in the nineteenth century. But any such move can also involve a choice of destination based on land availability.

Thus in Dar Masalit under the Ancien Regime, there is no sign that "control of land was both a sign of, and basis for social domination" (La Rue 1984:10). I believe that calling land an idiom of social relationships gives it its proper importance at the level of the commoners. External forces may have allocated rights to the land one lived on, but in local terms, society was fairly egalitarian and land was not a major concern.

As land has become scarce in recent decades, its importance has grown; in particular, the dependence of the right to possess land on its continued use has come to have a different meaning. As described in chapter 2, from the British conquest to the present, Dar Masalit has seen substantial immigration even as its territory has become firmly bounded. Inevitably, this has contributed to the development of land scarcity. Scarcity has also been caused in part by increased needs for land to cultivate export crops and make up for lost forest resources, and, in recent years, to counteract the reduced yields resulting from continuous cultivation and declining rainfall. Land scarcity is apparent in the Masterei area, especially to those who are forced to emigrate temporarily or permanently (as shown in chapter 4), but it has developed gradually. Because land can be kept under cultivation for long periods of time, because most farmers at the time of occupation were rotating among several fields, and because abandoned village sites were available to be reopened for cultivation, there was ample room for people to settle and farm in the short term.

As indicated above and in chapter 2, it was in the political and economic interests of local elites to encourage people to settle, and this policy was supported by the British and the Native Administration. In the long run, however, the increase in population meant that individuals neither rotated among fields locally, nor operated the former pattern of village formation and dispersion. The resulting reduction in productivity and flexibility were not sharply felt until well after most immigrants were socially absorbed into local communities.

The timing of this process varied throughout Dar Masalit, but the high level of internal mobility probably spread the increasing population over the available land in a way that roughly equalized scarcity. In the Masterei area, during the 1930s, 1940s and 1950s, numerous former village sites and agricultural areas were reinhabited or brought under cultivation by the residents of existing villages, which were growing in size. Good land near existing villages began to be scarce and rights of land use came to be more closely guarded and passed from parent to child. Even among farmers now over fifty years of age, who have primary use rights to the fields they cultivate, only 63 percent of their fields were cut from bush fallow; for those who are in their forties the rate drops to 33 percent, and continues to decline in younger generations (table 5.1. The data base of this table and other related analysis is discussed in more detail below).

Table 5.1
Fields cut from Bush according to Age of Farmer

	Fields Cut From Bush	Number of Fields Owned	Percentage Cut From Bush
Age Group			
Over 50	52	83	63
41–50	25	76	33
30–40	15	62	24
Under 30	8	53	15

Note: Based on fields under cultivation by their owners in the large sample; six cases of unknown age were excluded

Currently, the great majority of land under cultivation has been held in the farmers' families for one or two generations. A process related to fragmentation has taken place, but without as much actual division of fields as might be expected; in fact the size of fields owned by younger farmers is not significantly different from that of older farmers. However, whereas grandparents of today's farmers each cut three or four fields that they used alternately, these fields are now held by separate individuals who cannot fallow because they have insufficient land in total.

This process is made clear in the histories of the families of five village founders or early settlers whose ancestors cut lands at the end of the nineteenth century. They all had rights over several large areas, each large enough to permit rotation within it. In each family their children distributed these areas, and in some cases divided them into fields among themselves, and the children usually cut new fields in other places as well. Good lands conveniently located were scarce enough to be valued, but new land was still available for the children of the village founders. In the next generation, the grandchildren of the founders, who are now adults, distributed these fields among themselves and had little opportunity to cut new fields. Some got no fields; these included elder children whose parents needed their land to feed their younger siblings, as well as younger children who were last in line for gifts or inheritance from their parents.

Whatever the particulars were in each case, those who were landless either emigrated from Dar Masalit, married a person with land, or found a field in some other way. Among currently middle-aged or young adults, few of their fields have been fallowed since they have begun cultivating them. Most of the actual fields have not been fragmented to any great degree. However, the previous shifting adaptation to this environment involved each farmer in a rotation of cultivation over an area five to ten times as large as the average farmer currently cultivates. Because the rights in these lands are now held by a number of people who cannot rotate, there has been an effective fragmentation of the ownership of agricultural resources, in a way which is probably typical of shifting cultivation. Actual fragmentation at the field level may be about to begin; several cases were observed in which inherited fields were divided into two or more fields.

When land was abundant, the right to continue cultivating a field shared pride of place in the patterns of access to the land with the right to cut bush fallow, pending a permission that was assumed to be forthcoming. As bush became scarce, rights of continuity became the only important rights. Since fas rights were largely residual in character and expressed only when land was let fallow, they faded into insignificance, with a few exceptions. For example, in the 1960s, when mango planting was going on in the village wadi, some holders of fas rights were able to prevent tree planting or restrict it to themselves and their relatives. In one case, a young man had inherited a field which bordered the wadi from his mother; the sid al-fas had forbidden tree crops, but the man secretly planted trees among the grain next to the wadi. When this became known, the fas holder was supported by the village in taking away the field—except for the section with the trees. (As is later described, trees can be used to establish ownership rights.)

A few farmers still give a token gift of millet to their sid al-fas out of respect. However, for most farmers the sid al-fas is unimportant, and continuous cultivation of lands has made his position irrelevant. This change probably has contributed to the decline of the position of the maliks as well. For most purposes, land has become an individually held asset, which can be given, willed, or loaned. It still cannot be sold except in certain cases to be described below; neither can it be fallowed, at least not for more than three years, without it becoming liable to appropriation by another farmer. With these limits in mind, in the following discussion the person with primary rights to cultivate or dispose of a field is considered to be its owner. It is worth noting at this point that under the Sudanese constitution the government is the ultimate owner of all lands. In most of western Sudan land ownership below this level is considered by the government to be communal, which leaves the local community to determine the distribution of use rights, although the courts occasionally intervene.

Current Patterns of Land Access and Distribution

Information was collected from all families in the large sample concerning agricultural lands that they were currently cultivating or fallowing; fields not under cultivation by people in the families interviewed were excluded to avoid double-counting. Data were collected on four hundred forty-one fields, which number is reduced to four hundred twenty effective fields by weighting for polygyny; that is, the responses of a man with one wife in the village and one wife out are given one-half weighting. The weighted total area of large sample fields so claimed is 658 hectares, of which 72 hectares are fallow; these include a high proportion of abandoned lands with hard soils, useless under current rainfall conditions. Only 13 hectares of goz were let fallow in 1978. The fields are cultivated or fallowed by two hundred sixty-six farmers in one hundred sixty-nine families of the large sample. Information concerning access was recorded for three hundred ninety-five fields, of which two hundred eighty are cultivated or fallowed by their owners, and one hundred fifteen or 29 percent are cultivated by non-owners. For the owner-cultivated fields, farmers were asked how they obtained ownership; for the others, users were asked how they got access to fields and what their relationship was to the owner. Responses are listed in tables 5.2 and 5.3.

Table 5.2
Sources of Ownership of Owner-cultivated Fields (large sample)

	Number of Fields	Percentage
Inherited From		
Father	28	8
Mother	23	10
Other	5	2
Total Inherited	56	20
Given By		
Father	55	20
Mother	37	13
Other Relative	13	5
Husband	12	4
Nonrelative	4	2
Total Gift	121	43
Cut From Bush	100	36
Other Source	3	1
Total	280	100

Over 70 percent of fields are cultivated by their owners, and the most important source of ownership, most commonly from parents, is a gift. When parents have more than enough land, there is a presumption that if possible they will help a child who is just getting started by giving him or her a field. As one's children move out, one generally needs less land and can afford to give some away. By giving one's child a field, one encourages him or her to stay nearby. Fields are also given to relatives and others because they need land and the owner has some to spare, and some husbands have also made gifts of land to their wives. Almost all farmers continue to cultivate until they die, but, as they age they reduce the area they plant, giving land away in the process. Thus, less than half as much land has been inherited as has been received as gifts.

The other major source of ownership is cutting from bush fallow, which is becoming a relatively rare source. Currently, any land that has been fallow for three years is considered to be uncultivated (*bu:r*) and

Table 5.3
Sources of Access to Fields other than Ownership

	Number of Fields	Percentage
Loan From		
Husband	29	25
Father	14	12
Mother	7	6
Wife	3	3
Other Relative	11	10
Non-Relative	19	17
Total Loaned	82	71
In Trust From		
Husband	11	10
Father	7	6
Brother	3	3
Sister	3	3
Wife	1	1
Other Relative	4	3
Non-Relative	4	3
Total in Trust	32	28
Other Source	1	1
Total[a]	115	100

a Totals are inexact due to rounding of weighted fields

available for anyone to cut; it seems likely that it took longer to lose one's rights in the past. Owners who find themselves unable to farm can safeguard their rights by planting a row of millet around the field, even if they do not weed it; this is considered an acceptable use of a loophole in local practice.

Non-owners get access to land primarily in the form of loans and also by what is called "amana" (*'ama:na*, deposition in trust). The latter term has moral and religious associations which connote that the user is to be the faithful agent of the owner. In practice, it is generally applied to the fields of emigrants, who usually do make specific provision for their fields, and it recognizes their right to resume cultivation of them upon their return. Parents are major lenders of land to their children, but the largest number of borrowed fields is cultivated by the wives of the owners. Husbands are more likely than parents to extend land as a loan (*sulfa*) rather than a gift (*hadiyya*), presumably because they may divorce or remarry and wish to reallocate their resources.

Nevertheless, because use brings with it certain rights, it is often difficult to maintain the status of land as a loan, or to take it back. In one recent case, a man loaned a field to his daughter and her husband, and they used it for several years. When he wished to take it back, they resisted and the village supported them. Eventually the man took his son-in-law to court, and lost. The court upheld the principle of continuity of use, and the general flow of land from elders to the young. Also, in a number of divorce cases where a man had loaned his wife a field it remained with her (especially if she was raising children of the marriage).

It is also worthy of note that a few fields that are considered gifts by the current cultivators are still considered loans by their previous users. Thus, the line between loan and gift can be difficult to maintain. The use of the term "amana" may be a response to this situation by labor migrants, but it has not prevented them from losing land as well, as is described below.

The principle of continuity of use is also applicable in the case of inheritance. If there is any land whose status is ambiguous, concerning whether it is a gift or a loan, it must be settled at the death of the presumed owner. In the sixteen cases I recorded, fields almost always passed to those who have been cultivating them, if they were children of the deceased. It is often the case that an elderly person cultivates jointly with a daughter, and in cases like this the daughters have received the fields.

In one recent case, a problem arose when a young woman died (age twenty-nine) and she had been cultivating, with her husband, a field belonging to her mother. He continued to cultivate it for two years, in spite of his wife's mother's protests, and then gave it back. However, in an older case a widower went to court and was awarded title of a field that he and his wife had borrowed from her mother under similar circumstances. The duration of cultivation and the need of the various parties were said to be important factors. The future inheritance of a field may also be specified verbally by the owner before witnesses.

Notably absent are the purchase and sale of agricultural land. Among villagers, I recorded only one purchased field and this is a wadi field in Buga suitable for orchards. However, certain types of land are bought and sold in the Masterei area. Following practice elsewhere in Sudan, plots of wadi land become the property of the persons who plant fruit trees on them. The trees and land can then be sold, separately if desired. In Buga, wadi fields of up to one hectare have changed hands. Home sites have occasionally been sold in the sample villages in recent years, although it is exceptional; however, this practice is normal in Buga. Sites for shops in the marketplace are also auctioned off by the Rural Council and may be sold privately. Thus, sale of land exists; nevertheless, the overwhelming majority of fields are ordinary agricultural lands which are not subject to purchase and sale. In spite of the fact that use rights in these can be maintained and transferred, land ownership is still communal to the extent that an individual cannot alienate land from the group, nor can he or she assign rights to it in a way that is not acceptable to the community.

This communal aspect of land ownership has prevented individuals from accumulating areas of land very much larger than they can cultivate. This would of course be totally changed if land were adjudicated and placed under individual title. To date there has been no such policy, although the issuance of title deeds as the result of court cases has affected a small number of fields. I did not observe any test case in which title deed holders have attempted to sell land.

I have made the argument that patterns of land use and access have changed from a system of shifting cultivation in which most rights have been acquired by cutting bush, to a system where land is under continuous cultivation and acquired by one individual from another. This process, at least in its latter stages, is documented below in a cohort analysis of large sample fields according to the ages of their owners. I have also presented the effect of these patterns of access, in combination with other factors, on male and female land ownership.

In table 5.4 the three hundred eighty-five fields of known access and user's age are grouped into age quartiles, with approximately an equal number of fields in each (overrepresentation of ages thirty and forty due to approximation prevents better division). As I have mentioned previously, acquiring land by cutting bush shows a marked decline in younger cohorts. Access through gift is fairly stable in the three younger cohorts.

Inheritance is less important for the young because more of their parents are still alive; on the other hand borrowing is a more important source of land for the young, because they often do not own enough, or any, land. Many of these fields will eventually acquire the status of gifts or be inherited.

I have previously pointed out that land rights are obtained and maintained through land use. I have also pointed out in the last chapter that males are heavily engaged in labor migration. Because they are absent much of the time, it is difficult for them to acquire rights in their parents' land or maintain rights over their own. Women

Table 5.4
Sources of Field Access by Age Cohorts (number of fields)

	Age Cohort			
	Over 50	41–50	30–40	Under 30
Source of Access				
Owners				
Inheritance	14	20	10	12
Gift	14	31	37	33
Cut From Bush	52	25	15	8
Other	3	1	0	0
Non-Owners				
Loan	7	12	30	31
Amana	2	3	13	14
Other	0	0	0	1
Total[a]	91	91	104	99

a Rounding of weighted numbers causes some sums to be inexact

are much more likely than men to be present and cultivating in their adolescence and in the early years of marriage. Because they are present, need land, and have farmed with their parents as teenagers, young women are far more likely than men to receive land as gifts when they marry. The major trends of female land ownership are shown in table 5.5; as gifts have become the dominant form of land access, the proportion of gifts being made to women has also increased, from 57 percent to 79 percent. Also, among older cohorts, men have inherited most fields; among younger cohorts the majority are inherited by women. Men continue to cut approximately two-thirds of fields from bush, but these represent only 15 percent of owned fields in the youngest cohort, compared to 63 percent in the oldest.

Table 5.5
Female Percentage Ownership of Fields Acquired from Three Sources, by Age Cohort

	Age Cohort			
	Over 50	41–50	30–40	Under 30
Source of Access				
Inheritance	36	40	60	59
Gift	57	68	73	79
Cut From Bush	37	24	33	25

As a result of these processes, the pattern of land ownership by sex has reversed. Whereas in the oldest cohort men hold 62 percent of owner-cultivated fields, in the youngest, women own 66 percent (table 5.6). Among non-owner cultivators, 70 percent of fields are cultivated by women in spite of the fact that at least 65 percent of them are owned by men (table 5.7). Many of these fields are presumably in transition from male to female ownership, by the processes described previously.

Table 5.6
Owner-cultivated Fields by Sex and Age of Owners

	Male		Female		Total
	Number	Percent	Number	Percent	Number
Age of Owner					
Over 50	51	62	32	39	83
41–50	41	54	35	46	76
30–40	24	38	38	62	62
Under 30	18	34	35	66	53
Total	134	49	140	51	274

Note: Chi square significant at 0.004 level

Table 5.7
Relationship of Owners to Non-owner Cultivators according to Sex of Cultivators

	Sex of Cultivator	
	Male	Female
Owner's Relationship to Cultivator		
Spouse	4	35
Mother	3	4
Father	8	13
Sister	0	3
Brother	1	3
Other Relative[a]	5	9
Non-relative	12	11
Total	33	78

a Sex of owner was not recorded for the categories 'other relative' and 'non-relative'

Thus, the traditional patterns of land access, in an environment of land scarcity and male emigration, have the effect of reinforcing a new sexual division of labor in which women are tending to greater specialization in agriculture, while men are less and less engaged in agriculture, and more dependent on the fields of their wives. The majority of fields are still owned by men, but the cohort analysis suggests that women will own and cultivate more land in each future decade. There is a feedback effect as well; the less land men have, the less likely they are to live in Dar Masalit, and, thus, they become less likely to acquire land. The division of labor is leading to a division of the population into female farmers and mothers in the west, and male migrants spending at least some portion of their time in the east.

The fact that women control much agricultural land enables Masalit women to have a measure of personal independence which they value, but it does not provide the basis of prosperity. The feminization of agriculture results directly from the abandonment of local opportunities by men who find better opportunities elsewhere; women are less able to emigrate independently (compare Cliffe and Moorsom 1979). It has been argued that agricultural productivity has declined due to overuse of fields and reduced rainfall. Women are also hampered in agriculture by conflicting domestic responsibilities which result in less per capita groundnut cultivation and lower yields. In addition, land scarcity continues to be a problem for both men and women, and this problem is aggravated by an unequal division of land.

The amount of land under cultivation, including all that is owned or borrowed by all members of families, is shown in figure 5.1. There is a strong clustering around the median value of 3.1 hectares, and while 18 percent of families have more than 5 hectares, only three percent have less than 1 hectare. This must be interpreted in terms of the adequacy of land holdings to meet people's needs. Millet requirements for basic consumption in this region are usually estimated in the vicinity of 250 kg per person, including adults and children (Barth 1967a; DeWilde 1967b:344; Faulkingham 1977). As previously shown, millet yields per hectare have averaged approximately 400 kg in a moderately poor year and 600 kg in a moderately good year. At 500 kg/ha, a family needs 0.5 ha per person to meet its basic millet consumption needs, on the average. As shown in figure 5.2, 14 percent of families do not have 0.5 ha per capita, or enough land to meet their basic millet requirement in an average year. A full analysis including demographic variation within families is beyond the scope of the present work, but preliminary results indicate that the trends to be discussed are even more strongly supported by such analysis.

In addition to millet for family consumption, people need millet or groundnuts to sell in order to buy food items, clothing, and other market goods, as well as to pay taxes. Again, a full analysis of

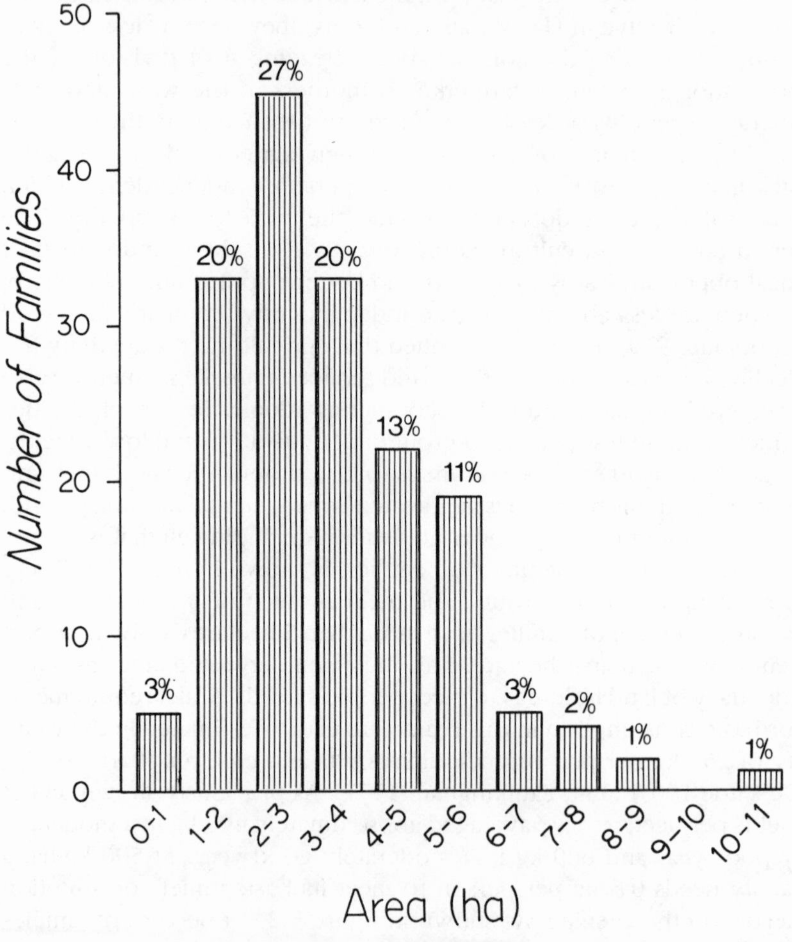

Figure 5.1. The distribution of agricultural land under cultivation by family. (Mean = 3.4, median = 3.1, S.D. = 1.8.)

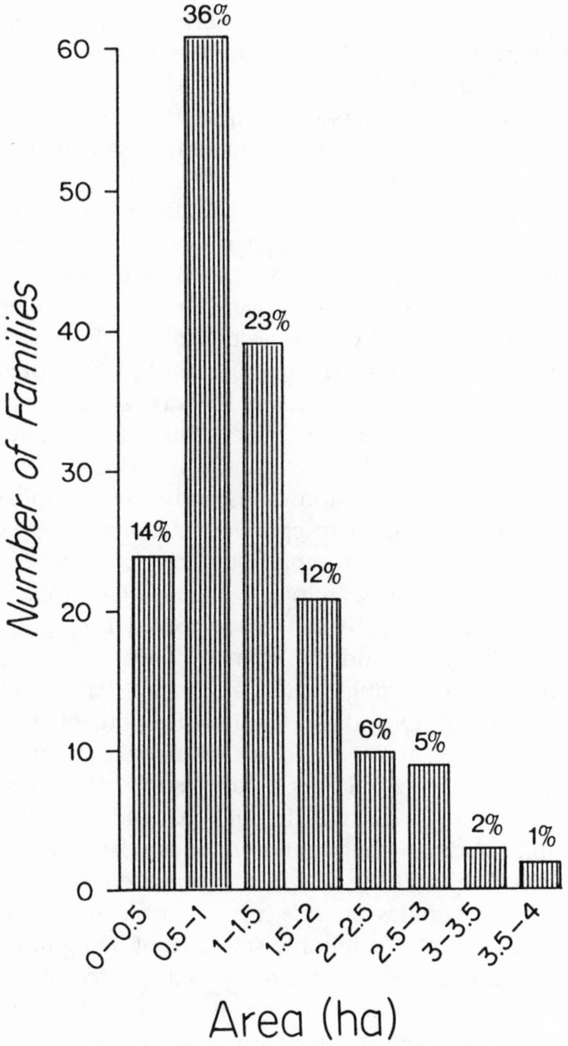

Figure 5.2. The distribution of agricultural land under cultivation per capita by family. (Mean = 1.2, *median* = 0.98, *S.D.* = 0.76.)

household economics is beyond the scope of this work, but roughly speaking a family needs LS 50 per capita yearly to live at a modestly comfortable level, or LS 15 per month in an average family of 3.6 members. In the previous discussion of returns to agriculture, it has been found that the worth of millet yields under the observed conditions ranged on average from LS 35–54 per hectare, while for groundnuts the range was LS 59–124. Taking the midpoints of these figures, they indicate that a family would need 1.12 ha under millet or 0.55 ha under groundnuts per person to meet this level in a typical year. Assuming an equal division, approximately 0.84 ha/person is required to meet these cash needs.

Including millet consumption needs, therefore, a family needs approximately 1.3 ha/person to meet this standard. Only one-third of families have this much land, and can thus provide for their needs through agriculture alone. Even if we assume that families can provide half of their cash needs by nonagricultural activities, only 52 percent of families have sufficient land, 0.92 ha, for this level of consumption. Under the assumption of moderately low rainfall, that is as in 1978, the average land requirement to meet this same standard through agriculture would be 1.6 ha/person, which exceeds the cultivated area of 78 percent of the population. Thus, most of the population is living very close to the minimum acceptable consumption level, and as rainfall declines this proportion rapidly increases.

Furthermore, land scarcity is increasing, based on a cohort analysis of land holdings by age. If we consider a family's 'age' to be the mean of the man's and the woman's ages, or the age of the sole adult in the case of a single man or woman, half of all families are under forty-five. Among these families, 82 percent do not have 1.3 hectares per capita, that is, enough to meet consumption and cash needs under typical conditions, compared to 51 percent of families forty-five or over. In spite of the fact that older farmers have given considerable lands to their children, mean land per capita among farmers forty-five and over is 1.43 ha, compared to 0.95 ha among the younger half of families. At this level, most younger families in Dar Masalit are restricted to a humble standard of living in the best of circumstances, unless they have a substantial source of nonagricultural income. As has been shown previously, the families most pressed for land are the most likely to have some members emigrate, which increases the land per remaining family member and occasionally produces remittances as well.

Not all families are experiencing land scarcity as a threat to their minimal consumption needs; 27 percent of families cultivate more than 1.5 ha/person, and 14 percent cultivate more than two ha/person (figure 5.2). These include people who inherited large tracts and kept them under cultivation, as well as some farmers who cut substantial fields themselves before bush lands were exhausted. In addition, as discussed above, merchants or other people with cash are often able to borrow land for groundnut cultivation. In the light of our discussion of land rights, it can be appreciated that a merchant is a safe borrower, lacking the kinship basis for a claim to permanent rights; furthermore, their cultivation of groundnuts 'cleans' the soil of weeds. Merchants and others who cultivate groundnuts with hired labor also contravene the trend to increasing female control of land; due to their strong domestic position, merchants and other men with cash incomes can often get access to the land of their wives and use it to cultivate export crops.

Thus, certain people have been able to keep considerable areas under their control, either as individuals or as families. Accumulation is limited by the general demand for land and by local patterns of access; only 17 percent of families have more than five hectares of land, and only one family has more than nine hectares (figure 5.1)—which is far below the levels found in mechanized or pump schemes in the eastern Sudan. Nevertheless, by local standards five hectares can be the basis of a secure and very comfortable life, especially if one can recruit labor for groundnut cultivation on part of it. By growing groundnuts on two hectares and millet on three, such a family can feel secure in their ability to feed themselves even in poor rains, and obtain enough cash for their basic needs in an average year from agriculture alone. If one has the cash to hire labor, such substantial land ownership or borrowings of land can be instrumental in a process of capital accumulation, as local merchants have discovered.

Thus, the nature of land as an asset has changed radically in recent decades. From essentially being a free good, the control of which has been limited only by the amount of labor one has had available to cultivate, land has come to be a limited good. For some people, land shortage has made it impossible for them to live in Dar Masalit, while for others, small land holdings confine them to a life on the margin of subsistence. For these people, their land resources limit the amount of labor they can expend in their own agriculture, reversing the previous relationship of land and labor. However, for those with access to larger amounts of land, labor is still an important constraint; they must be able to mobilize sufficient labor to cultivate the land in order to profit from it, and for that matter simply to keep it. The techniques for labor mobilization and the nature of labor as an asset have undergone changes as profound as those involving land, due to the relative scarcity of land, labor migration, and the use of cash. I now turn to a discussion of access to labor in the Masalit economy.

Labor

Farmers tap a number of sources of labor in completing their cultivation. Most labor is personal; that is, farmers working on their own fields. They may also get or give varying amounts of labor on a 'free' basis within their families. Beyond the family, labor exchange of a number of types exists, as well as wage labor. All of these have existed in some form since the precolonial period, but they have changed in character and in relative importance with the integration of Dar Masalit into the global economy. Other forms of labor control, such as slavery and corvee, have been eliminated. The various modes of labor recruitment are discussed in terms of their current and previous places in the Masalit economy, and the process of their transformation.

In both past and present the basis of Masalit agriculture is and has been personal labor. As was pointed out in chapter 4, individuals cultivate independently to a large extent, and almost always allot responsibility on a personal basis for each field. The returns to cultivation are usually under the control of the primary cultivator. Nevertheless, consumption within the family draws on the production of all members, and there is to a large extent a pooling of consumption especially in the case of food. Spouses recognize this joint aspect in the degree to which they lend land to each other and assist each other in cultivation. The analysis of the domestic economy and intra-familial labor allocation is too complex to be considered here; therefore, the quantitative analysis of data from the large sample is restricted to the family level, while the distinctions between male and female farmers' strategies and between those of adults and children are described in more general terms.

In chapter 4 labor requirements have been discussed for various crops. Labor is most scarce in the peak season, namely the period of the first weeding of millet, and of the first weeding and planting of groundnuts. It has been pointed out that in terms of actual labor expended in very full days, millet requires seven days per hectare in this period while groundnuts require fourteen days per hectare. If 18 percent of each hectare (the village average) is planted to groundnuts, 8.3 days per hectare are required in this season. This assumes a grueling pace and neglect of all other duties, which is not practical for an extended period. If we assume that every fourth day is not expended in agricultural labor, then eleven days per hectare are required in this season. This season spans four weeks, although farmers try to have millet weeded within the first three weeks and groundnuts within the first two.

At this rate adults can cultivate just under 2 hectares apiece in the peak three weeks. Fifty percent of all families have less than 2 hectares under cultivation per adult, and 30 percent of families have 1.5 ha or less (figure 5.3). For these families completing their cultivation is not usually a problem. However, even in this range other sources of labor can be desirable and sometimes necessary, depending on one's circumstances. Working less oneself is always attractive, especially if one is old or sick, and timing may also be improved by getting the work done more quickly. With larger areas or higher proportions of groundnuts under cultivation, labor recruitment becomes increasingly important, and getting the work done at all requires help. At eleven days per hectare, a man and woman with five hectares or a single adult with 2.5 ha need four weeks to finish, which extends into the last possible moment for weeding if they restrict themselves to their own labor. As shown in figure 5.3, 33 percent of families have more than 2.5 ha per adult. These farmers supplement their own labor in a number of ways to solve these problems.

In addition to one's spouse, adults can draw on the labor of their children. In principle mothers have exclusive rights to their children's help, and in general children do help their mothers much more than their fathers. This partly offsets the disadvantage women have due to conflicting domestic tasks, but this is only applicable when the children are of an appropriate age. Girls are of greatest help to their mothers just before they marry, which is said to be the reason that the girl's mother receives the greatest share of the bridewealth, as well as the brideservice of her new son-in-law. It is also considered suitable and friendly that children occasionally help their fathers, and this is especially true in the case of adolescent boys. At this age, boys interact more with their fathers in general than they have before, and also come to depend on them for their increasing cash needs. Sometimes

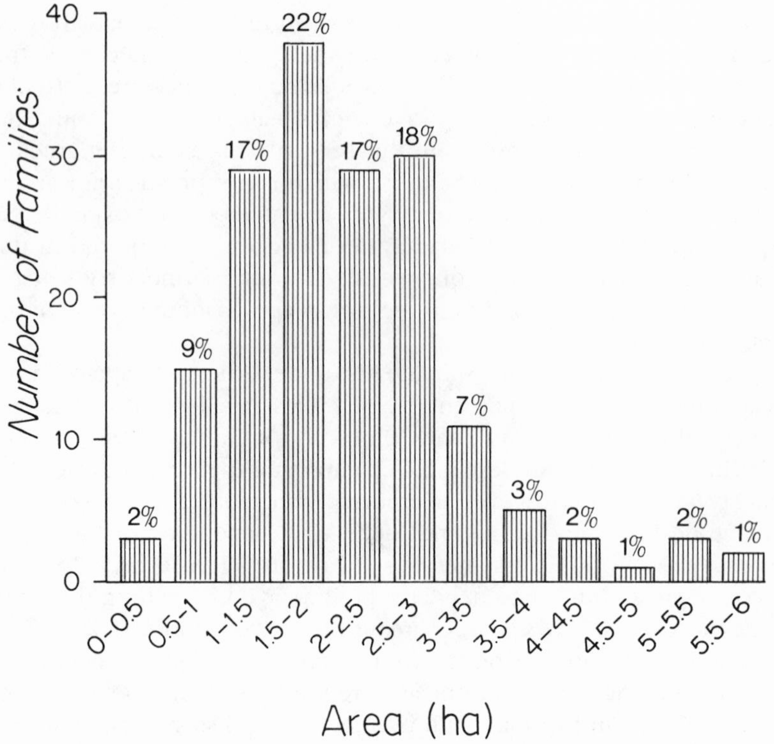

Figure 5.3. The distribution of cultivated area per adult by family. (Mean = 2.2, median = 2.0, S.D. = 1.1.)

fathers hire their own sons for cash, and they may also recruit them through work parties, along with non-family members. Older children are frequently given a plot of their own to cultivate. (Five percent of cultivated land in 1978 was made up of plots farmed by children independently.) When they grow millet, the harvest is mixed with their mothers', but children usually keep the proceeds of their own groundnut cultivation to buy clothing or for entertainment. This relieves the father of part of his obligation to provide for their cash needs, while solving the problem of recruiting their labor.

These children form an important part of the overall labor force. In the large sample I have estimated the relative rate of agricultural work per individual in various age groups by the coefficients listed in table 5.8, based on observation and data from labor contracts. On this basis, 22 percent of the labor force is made up of children. If these children are all mobilized at this rate within their families, only one-third of families would have land under cultivation in excess of two hectares per unit 'producer,' (figure 5.4) and only seven percent would exceed three hectares per producer. However, there are other calls on their labor, as well as problems of recruitment. Adolescent males have the option of labor migration, as discussed previously; in addition this age group makes a disproportionately large contribution to the wage labor force and to work parties.

Table 5.8
Estimated Producer Coefficients of Masalit Farmers according to Age

Age	Producer Coefficient
0–8	0
9–13	0.3
14–20	0.7
21–70	1.0
Over 70	0.8

In part because they have these options, and in part because their parents may be in a poor position to offer their children much in the way of reward, the labor of adolescents, especially males, often eludes their parents. Parents complain that the level of respect and obedience is not what it used to be, and while this opinion is undoubtedly due in part to the change in perspective that comes with age, it agrees with reports from the eastern Sudan of intra-familial strains resulting from market integration (Duffield 1981:66–67; O'Brien 1980:393, 458) and it is credible in terms of the change in circumstances of the young. If their fathers cannot give them what they want, or if they are too demanding, they can go elsewhere in Dar Masalit for the rainy season and earn enough money for their immediate needs, with food and shelter provided. Alternatively they can leave and be independent in the Nile Valley. The young are not as dependent on their parents to arrange their marriage as they used to be, and they usually cannot expect a sizable parcel of land until later in life.

Thus, it is probably true that the young, particularly adolescent males, are somewhat less enthusiastic about helping their parents now than in previous generations. In addition it has probably always been true that children have much more interesting things to do than work

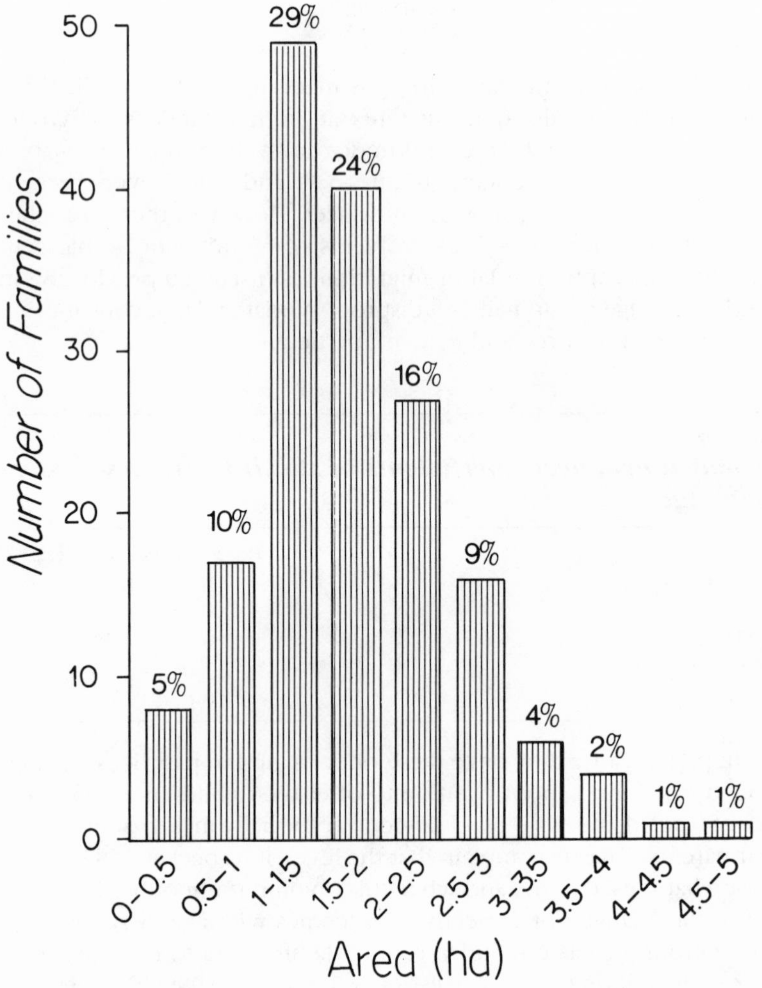

Figure 5.4. The distribution of cultivated area per producer by family. (Mean = 1.8, *median* = 1.6, *S.D.* = 0.84.)

for their parents, and furthermore children old enough to be good workers are present in a minority of families. Thus, familial labor, while an important form of labor recruitment, has its limitations. These have been increased by market integration, so that the labor of youths in 'demographically rich' families is diverted to migration and wage labor instead of production of a surplus within the family.

Beyond the level of the family there are several patterns of labor exchange and donation. Many of these fall within the realm of the "grants economy" (Boulding 1973), in that they are carried out without reference to the exchange value of the labor involved. In this respect labor exchange beyond the household resembles exchange within the household, which is carried on in an idiom of generalized reciprocity. At least in principle, labor given as assistance to co-villagers or others with whom one has personal ties is not counted, measured or compensated, in contrast to labor for hire. " 'Generalized reciprocity' refers to transactions that are *putatively* altruistic, transactions on the line of assistance given and, if possible and necessary, assistance returned" (Sahlins 1972:193–194; emphasis added).

Labor exchange and donation are carried out on a number of levels. The smallest and least formal of these is simple assistance on a one-to-one basis. This most commonly occurs among close kin, such as mothers and daughters, but neighbors and friends can be expected to help each other if they find that one of them is in special need, and if their personal responsibilities are not pressing it is common for them to assist at other times as well. Mutual aid is so general and unremarkable from the point of view of the villagers that data collection on this issue was rather difficult to carry out; without considerable prompting few people have considered such assistance worthy of note. Nevertheless it constantly presents itself to the outsider; one continually encounters neighbors helping each other to shell nuts, make beer, churn butter, or carry out any number of other tasks. A clear affirmation of the value of mutual aid is seen in the weeding season when it is considered bad form to walk on a path without carrying a hoe, because it is expected that one stop and help, even if briefly, at any field where one encounters another farmer at work. Even those on horseback en route to market often dismount and lend a hand until the farmer insists that they leave.

On a more formal level are institutions of rotating group labor and work parties. The former are somewhat limited, usually being restricted to groups of young men or women who agree to take turns cultivating each others' fields. The latter is the more common form of work party or *nafi:r*, which is not a rotating affair in which turns are taken, but rather an open ended and flexible institution of mutual assistance. The general procedure is as follows. If a person decides to seek the assistance of a group in some endeavor, they decide on a date and invite kin, friends, and neighbors (including farmers with neighboring fields). If the host is a woman, she makes beer or other foods for the occasion; a man usually asks his wife, and possibly his sisters, to do so. Frequently kin or neighbors contribute beer or help in the preparations. A work group may be restricted to drinkers or non-drinkers, or include both; while beer may suffice for drinkers, sugar, tea and nonalcoholic grain beverages are usually readied for non-drinkers. Either group may be treated to special foods or meat if the occasion is particularly festive.

On the appointed day, the group usually convenes in the early afternoon, sometimes after getting started drinking the beer in the morning. The people work together in separate male and female groups, and the participants often compete or urge each other on.[4] There may be breaks for beer or tea at several points, and after the nafir the group finishes off the refreshments. There is plenty of opportunity before, during and after the work to talk and joke, and ideally a good time is had by all, while the host gets a large piece of work done.

Nafirs are used for many types of work. Almost all houses are built with the help of a nafir at some point, usually in the final stage when the roof is raised. Some houses are moved by groups as well. These are dry season activities which take place when both time and grain are plentiful, and they are a good excuse for a party; the work involved in raising a roof is fairly brief. In the agricultural season, nafirs are not usually called until at least some of the villagers have a little extra time, which is not the case until near the end of the first weeding. At that time there are usually a number of parties in which those who are behind in their work take advantage of the good spirits of those who have finished their weeding earlier. Work parties continue through the season of second weeding, which is somewhat less intense, and in which optimal timing varies from field to field. In the period of harvesting and threshing there are a large number of nafirs, because the work is very arduous and boring when done alone, and also because there is a relative abundance of food and money at the harvest, and people are willing and able to put on a good party. Because the forest has been greatly reduced, birds are not a problem in most millet fields, and one's harvesting can be postponed while one attends the nafirs of others.

From the point of view of the host, the nafir has a number of advantages. Most importantly, the host recruits a large amount of labor for a fairly low cost; furthermore, the cost may be shared by one's spouse or other relatives who provide beer or food. It can also be the occasion for a pleasurable gathering of friends. However, this mixture in the nature of the work party leads to a certain unpredictability of results; if the party becomes too lively, little work gets done. The host has to be careful not to be too generous! Farmers also agree that work party labor is often not of good quality; for example, during hoeing the plants may be nicked, or during harvest some of the crop may be left behind. Finally, one cannot know with certainty in advance what the response will be to one's invitation. One may prepare too much or too little beer or food, either one of which might prove detrimental to the productivity of the group. The weather might be bad on the day planned, or someone else may call a nafir on the same day, in which case the group will divide its time and double its appetite. Because the nafir is not a contractual form of labor recruitment, and involves people beyond the domestic group with whom one's relationship may be somewhat ambiguous, the success of a nafir is partly a test and measure of the strength of one's personal relationships and the balance of obligations in them, and partly a matter of luck.

Those who are invited to a work party can make excuses if they cannot or do not want to attend. This can be difficult, however, for close relatives and neighbors, and particularly for married sons and sons-in-law, who have a moral obligation to help. Thus, a farmer with married children may choose to have more work parties than others in order to exploit these unequal personal relationships. Fathers may also use the work party to get help from unmarried children, who ordinarily give most of their time to their mothers, or spend it in leisure activities. Sheikhs or merchants with people who depend on them may use nafirs to get some labor from those who owe them favors. However, most personal relationships that are invoked in this institution are relatively symmetrical. Neighbors and field neighbors help each other, especially co-residents in the bush camps. Siblings and cousins in one's village can usually be counted on. These ties and the obligation to assist are strengthened if the host of a work party has helped in one's own work party in the past, although this fact should remain unspoken.

One important source of labor for nafirs is the adolescent males of the village, who tend to enjoy working in groups and to appreciate a good party. As mentioned above, when children get older their labor becomes somewhat problematic for their parents to obtain. Adolescents have free time and their own set of priorities; while not averse to work, they prefer a party, and a work party is not a bad compromise. The sociability, free beer, and possibility of encountering or impressing the opposite sex all encourage their participation. Some parents are able to persuade their children to recruit a group of adolescents for a work party. However this age group is somewhat unpredictable, especially since they are rarely bound by ties of obligation to the hosts.

It is said that in the past, the young men under the wornung (see chapter 2) formed a well organized and disciplined part of work party labor, and Kapteijns states that young men and women used to work in groups in exchange for goats, which they ate at their own festivities (1985:30). Adolescents now have the option of working for money, and they may have fields of their own; the number of adolescent males is also reduced by labor migration (compare Moore 1975:276). The resulting decrease in the effectiveness of nafirs in recruiting adolescents has probably diminished their overall importance in the Masalit economy, but they continue to have some importance.

The ideology of the nafir is one of mutual aid, neighborliness and sociability. People feel that they are doing the host a favor by attending a nafir, and they do not consider the food served to be compensation; it is merely a token of appreciation by the host. The only true compensation for attending a work party would be the host's attendance at one's own work party. Nevertheless there are imbalances in the exchange of labor carried out in work parties. Adolescents, for example, have no chance to receive labor in exchange for their own because they have no fields, or very small ones. Thus, the nafir acts in part as an institution to recruit youthful labor for the fields of adults. In addition, the nafir is used without an expectation of equal return by farmers who are unable to complete their cultivation because they are old, sick or overburdened with domestic responsibilities. Kapteijns reports that this welfare aspect of the nafir was also present in the nineteenth century (1985:31, 42). Finally, as indicated above there is an inequality in nafir participation based on kinship, power and wealth. In general the wealthier farmers cultivate larger areas, and therefore they are in need of labor. Most of the wealthier farmers act in a way that is considered at least minimally socially acceptable for them; they offer more hospitality than other villagers, make larger contributions to collections for festivities or wakes, and they help their poor relatives and neighbors. They also may be able to use their name or influence to help villagers in local affairs of various types. As a result, some of them are able to attract large numbers of people who owe them favors, (albeit at a higher standard of hospitality than is expected when average or poor villagers host).

As many writers have pointed out (for example, Nadel 1947:54–57; DeSchlippe 1956:148–163; Vincent 1971; Moore 1975;

Saul 1983), this is a pattern by which those with a surplus can maintain or increase that surplus at the expense of those who are short of food, and who give labor in order to eat what the host provides. Pierre DeSchlippe suggests that this mechanism would be most effective in years of food shortage. However, although nafirs do contribute to the labor used by wealthier farmers, and I suspect that they were an important mechanism of inequality in the past, this model is not entirely appropriate in Dar Masalit today. First, those villagers who are short of food are much more likely to work for money to get it, because they get more sustenance for their time, and they can use their earnings to buy grain for their families as well. Second, the wealthy can afford to hire labor, and they do so particularly on critical tasks such as the first weeding. Nafir labor is considered to be of lower quality than hired labor, and, as land has become more scarce, farmers with enough resources to hire labor choose to do so for yield-determining jobs (similar observations are reported by M. P. Moore 1975:283 and Hans Hedlund and Mats Lundahl 1984). They resort to nafirs most often at the harvest season when paid labor is somewhat scarce, mainly because the poor are no longer in urgent need of money. At that time the nafir is a means of labor recruitment that is less desirable than hiring labor, but which is more feasible.

In the past under conditions of relative land abundance, the nafir was probably of greater importance. Kapteijns points out that if the malik held a nafir, it was bigger and more festive, and more work was done (1985:42). Probably this also applied to the work parties of the sid al-fas and the village founders. Work parties were probably the most important supplement to familial labor for those who wished to accumulate an agricultural surplus, for several reasons: the land cultivated depended on the amount of labor one recruited; it was not as essential to make optimal use of a limited quantity of land; and hired labor was relatively rare and expensive (see below). The surplus produced was used in hospitality and generosity, as well as to support retainers, all of which increased both one's reputation, and one's ability to recruit labor in the future.

Work parties continue to recruit labor for the wealthy in an unequal manner, but in this respect they have been superseded to a large extent by wage labor. However, the demand for work group labor by the poor has apparently increased; there are more widows and divorcees with families to support, due to male emigration, and the minimum amount of cultivation for subsistence has increased due to new cash needs and lower agricultural productivity. It is difficult to say whether nafirs are becoming more or less important overall, but they are probably playing more of a welfare role and less of a stratifying one than they did in the Ancien Regime. The Masalit case supports David Guillet's (1980) argument, that market integration does not automatically result in the disappearance of this form of labor recruitment. Although their labor force has been reduced by the emigration of young men to the eastern Sudan, in this case it appears that nafirs persist because they draw, at least in part, on different groups of laborers than wage labor, and they invoke local values which continue to be respected.

Hiring labor is the alternative to the nafir for recruiting extra-familial labor. Laborers are usually hired on a piece basis, in which a price is agreed upon for the completion of a specific job. Hiring on a daily basis also occurs, but rarely. Wages are fairly uniform over the Masterei area, being a topic of conversation throughout the agricultural season, with workers and employers constantly comparing notes. Workers always appear to be scarce when employers want them, but this does not appear to stimulate competitive bidding for labor which would drive the price up to its marginal value. As shown in chapter 4, the economic return to hiring labor is quite high, and hiring out is costly to the worker in terms of future production if he or she has fields.

Villagers were in agreement that weeding for someone else indicated poverty for an adult, because no one neglected their own fields to work for money unless they were in need of food. It is true that some agricultural laborers were short of land, which reduced their opportunity cost, but this is not always the case; a number of workers clearly neglected fairly extensive fields in order to get money for food.

In 1979 with the help of assistants and friends in diverse parts of the sample villages, I attempted to record all cases of villagers hiring laborers or working for someone else. I estimated that no more than 20 percent of contracts went unobserved. Of the two hundred ninety-two cases, the total amount paid was recorded in two hundred fifty-seven; the grand total for these cases was LS 422. My presence distorted the market somewhat; nineteen percent of this total was paid by my two assistants, who were given extra funds in the agricultural season in order to hire labor, and thus, to be available to work with me. Hired labor made up a small proportion of total village labor; for example, less than 6 percent of the area cultivated in the peak season was weeded by hire, although this work earned more than half of all wages paid. However, hiring was of some significance to subsets of the village population who either employed or worked extensively.

Adult men were employers in two hundred seventy-two contracts, and adult women in the other twenty. In 15 percent of cases, employers were non-villagers, while in the other 85 percent they were members of forty village families. Of these forty, twenty-eight spent less than LS 10, while only six families spent over LS 20 (table 5.9), including my assistants. Excluding the latter, 52 percent of all wages were paid by merchants and 19 percent by jammala (transport workers with camels).

Table 5.9
Amounts Paid to Hire Labor in 1979

Total Paid	Number of Families
Up to LS 5	21
LS 5–10	7
LS 10–20	6
Over LS 20	6

In 38 percent of the contracts, workers were non-villagers, which indicates that the village was a net employer in 1979. (This may be an artifact due to more complete recording of work done on village fields than elsewhere, but it is probably a true result of the high number of merchants in the sample villages and their absence in other nearby villages.) Workers in 57 percent of contracts were female. In half of all the cases, workers were children or adolescents; these contracts tended to be smaller. In general, workers came from poor families, but a few children of well-off families also worked for wages. Village workers came from forty-five families, and the amount worked varied widely. In twenty-five families total earnings were LS 3 or less, often being a source of pocket money for young people. Ten families earned LS 4–10, while ten earned LS 11–16. In eight of the latter ten cases there was no husband present, illustrating the difficult economic situation of single women. Families who worked for wages to this extent were selling enough labor to weed two or more hectares, which significantly compromised their own ability to cultivate.

Weeding for hire was usually done to buy food. In chapter 4 it was estimated that an able-bodied adult working on a contract basis in agricultural labor earned about LS 1.00 per full day of energetic work in 1979. At prices then current, this bought four *kora* of millet, or approximately 10 kg; for a family of two adults and two children, this was approximately enough millet to subsist for four days. Thus, if a farmer found his or her grain supply exhausted as the rainy season began, agricultural labor was feasible as a source of food; it did not provide for tea or clothing, but by working for eight days per month one survived until the harvest began to come in. That is, wage labor got one through July and August; then in September the early grains in the garden plots ripened, and in October one harvested selected ears of grain in the fields. If one had been able to plant groundnuts one harvested them and bought grain at that time, or one harvested groundnuts for money.

However, the sacrifice of two weeks in the weeding season is costly. If three out of four days are available for farming, and one-third of these are spent on the fields of someone else, this seriously undermines one's ability to attain self-sufficiency on one's own farm, and certainly makes labor-intensive crops such as groundnuts difficult to grow. The level of the wage is such as to maintain the laborer and permit enough time for some cultivation, but not enough to make it easy to escape from the cycle of poverty.

This was in striking contrast to the patterns of labor hiring that obtained in previous times. In the Ancien Regime and in the early colonial period, hardship came to everyone occasionally; there were many stories of droughts, locust plagues, raids, and other disasters which caused local and temporary conditions of famine. At the individual level, livestock or wildlife might have destroyed one's field in a given year, a new field might have turned out poorly, and illness or other factors possibly resulted in a temporary shortfall of grain. Hunting and gathering were possible to make up for a poor harvest, and farmers also attempted to have at least one year's grain supply in storage. This was not always feasible for young adults with new households, and it did not protect one from an extended period of famine.

As a last resort, one could rely on selling labor; if not locally, then one could travel to an area that had escaped disaster to find work. According to Kapteijns (1985:30), the standard rate of pay was six *midd* of millet per day, or approximately 22.5 kg. My informants confirmed this rate as a minimum in the 1920s and 30s, with some reporting ten *midd* per day (37.5 kg). At this rate, as contrasted with the equivalent of a 10 kg per day rate current in 1979, a worker could obtain subsistence needs in a relatively short time, and still grow enough grain to feed the family in the next year.

Apparently the compensation paid to laborers has declined dramatically in recent years. There are a number of probable explanations. First, the bargaining position of the worker is relatively weak.

Whereas in the past, there existed the possibility of hunting and gathering, now the dependence on millet for basic subsistence is very great; supplementary foods such as sugar, oil and meat are luxuries rather than staples. Thus, the person without millet must either work or leave.

Second, young workers undermine wage rates. The recruitment of labor was formerly divided, in that the young worked under one system while adults worked under another. Kapteijns reports that young men and women were recruited as a group for a job, in exchange for goats. They had no reason to want millet, in which adults were paid. Currently, however, young people whose parents may or may not be in need are able to work for cash; because their responsibilities are less than those of adults, and their basic food and shelter needs are met by their parents, their calculation of an attractive wage is different from adults. Low wages are a preferable alternative to working for their parents for free. However, they perform the same jobs as adults, and since the work is paid by the piece the fact that they are somewhat slower does not make them less desirable as employees.

Third, the purpose and effects of hiring labor have changed. In the past, adults either worked at nafirs, or they worked in exchange for millet as described above. Both were considered part of reciprocal exchange within the community, according to Kapteijns, and, thus, were not supposed to increase one person's fortune at the expense of another. Work for grain only deprived the person in need of a little extra labor in a single year. The institution was in part a kind of charity. There was not, after all, much chance of profit through selling one's surplus grain, and by using it locally in this way one enhanced one's prestige.[5] Besides, the exchange rate was probably comparable to the marginal value of the labor received (at least it would be, based on the current returns to labor calculated in chapter 4), and so the hirer neither lost anything material nor did he gain.

With the development of an export market, however, it has become possible to benefit in a different way than any that existed in the Ancien Regime. Employers now have an incentive to keep wages as low as possible, because their profits can be used to consume new types of goods or invest in new kinds of enterprises from outside the local area. The prestige of being a local benefactor is sacrificed for the concrete wealth available through hiring labor for profit. The resulting decline in the daily rate of compensation for agricultural labor is one of the most striking results of Dar Masalit's integration into the global economy.

The effect of the current practice is to make it difficult to escape the cycle of poverty. Even with small lands, a family in which one member has a good source of cash income can survive in Dar Masalit. However, as pointed out in the previous chapter, the market for low-capital products or services is lowest in the rainy season, and a family with a food shortage may be forced to depend on agricultural labor in the months of weeding even if they have a craft as a source of income. If this occurs in one year, after a bad harvest or an unlucky incident, it cannot be overcome with a brief stint of labor or through intensified hunting and gathering; it requires a substantial part of one's weeding time. The exchange of labor for food was formerly considered a nearly equal exchange among near-equals, which anyone might have to resort to in a bad circumstance. Now it is considered an act of desperation, and its effect is to reduce the future income of the needy while increasing the future income of the wealthy.

Clearly the position of labor, and one's own potential for labor, as an asset in the Masalit economy has undergone a profound change. It has certain parallels to Marx's model of the alienation of labor, in that the free individual who works can now be separated from the surplus value that he produces, and this is accomplished without the creation of social relationships of patronage or obligation, which might provide security or compensate the employee in some way. The relative weakness of labor is due in part to the fact that land has become scarce, and one cannot employ one's own labor to acquire as much land as one wants in the way that was formerly possible. Thus, those with less land are in a position of need. However, this weakened position, and more importantly the alienation of labor are more closely related to the introduction of a new productive asset—money.

Cash

In the section on trade, the introduction of cash to Dar Masalit was discussed. In the Ancien Regime, commoners obtained what few imports they acquired through barter. There were fixed prices in the market, and certain goods such as grain, salt, cloth and amber beads acted as measures of value that had some of the functions of money. Among the regional elites, there was also a certain flow of internationally recognized currencies such as the Maria Theresa thaler. The circulation of these currencies presumably increased in Dar Masalit under the Masalit sultanate, since it was directly engaged in international trade, but at colonial occupation cash was still a rare item for all but a small part of the Masalit population.

During the 1920s the occupation government moved to a policy of tax collection in cash (Sudanese currency), but this did not bring about its general usage in the Masalit economy. As previously noted, in the rural areas cash was a commodity with the peculiar value of satisfying the occasional requirements of the authorities. This commodity was obtained by exchange with foreign merchants and soldiers of the Geneina enclave, as well as the sultanic elite. The goods that could be exchanged for cash were the same goods formerly demanded as tribute by the Masalit and Fur rulers: livestock, grain, ivory, honey, and others. The need to obtain cash concerned Masalit commoners two times per three years, when taxes were due, and rarely otherwise.[6] Conversely, by establishing a large cash income for the Masalit Sultan, the British caused him, his family and those he favored to be closely bound to the Geneina enclave and the larger Sudanese economy.

The rural areas became more involved with cash after the Second World War, when the policy of increasing the circulation of consumer goods such as Manchester cloth, Indian tea, and sugar was applied in Dar Masalit. By the 1950s cash was commonly accepted as a medium of exchange for these import goods. The increasing use of cash was accelerated by the return of labor migrants from the Nile Valley, with new cash resources and new standards of consumption. Cash and the things it could buy did not form a separate sphere, as defined by Paul Bohannan and George Dalton (1962:3–7), for several reasons: cash-goods were not mutually exchangeable; cash was acquired through the exchange of subsistence goods; and such transactions did not have any moral component as required by the description of conversions between spheres. However, there was a practical division between the goods one produced, which one could sell for cash, and the goods which one could only acquire with cash. Meanwhile, the local exchange economy of Dar Masalit continued to operate on a barter basis, and for the most part people produced their own consumption needs. Both the cash market and the local barter market continued to be peripheral to the local subsistence economy.

As in any dual economy, productive activities were changed by the cash market. Tea was an addition to consumption, and, thus, required the production of a surplus of products that could be exchanged for it. Imported cloth was a substitute for a local product, which resulted in more production of goods for exchange and less cotton cultivation and weaving. Similarly sugar, spices, needles, soap, shoes, utensils and other consumer items from the cash economy were acquired only through an intensification of production and a reallocation of resources in response to the demands of the cash-oriented enclave. Thus, even though cash remained merely a medium of exchange for a limited set of optional goods, consumption in the cash economy began to transform productive activities in the subsistence-based rural economy.

At the present time, the cash market continues to play this sort of peripheral role in the lives of some of the people, particularly those who are too poor to purchase any imported goods except those that are absolutely necessary. For them, cash is still a commodity or a special purpose money. However, for the majority of the population, cash has gone on to acquire the functions of general purpose money—as a standard of value, mode of payment, and means of exchange—in a much broader range of circumstances than was formerly the case. Now exchange of money occurs among rural Masalit, and not only merchants. Farmers use money to hire other farmers for labor, transport, and sewing their clothing, and they buy and sell crops, livestock, meat, baskets, beer, furniture, etc. from each other.

Cash has become necessary for the essentials of life as well as luxuries or substitutes. With the elimination of local cloth manufacture, clothing must be bought for cash. As land becomes scarce, food must be bought. As the forest is cut down, building materials must be bought from those with camels. As elsewhere in the Sudan, cash is coming to be included in bridewealth. No one can choose to stay out of the cash economy, because the environment of everyone has changed to make this impossible, whether or not they approve of it. The market situation of rural Dar Masalit is now intermediate between that of the peripheral market and the third of Bohannan and Dalton's types, "in which the primary source of income for sellers and producers is the market in the sense of a transactional principle. In such a society, livelihood is acquired by first selling something, which means that not only products but the factors of production as well (particularly land and labor) come to be subject to the operation of the market principle" (Bohannan and Dalton:2). At this point, the sale of commodities and of one's labor, especially through migration, in order to buy other commodities has certainly increased.

However, the extent of direct market integration is still limited; land is not on the market and only a small proportion of local labor is hired labor. Furthermore, there continues to be a good deal of production for use. Firewood and water are still collected for one's family in villages, if not in towns, and one does one's own building, hunting and gathering. Most importantly, the essential food of the Masalit diet—millet—is generally supplied by one's own cultivation. Everyone grows enough or nearly enough millet to meet basic consumption needs in most years.

This self-sufficiency is inevitable because local wages are too low and the working season too short to allow the existence of a rural proletariat, or even of a group of farmers who depend on selling their labor to supply more than a small fraction of their needs. Most families where adults work for wages can produce enough millet for basic consumption for ten months at least, which maintains them until the beginning of the next rains when work is available. If they do not have this much millet, they must go into debt if they wish to stay in Dar Masalit. When a family's situation is this bad, some members usually emigrate so that the available food will last. It is not practical for the poor to cultivate groundnuts in order to sell them and buy millet, because the yields in groundnut cultivation are quite variable, and the prices of groundnuts and millet are unpredictable. Groundnuts are grown to supply cash requirements, in which one has somewhat more discretion.

It can no longer be said that the use of cash is entirely an option or a luxury. Clothing, meat and agricultural tools, for example, are only available for cash in the market, although village merchants will calculate millet or groundnut equivalents and 'barter' for their goods. However, there is considerable variation in the quantity of cash that individuals or families have at their disposal. For those who are short of millet, its purchase is of course of prime importance. With more cash, one can clothe the family at a minimal standard and buy meat, tea, and sugar. Beyond this level, the more cash one has at one's disposal, the more flexibility and choices one has. In consumption it is certainly preferable to have more than one new set of clothing per year, and to wear Japanese or Korean polyesters and blends rather than cotton seconds from Pakistan. Meat, oil, butter, red pepper, coriander, salt and other spices, and plenty of tea and sugar are all desirable consumption goods that require cash, and the use of these items has increased greatly in recent decades. Expensive items like radios and tape recorders are now affordable to a handful of villagers. With money, one can also buy leisure; that is, others can be hired to take over some of one's weeding, gather building materials, or do other jobs.

The above uses of cash, both in purchases of imported goods and in local exchanges, are all examples of commodity—money—commodity cycles, or Marx's C-M-C (1977:200). This is, the money acquired by sale of commodities such as groundnuts, one's own labor, or services is used for the purchase of other commodities. Those with enough money to consume at a high level can also use their money in an M-C-M cycle; that is, as investment capital. In the previous chapter, the main opportunities for investment in Dar Masalit at the present time have been discussed: reproductive livestock, camels for transport, sewing machines, and trade. Livestock act as savings, to a large extent, just as they always have; however, whereas they formerly were used to trade for grain in times of famine, or to pay tax and ceremonial obligations, they are now easily convertible to cash, and they can act as a store of cash accumulated through trade or other means. Camels and sewing machines are expensive items that are used by non-merchants to obtain high incomes for the purchase of consumer goods. The highest levels of trade are the most capital-intensive enterprises, and at this point money provides more options for its use—such as investing in agriculture, retail goods, or crops—in addition to those already discussed. Just as there are more consumption choices available to people with more money, there are more investment choices as well.

Thus, the nature of cash as an asset has undergone a profound transformation in the colonial and postcolonial period. While it was formerly a rarely needed commodity, it has become a general purpose money which can be used as capital. There are other assets and resources in the Masalit economy, but the three so far discussed—the traditional land, labor and capital—are sufficient to proceed to the interpretation of changes in the meanings of these assets, and their effects on the nature of inequality in wealth and power.

Inequality, Past and Present

Power and wealth are based in large part on the control of productive assets. Therefore it is inevitable that changes in the functions and availability of these assets are associated with changes in the nature, source and extent of inequality that exists in a given society. In the Masalit case, the relative scarcity of land and labor in the past has been reversed, and both have come to be subordinated to capital. Below, the effects of these shifts on the determination of inequality are examined. In addition, as outlined in chapter 2, there have been changes in the position of Dar Masalit within larger political entities, and these have also affected the local structures of inequality.

Inequality, both past and present, is most easily considered in two categories. There is the obvious superiority of political elites, reinforced by offices or official statuses, over commoners and slaves. This involves a hierarchy which permeates Dar Masalit and, except in the period of independence, has joined it to an external hierarchy. On the other hand, there is the less obvious inequality of influence among commoners, which is of local importance. Both of these have been affected by the changes in assets discussed above, and each are discussed in turn.

In the Ancien Regime, the political elite was composed of the Masalit maliks and furshas who were part of the Fur administrative hierarchy. After Masalit independence but before colonial rule, many of these were reduced in power and replaced by an elite directly responsible to the new Masalit sultan. In the colonial era, the maliks and furshas were employed as an administrative hierarchy under the sultan, who was officially responsible to the governor of Darfur province. All officials, with the exception of the sultan himself in the period of independence, were responsible both to their constituents and to their superiors, and required some degree of support both from above and below.

In the precolonial period, the political elite was distinguished by their economic position, which was part and parcel of their offices. "The rulers did not monopolize the means of production, but controlled the agricultural surplus, which was extracted from the commoners (in kind) through regular taxation and *ad hoc* demands, and which was consumed conspicuously, redistributed, or exported abroad" (Kapteijns 1985:8–9). This consisted of grain, livestock, cotton cloth, and other staples of life. The elite also had slaves who worked on the production of the same staples and freed their masters from labor. Thus, the wealth of the elite was based on their control of people, either as subjects or as slaves (compare Sahlins 1972:92–93).

With their supplies of the local necessities of life, the elite could afford to provide ample hospitality, support retainers, and assist the needy, all of which enhanced their reputation and influence. Furthermore, they controlled almost all import and export goods. The malik "received in his house the ivory of the elephants, the horn of the rhinocerosses, the feathers of the ostriches killed or found dead in his *dar*, and the runaway slaves and stray animals (the *hamil*) captured in it" (Kapteijns 1985:4).

Under the Ancien Regime, maliks sold some of these to the foreign traders while passing on a portion to the Fur overlords. During independence the sultanate took firm control of foreign trade. In both periods the ruling elite alone had the right to consume most imported goods received in exchange for export goods. Direct contact with foreign trade was limited to this group, and commoners were excluded.

Colonial policies undermined the former bases of political power and also made possible the emergence of an elite deriving its power from the possession of capital, rather than the occupation of an office requiring some form of consent. Colonial rule eliminated slavery and most of the trans-Saharan trade. The system of taxation and customary dues was replaced by a money system, which left little in the hands of local rulers for redistribution. The sultan and eventually the furshas and maliks were compensated in cash, which they could spend on imported goods for their own consumption. The trans-Saharan trade was replaced with an enclave of foreign traders in Geneina who mediated commerce with the Nile Valley.

Thus, at first, exclusive consumption of import goods by political elites continued, and they still relied upon their offices to supply the basis for a high standard of living. The sultan and some of the furshas also invested in trade, which gave them an independent source of income. This became especially true in the postwar period, when the increase in commerce in the Dar provided many opportunities for entrepreneurs to profit. However, at this time there were others who took part in this commerce, including both Masalit and non-Masalit without political position. They built up the small towns of the Dar as trade centers mediating between rural people and Geneina, and the merchants soon outnumbered the political elite. High-status goods came to be consumed by rich commoners and foreigners, and even by the general population, albeit in smaller quantities. Thus, the symbolic distinction between commoners and rulers broke down. As capital became the determinant of wealth, rather than control over people or land, the office of fursha or malik became less important than the accumulation of capital in determining one's position in power structures of Dar Masalit.

Under the current policy of dismantling the Native Administration, this process has taken another step. Those with capital, whether or not they are members of a political elite, continue to have wealth and influence, while those with nothing but a title now join the commoners unless they obtain a position in the new system. In the new structures of national politics, namely the rural councils, cooperatives, and courts, merchants are well represented, side-by-side with the wealthier members of the old elite. Their political equality is now given full recognition; in time their superiority should become clear.

A comparable process has taken place at the local level among commoners. I have discussed above the relative positions of big men and followers among the common people, who made up the vast majority of the population. It has been pointed out that in the past, influence over people was primary, and influence was won through work, generosity, and personal qualities. Land was abundant, and, thus, control over it was not the basis of inequality. Among the commoners of any region, some individuals had the desire and ability to become influential and develop a reputation. They were not rewarded by the consumption of import goods, since this was above their station, but they enjoyed some satisfactions of prestige and success.

One could aspire to a large family, two years supply of millet in storage, a horse, animals to provide milk, butter, and security, and clothing of local cloth in good repair. If one were a village founder, or an able and generous helper of those in need among neighbors and relatives, one could expect to have the support of family and friends in local disputes or celebrations, and the respect of the community in group deliberations. There was a certain security for the poor in this relative exaltation of some commoners, because they could establish personal relationships (as clients of a sort) with those who were better off, and invoke the common values of mutual aid when they needed help.[7]

The penetration of the market economy was associated with substantial changes in these local patterns of inequality. With the promotion of import goods on the public market, and the return of migrants accustomed to such goods, new consumption possibilities opened up for the better-off commoners, which were alternatives to generosity (compare Nadel 1947:82–83). Millet stores and animals could be sold to acquire new goods, although this has also reduced the security of the community. Values of mutual assistance were (and still are) respected, but it appears that nowadays less wealth is devoted to assistance than to personal consumption (although this would be very difficult to quantify).

Of greater long-term significance are new investment opportunities. Whereas formerly a well-off Masalit was dependent on others for his position—being rewarded by prestige, respect, and perhaps labor in work-parties—now he finds it possible to invest in an enterprise under his own control, such as a camel, a sewing machine, a trip to the Nile Valley, or a trading venture. That is, he can invest in himself rather than in the community. Finally, because land is no longer abundant and villages no longer move, it is not possible to obtain a position of local influence through the village-founder route previously described. Those ambitious for wealth or prestige must seek to elevate themselves in terms of the market economy which is now dominant.

This statement requires some modification. There are still Masalit who are wealthy in 'the old way.' In the sample villages there are two old men with livestock holdings comparable to the biggest merchants.

One explained to me that he and his wife had two large fields, and cattle to keep them fertilized; year after year they grew millet—and no groundnuts, he was proud to say. If he needed cash he sold some butter. His family ate well, and when asked about his millet supply he said, "Praise be to God." (This is not an unusual answer to such a question in Sudan, but I later verified that his stores were ample, and he had good reason to be grateful to his maker). The other man was considered something of a miser, but nevertheless he acquired his wealth in livestock through work and savings over a long time. These two were unusual, however, for the new way to wealth in the village is through commerce. As described above, trade can be a very lucrative business by village standards, and the new wealth is concentrated among a handful of young merchants.

There are still ways to attain local prestige and influence that do not require capital. Religious study is a respected pursuit, and relatively learned villagers enjoy a measure of esteem and personal satisfaction, if not wealth. Speaking well and being judicious and persuasive in a group discussion is a talent that has not lost its value in the new order. Neither have singing, drumming, brewing, dancing or good humor and comradeship. Yet there is a difference.

Ambition was valued in the old order, and one earned respect in a community through it as well as through any other talent, as long as one was not antisocial. Now, the reward for being ambitious (and lucky) is in a class by itself; if one can get some money and invest it in trade there is a tremendous profit potential. The world of money and the world of sociability are divided in a way that undermines local social values and strengthens materialistic values.

Furthermore, those who are successful can no longer be assumed willing to help a fellow-villager freely in time of need. Now, it might be counted as generous to extend a loan, even if it is to be repaid by crops or future work in the lender's fields, and valued below going rates at that. One does not expect generalized reciprocity from the new elite; one speaks in the idiom of balanced reciprocity or the *quid pro quo*, but even then the true determinant of exchange rates is supply and demand. Capital is precious and scarce; those who have it can demand a high rate of return, and still consider a transaction quite fair or even generous.

The poor, then, cannot look to the well-off for as much generosity as was formerly the case, nor for land. If one is short of land or temporarily short of food, wage work in agriculture is hard to avoid. With small land holdings one could do well with a good source of income, such as a camel; however, the cycle of poverty inherent in agricultural labor makes such an acquisition very difficult. The poor farmer must neglect his own farm to get food, and he or she can scarcely hope to raise enough groundnuts to buy a camel.

As Galal-el-Din points out: "Poverty existed in both the present and the past. What is new is that the traditional societies have lost the balance and the customary security with which they were endowed in the past" (1978:92). Not only do the poor have to bargain for their subsistence when the community as a whole is not lacking; they also cannot expect their condition to be temporary. Thus, just as there is a difference between the new wealth and the old wealth, there is an important difference between the new and the old poverty. It is no wonder that migration is attractive, even though it is unlikely to change one's situation, when the alternative is life at a bare subsistence level with no escape in sight. Such a condition was formerly reserved for slaves, but they at least had some security.

Classes, Nascent Classes, or No-classes?

An analysis in terms of inequality in consumption misses much of the dynamic aspect of socioeconomic change, including the development of relationships which are the basis of inequality, and of new interest groups which may play important political roles in the future. Class analysis takes these aspects into account and allows for another perspective on the social and cultural dimensions of economic change. In the Masalit case it is questionable whether a full-scale class analysis is justified. Nevertheless important processes which will determine the position of Dar Masalit in the world economy in the future, and the position of various groups within Dar Masalit in that economic structure, can be better understood in terms of certain aspects of the class structure model, even though classes are not fully developed at this time.

Lionel Cliffe has argued that "the task of isolating classes in Africa or, more exactly, tracing their dynamic, is thus best seen as part of what is involved in the process of *articulation of modes of production*: of capitalism with historically and geographically specific and varied modes" (1977:197). His method is to consider emergent classes in terms of the local mode of production before market integration occurred, on the one hand, and "the different role that different rural societies were expected to perform in the capitalist economy" (Cliffe 1977:200) on the other. This approach has the advantage of suggesting broad generalities in the process of incorporation while appreciating local diversity and the effects of local action on the emergent structures. In any particular case these factors must be supplemented by analysis of exogenous variables, such as climatic change and immigration in the Masalit case, and one must also take into account changes in policy over time.

In some cases, the emergence of classes, or of relations of production typical of classes, is unambiguous. For example, where a precapitalist chiefly class obtains extensive rights over land, and farmers become a rural proletariat, the discrimination of an emerging class structure is not difficult. Where the two groups engage in open political struggle over the control of the land, a full-blown class structure at the local level is easily observed. The local relations of exploitation which defined the precapitalist situation are transformed, but continue to involve the same actors and the same community.

However, where colonial policy encourages or allows the elimination of local precapitalist relations, and furthermore where capitalist relations of production transcend previous community boundaries, then local relations are not an adequate determinant of local class structure. Mark R. Duffield faces this problem in his study of Maiurno (central Sudan). Although his subject is the transformation of the rural class structure, he finds it necessary to define class membership in terms of the role of the actors in the world market (1981:75–81). While there is a certain amount of hiring and lending within the community, which is indicative of position in the new class structure, it is a small part of the overall activities of the new "petty-bourgeoisie"; they hire most of their laborers and make most of their investments outside the community. Local relations of production have been transformed, but this is only a part of a larger transformation. In practice, Duffield's definitions of class, based on occupation and income, resemble census-type definitions of class as a characteristic of individuals rather than as a structure of relations. However, by combining this approach with analysis of the role of these occupations in the world system, especially in terms of exploitation and the accumulation of capital, it is possible to understand the new structure of class relations and the bases of conflict.

In the Masalit case, the problem of changing community boundaries takes another form as well. Laborers do not confine themselves to Dar Masalit. By emigrating to work directly for the national bourgeoisie, they place their families and communities in a position of indirect exploitation by an external class. This occurs simultaneously with the development of local structures of exploitation based on community production and exchange with local merchants. These processes reinforce each other in certain ways, as previously shown, and at a deeper level they are part of the same process of incorporation into the world market. Yet, the overlap of social units within which exploitation takes place makes the description of class structure more difficult.

The definition of the proper unit of analysis would seem to be an inherent problem in a local study of the emergence of classes which, by their very nature, transcend local boundaries. If integration into the world economy is the source of a class structure, then the interface of local exploitative relations with larger scale extractive relations plays an important role in the definition of classes. The ultimate unit of analysis is the entire world, and it is possible to oversimplify the spread of the market by looking only at this largest scale, for example, by focusing on the extent of industrial development and the proportion of the world labor force working in wage labor. The majority of the world's people participate in the market through diverse structures of exploitation on a smaller scale, in which class relations are not always so obvious.

Another issue which is somewhat difficult in a transitional situation such as this is that of class consciousness. It is often only possible to consider the existence of "objective conditions of class," "nascent class," or "class-in-itself" (Feldman 1975; Vincent 1982:232–262; Wright 1982) in the absence of self-aware classes capable of political action. Joan Vincent finds a situation of "no-classness" in the Teso (Uganda) community at the present time, a condition of exploitation without class consciousness and struggle. She argues that this is a typical reflection of the contradictions facing local communities in transnational capitalism (Vincent 1982:259–262). In Ismani (Tanzania), Rayah Feldman also finds that neither capitalist nor non-capitalist farmers recognize their joint interests and act as classes (1975:161). A number of factors mask conflicts of interest and discourage awareness of class relations at the local level. These effects would of course be compounded by the emergence of classes whose spheres of activity go beyond the local community.

These problems are faced in the consideration of class or nascent class in rural Dar Masalit. Both the criterion of relations of exploitation and that of consciousness are somewhat ambiguous in the Masalit case at the present time. However, the delineation of classes is not an end in itself. One attempts a class analysis to understand the dynamics of the local situation, and to discern conflicts that might be emerging. It may be useful to attempt to describe a class structure in the Masalit case, at least looking for relations of exploitation and possible bases for class consciousness to develop. Some insights may be drawn even if Masalit political economy is not a model of well-defined class conflict.

The precolonial class structure of Dar Masalit was one in which the political hierarchy and the economic hierarchy were one and the same. This was true in the Ancien Regime, in the period of independence, and in the first quarter century of colonial rule, even though the nature of the political elite continually changed. The elites of each period absorbed part of the surplus by collecting taxes and other forms of tribute from the general population. During the colonial period, in Cliffe's terms Dar Masalit was a "quiescent area," in which "the main aim of colonial policy was to maintain social control until there was a need for their "labour-power or their land" (1977:201). In the Masalit case there was also the purpose of maintaining a stable border with French Africa. The area was not developed as a source of labor or exports, and therefore no policy with major effects on productive relations or control of productive assets was purposely applied in Dar Masalit.

I previously described the postwar period as a time of rapid economic change in this area. Whether by design or as a result of policies carried out at a national level in Sudan, Dar Masalit was integrated into the colonial economy in three ways: as a market for imported goods, as a source of exports, and as a labor reserve. For these purposes, a population of farmers with small holdings was apparently satisfactory to the authorities. They were willing to self-exploit in order to produce a surplus of marketable crops, and they also acted as migrant laborers who would return home in large numbers when they were not wanted. There was no adjudication of land or other policy directed at changing the control of productive assets.

However, the increasing flow of money and the opportunities for profits in trade had a more important effect. Traders from the Nile

Valley had been numerous, but they were soon joined by local people who had accumulated enough money to use it as capital. The high-capital occupations of transport, sewing and trade, especially the latter, have become the most important sources of wealth in Dar Masalit. As for the old elite, sheikhs now are usually poor villagers, maliks are forgotten, and the furshas and the sultan are overshadowed by the new merchant elite. Thus, in this case the precapitalist hierarchy was supplanted rather than transformed.

The population of non-Masalit traders, based in Geneina and the towns of Dar Masalit, has some characteristics of a class relative to the rural people, as the local branch of a national petty-bourgeoisie. They do not generally engage in direct relations of production with the Masalit, but rather accumulate the products of the self-exploitation of the peasantry. They exploit the peasantry in the technical sense by accumulating surplus value through their commerce, and also in the visceral sense, by demanding high rates of profit on goods imported and exported. They and the rural Masalit are fairly well aware of their divided interests, but antagonism between them is usually expressed in terms typical of town-countryside interactions around the world. Farmers sometimes express their feelings that the city merchants are dishonest and exploitative, but there is little they can do about it; merchants often find the rural people ignorant or rude, and therefore deserving of ill treatment. Thus, there are relations of exploitation, and perhaps one could say a degree of consciousness of those relations.

However, to a large extent Geneina remains an enclave, and its existence is not predicated upon the export of groundnuts or sales of consumer goods to peasants. Most merchants are oriented to the urban market, which includes large numbers of government officials, bureaucrats, soldiers and police, as well as the staff of schools, health centers, and others. Geneina was a sizable city well before the rural areas were an important market or source of export goods. The development and transformation of the Geneina class structure is most closely related to national processes of urbanization, and is beyond the scope of this study. But if exploitation of the rural population is of minor importance to them, the key to the class structure of Dar Masalit is not likely to be found here.

In the rural areas, particularly at the village level, the use of class analysis encounters certain problems. Rural merchants are also farmers and members of communities of farmers. The differences in wealth and economic activities are very small in comparison with the degree of differentiation at the national level, let alone the international. It is precisely because of this that such local differentiation can be easily ignored in a large-scale study. However, from the perspective of the village there is a clear difference in the situations of a land-poor farmer who tans hides, one who uses his camel to sell firewood in the market, and one who has built a shop and buys groundnuts from his neighbors. The question remains whether this differentiation can be profitably examined in terms of class relations and class consciousness.

The most distinctive new elite is of course the merchants. The larger merchants discussed in chapter 4 have seen their trading capital multiply at a high rate, and now have assets worth thousands of pounds; few other villagers approach that level. They obtain high incomes as profit on their capital, and although most of it is reinvested they and their families enjoy a high standard of living, with plenty of clothing, and desirable foods. They act as major employers of other villagers, as described above, and make handsome profits on their labor.

However, hiring is not an adequate defining feature of class relations in this case for several reasons. First, and most importantly, hired labor is a small part of village agricultural labor, and also constitutes a minority of the labor expended on merchants' fields. It is highly questionable whether the existence of farm laborers is an essential condition for the existence of merchants, which Lenin took as a defining feature of class relations in Russia (1964:110). Second, many villagers who are not merchants hire labor to supplement family labor; for that matter, the poor hire the well-off to transport their crops (compare Bernstein 1977:68). Third, while adult labor indicates economic need, children of well-to-do families may also hire themselves out to get money for personal use. Finally, the majority of village families do not engage either as employers or employees in any labor contract whatsoever. Thus, although the merchants differ from other villagers in their greater use of hired labor, this cannot be the defining relationship of exploitation between them and the villagers. Neither, at this point, is shail (credit), because it involves few villagers.

At this time the defining activity of merchants as a class relative to other villagers is commerce itself. While the role of trade in accumulation, and therefore in the development of industrial capitalism, was discussed by Marx (Hansen and Shulz 1981), trade as a form of exploitation has received less attention. Lenin refers to it (1964:175), but does not develop it. However, insofar as merchants accumulate profits which do not come from thin air, and do this through exchange with producers, this would seem to fit the most orthodox definition of exploitation. By using their capital in trade, mediating the flow of imports and exports, merchants are able to accumulate a part of the surplus value produced in agriculture. Every villager deals with merchants and is touched by this commerce, and it is certainly the case that the existence of customers is essential to the merchants' existence. Thus, in terms of objective conditions, deferring the issue of consciousness until later, one can argue that the new village merchants and the rest of the villagers have an objective structure of class relations, at least.

A second group that can be considered distinctive is composed of those men engaged in high-capital occupations; that is, the jammala (camel workers) and the tailors. These people have invested money in a camel or a sewing machine, and in the case of tailors they have invested a substantial period of time in an apprenticeship. In return, they are able to command a high price for their services, which in theory could be broken down into a wage for themselves and a rent for their equipment. To pay for one hour of their work a villager would have to work approximately two hours in his or her own field or three to ten hours in a low-capital craft. Although not as straightforward as one might like, insofar as the capital investments of the tailors and jammala make possible their accumulation of value, it seems reasonable to call their exchange with other villagers a relationship of exploitation; this would certainly fit with John E. Roemer's (1982) formulation, which is more flexible than most. Furthermore the tailors and jammala on the one hand, and villagers without capital on the other, are necessary to each others' existence. Tailors and jammala also play a crucial support role to the merchants' activities. Thus, the tailors and jammala can also be construed as a class in relationship to other classes.

In part because they can afford to hire labor, as a group tailors and jammala grew more groundnuts per family than other non-merchant villagers. On the average they grew 0.99 ha of nuts per family in 1978, compared to 1.39 ha grown by merchants and 0.53 ha by other villagers. They were somewhat more likely than other villagers to hire labor, but only 38 percent of them did so in 1978, and for smaller areas than merchants. (All merchants hired labor and 23 percent of other villagers did so.) By contrast to the merchants, the jammala and tailors are not engaged in a significant cycle of capital accumulation; most of their incomes are spent on commodities for their own and their families' consumption. They do save—on the average they own 45 percent more livestock per family than villagers who are neither merchants, tailors nor jammala, but this is a difference of only about two cows. Their herds are much smaller than those of the large merchants.[8] Thus, jammala and tailors are fairly well off on the average, but the differences from other villagers are relatively small.

Among the one hundred fifty-five families that do not include merchants, tailors or jammala, there is internal differentiation as well. Of one hundred forty of these families that are in the large sample, thirty-two hired labor in 1978, while at least twenty-two had a family member work as a laborer. Those that hired labor had 21 percent more land under cultivation, including twice the area of groundnuts (0.86 vs. 0.43 ha), than those that did not hire. They also owned an average of 30 percent more animals. Some members of these families act as sabbabis or small traders with varying amounts of trading capital, while others rely on large land holdings or livestock to provide a good income. Thus, it is reasonable to consider that a 'rich' peasantry exists who cannot be distinguished as merchants, jammala or tailors, but who nonetheless employ capital in a way that allows them to profit from their relations with other villagers. I cannot define and characterize them more precisely, but it is important to point out that there are rural Masalit with capital in addition to those who work in the well marked high-capital occupations.

Another kind of exploitation is relevant here but is not usually considered in Marxist analysis—exploitation of the environment. If exploitation is defined as the accumulation of surplus value produced by labor alone, the natural environment can only be considered indirectly. However, where a society holds land communally, and similarly obtains access to forest resources by virtue of communal possession, then individuals have the value of these assets available to them as well as their own labor power. Where a new political economy emerges which permits the accumulation of these values, this can be an important part of class relations.

Richard W. Franke (1982) has argued that societies of the West African Sahel with powerful ruling classes experience degradation of their environment, and as a result of their food production systems, while other societies which are relatively egalitarian have sounder environmental adaptations. Duffield (1978) has described a case where the exploitation of formerly communal lands by those with money to invest has produced substantial profits, which they have invested in the commercial sector; the land was sold to poor farmers when the returns declined. These patterns are repeated in one way or another throughout the world, and need to be incorporated into our understanding of class relations.

In the Masalit case there are two important ways in which the upper classes benefit from over-exploitation of the environment: the abuse of farmland and the arrogation of forest resources. With respect to farmland, the most serious danger is posed by groundnut production. I have argued that groundnut cultivation promotes erosion and reduces the phosphate content of the soil. Groundnut cultivation, however, is indirectly the main source of income for merchants and jammala, who can accumulate the profits resulting from its production and use them in consumption or other ventures. A part of their profits are a result of the value of the labor involved, but they also are drawn from the value of the nutrients of the land, which are being exported. This process is at an early stage, but if groundnut production continues to increase with the suggested environmental consequences, the result will be an impoverishment of the farmers through the deterioration of their farmlands, associated with accumulation of capital by merchants, who can then take their profits elsewhere.

At a much more advanced stage is the depletion of forest resources, described in detail in chapter 3. The development of towns has created a high demand for building materials, including the heavy timbers required for shops. The concentration of people has created a need for fences, as well as firewood, house materials, and fodder. Since the townspeople are not actually gathering these materials, they can use as much as they can afford to buy. This process is now extending to the villages, where merchants are building shops like those of the town. This contributes to a reduction in the area and density of bushlands, and losses of game and gathered foods as well. The wealthy can still afford to enjoy the consumption of these goods, and the jammala benefit because both townspeople and fellow-villagers pay them to find and transport forest products from an ever-increasing distance. For the poor, however, the loss of nearby forest impoverishes them in a particularly cruel way. It requires increasing amounts of labor to obtain the necessities of cooking food and building a house, and there is very little game, nuts or other wild foods available within reasonable distance to supplement their diets. Unlike the case of groundnut cultivation, they do not obtain any benefit from this sale of their part of a communally held resource.

I have outlined a simple three-tiered class structure that seems applicable to the rural people of Dar Masalit. There are merchants who buy from and sell to their fellow rural residents at a profit; there are tailors and jammala who use their capital to command a high price for their services, possibly joined with some small traders and other farmers who are relatively commercially oriented; and there are poor farmers who try to grow their own food and earn enough cash to get by through low-capital crafts or agricultural labor. While I have tried to emphasize locally relevant aspects of this structure, that is, relations of exploitation, it is also true that these groups are precisely defined by their relationship to the larger market. Merchants import and export, directly mediating economic flows with merchants one step higher in the national hierarchy; jammala transport the imports and exports, while tailors convert one of the main imports (cloth) into a commodity for use; and the majority of the population cultivate crops and carry out low-capital handicrafts, most of which are for local consumption. Thus, in this case the locally defined class relations are in agreement with a structure based on externally defined economic roles.

There are certain structural similarities between the position of the upper classes of rural Dar Masalit and the "lumpenbourgeoisie" as Frank (1972) called it, that is, the national elite who profit from the nation's interaction with the global market. The elites of the nation and of the village are both riding a current of change whose center is beyond their control; however, they are profiting by doing so. Of course the village capitalists are several "lumpens" removed from the national elite, who would consider them peasants indistinguishable from their fellow villagers. However, the village merchants and jammala share certain aspects of ideology with the national bourgeoisie, which add some validity to their characterization as a class.

It is typical of ideologies of dominant classes that they claim to fulfill basic human needs and wants for the entire population (Roberts and Brintnall 1983:326). In spite of their recent appearance, the merchant and high-capital elites of rural Dar Masalit have accepted many aspects of the national ideology. The value of trade, of course, is consistent with their lives; commerce and imports are seen as aspects of progress made concrete in consumption, the level of which can easily be compared with other parts of the country. Perhaps it is a leftover from the days of administered trade, but merchants and peasants alike consider the availability and prices of goods to be a direct reflection of the strength of the government. Village merchants, and to a large extent their customers, consider themselves to be doing a service to the community by making imported goods available, and handling the export of crops and livestock.

There are also interactions with Islam and Sudanese nationalism in the ideology of progress. The Masalit are Muslims and have been for centuries; however, as was pointed out in chapter 2, Islam has been practiced as a 'little tradition' in Dar Masalit. Islam has displaced local belief systems at a certain level, but many indigenous beliefs have been maintained in Islamic terms. For example, although witchcraft and divining are forbidden in orthodox practice, they are incarnated in an Islamic idiom in Masalit practice. These are responses to locally felt needs, as are curing, locust charming, and rain making. The adoption of a great tradition has not eliminated the needs of rural people for locally relevant practices, and the fekis have moved in to fill these needs in Islamic terms. The Islamic idiom has also been used for local values of reciprocity and neighborliness, and local Islam has accommodated the practice of drinking, a focus of sociability and value.

The Mahdist reformers attempted to work changes in Masalit practice of Islam, but their success was limited. However, with the development of contacts with the Nile Valley through trade and migration, Masalit have increasingly become aware of more orthodox practices of Islam. One aspect of this which is convenient for merchants, but probably incidental, is an increase in the amount of clothing considered necessary to be properly dressed. This is just one of a variety of practices and beliefs that are characteristic of "Sudanese metropolitan Islam" and which most Masalit now consider superior to their local practice.

The upper classes have taken the lead in adopting these practices, which gives them a certain degree of legitimacy as a superior group. The merchants are the most extreme case. Being externally oriented in their business, it is not surprising that they are externally oriented in cosmology as well. None of the merchants in the sample villages drink, and as a group they are among the most pious villagers. They are, however, oriented to Islam as practiced in the Nile Valley, rather than the local tradition of the fekis. They are interested in learning more Arabic, jurisprudence, correct behavior, and interpretation of the Qur'an, which are important in the great tradition of Islam, rather than the techniques and charms that the fekis use for local needs. They are adopting the pious practices of the Nile Valley, for example, naming ceremonies for their children, at least partial seclusion of their wives, and extensive evening prayer. It is likely that these men will make the pilgrimage to Mecca when they are able, and perhaps they will be the first villagers to have their daughters circumcised when they come of age. Within the great tradition of Islam, trade is a well accepted, honorable activity, and these men consider their work respectable. They consider their benefits both as rewards for their hard work, and blessings from God for which they are grateful. The jammala and tailors are also a pious group, and share in general this external orientation in trade and Islam. They and others feel that the merchants are to be admired, respected,and possibly emulated.

Thus, the merchants, tailors and jammala form an interest group as coreligionists in addition to their interests in economic development. As a result they frequently pray together, attend each others' ceremonial observances, and generally fraternize comfortably on the basis of a largely shared world view. They discuss Islam, political events of national significance, prices and availabilities of commodities, with confidence that these issues are of interest to all of them. Other pious villagers often join them. (I was not sufficiently sensitive to this issue at the time to note how the conversation changed in that context. As a general retrospective impression it seems to me that older fekis were treated with respect and patiently indulged, and younger pious men were fully involved in conversations on village events or religion but sat quietly in discussions of commerce.) There are certainly more pious villagers than the number involved in commercial economic relations, and Islam is not a well-defined 'insider cult.' However, it is one more element of external orientation that brings the elite classes of rural Dar Masalit together as a group, and helps them to conceptualize themselves as a progressive element of society.

This convergence of commercial activity, national identification, and religious interest brings the upper classes together, but also reduces the likelihood of the emergence of class consciousness based on economic activity. To an extent, religious orientations cut across the economically defined classes. Furthermore, merchants and jammala are also villagers, and are involved with their kin and neighbors in ties of generalized reciprocity and hospitality. Each merchant has a number of villagers who are grateful to him for assistance in some special situation or on a continuing basis. The village merchants are generally seen in a favorable light compared to the Buga merchants; they deal on slightly better terms with villagers, especially in shail arrangements, and are more understanding of the villagers' situations in general. People are often appreciative of the activities of the merchants, especially as they make trade easier for villagers; also, they perform some services, such as acting as bankers for them.

In addition, poor and rich villagers often share political and economic goals. Commodity prices, communications, government services, and other factors under external control are common interests of all villagers; all are farmers and commodity producers, purchasers of imports, and users of medical facilities. High prices charged and low prices paid by city merchants to village merchants hurt all the villagers and are resented. Thus, in many respects there is not an obvious divergence of interests between merchants and other villagers at the local level.

The position of village merchants is not so strong that they can afford to ignore the feelings of their co-villagers. They receive a good deal of respect, but the respect is conditional upon the merchants behaving properly by local standards. They must be generous in offering hospitality in their compound and at village events, and they must not neglect their social obligations as kin and neighbors. If they do not visit the sick, attend funerals (and keep burial shrouds in stock), help in work parties, and weed most of their own fields, they are subject to gossip and criticism that can ruin their trade. Villagers are very sensitive to the putting on of airs, and one man lost his customers, because the people considered him condescending when selling them sugar. (He complained about being disturbed for small amounts.) Also, farming is a symbolically important and highly valued activity. Hiring labor is accepted and envied, but the man who attempts to totally avoid farm labor is liable to criticism, and some Buga merchants are mocked for not weeding.

When people are angry with a merchant, there is a reservoir of resentment that can be opened. One feki stated that a merchant would not benefit from the pilgrimage to Mecca, since it was made with "*hag an na:s*;" that is, that which belongs to others (implying that his profits were not legitimate). Some drinkers are also hostile to merchants, considering their abstinence to be unsociable and mocking them among themselves. Nevertheless, such discontent does not often progress into public disagreement, primarily because there is no sympathetic forum. All agree that they are Muslims, and in the context of the most advanced information of which villagers are aware, it is the drinkers that are wrong and the merchants that are exemplary. The grumbling of the locally-oriented villagers cannot find a legitimate basis; they accept Islam as the standard, and are faced with higher authorities within that tradition who say that they are wrong to complain.

Thus, we have a situation where class relations are somewhat established in terms of the use of capital in one's interactions with other villagers, but consciousness of class relations within the village is very low, except for a bit of discontent which cannot be clearly articulated. There are other factors besides religious practice that contribute to this effect. I have already referred to Joan Vincent's position that this condition is typical of locally-oriented communities in the process of articulation with a wider market; in part class relations are ambiguous because local relations of exploitation are externally determined, and based upon the larger process of transnational capitalism. In Dar Masalit, the people are aware that the processes from which the merchants profit are determined on a scale much larger than the village; they do not hold the merchants responsible for those processes nor do they blame them for taking advantage of the opportunities presented to them, as long as they are reasonably fair to their fellow villagers. They are more likely to perceive the main conflict of interest to be between the Masalit, along with rural peoples of Sudan generally, and the national urban elite who form the government.

This case, as well as that of Joel Samoff and Rachel Samoff (1976), suggest that the conflict of interest between local exploiting classes and those closer to the core may be of greater importance to peasants than their immediate exploitation by merchants or employers. On the other end of the transaction, Christopher Chase-Dunn (1985) has suggested that a harmony between classes in the core is obtained through exploitation of the periphery. This is the sort of conflict of interests to which attention is drawn by a focus on unequal exchange, beyond the level of production. Does this constitute false consciousness? Or is it the case that in the world of today exchange predominates over production as a means of accumulation? It would seem difficult to answer these questions without quantification of value transfers in exchange, but it appears that many villagers do not hold their cousins and neighbors responsible for exploiting them.

Rayah Feldman, in a case where the elite are primarily commercial farmers, suggests other ambiguities. In her study, the main activities for surplus accumulation—hiring labor and being a landlord—are not distinctive, because many non-elite villagers practice them as well. They are not seen as exploitative when commercial farmers do them, even though the scale of their operations is quite different (1975:161–164). Similarly in the Masalit case, non-merchants also hire other villagers and engage in trade to a certain extent, and they do not consider these practices exploitative. Thus, class consciousness and conflict have not developed to any appreciable degree at the village level.

The lack of consciousness of class relations reflects the fact that there is not currently a struggle between the objectively defined classes; however, the members of classes still act in terms of their own interests, and there are inherent conflicts here that may become more apparent. In Dar Masalit, the most obvious possibility concerns the production of groundnuts. The profits of merchants at the present time, as well as the income of jammala and tailors, are based in large part on groundnut production. Merchants are also accumulating profits that need to be reinvested. In the absence of technological change, the only ways merchants can reinvest to increase groundnut production are through hiring labor and shail; thus, it is likely that both will increase in the future.

Another factor that limits the ability of merchants to invest at present is the communal ownership of land. Elsewhere in Sudan, land is registered, bought, and sold, permitting accumulation by those with capital. It is quite likely that at some point merchants of Dar Masalit, including town merchants and outsiders, will lobby for land registration in this area. This would be the final struggle between the old elite, charged with managing the land for their clans, and the new, citing progress and modernity. The probable result of such change would be dispossession, creation of a rural proletariat, and degradation of agricultural land, followed by outside investment of the profits generated.

Whether or not land registration occurs, the high rate of return to capital at the present time indicates that inequality of wealth will be maintained or increased in the future. Class analysis directs our attention to ask whether this structure of inequality can be perpetuated into the next generation. For the elites considered, the answer is clearly yes. Several jammala are actually young men with little accumulated wealth who are allowed to use the camel of a parent or parent-in-law; eventually they may buy their own. Among the merchants, sons are considered the best business partners one can have; only one village merchant has a son old enough to assist him now, and he is a great asset to his father. In towns it is quite common for sons of merchants to assist their fathers, and they expect to move into the business one day. Capital is easily transferred, and this process allows for the transfer of training and clients as well.

Education is one important means by which an elite can invest in their children's future (Feldman 1975; Samoff and Samoff 1976). Elsewhere in Sudan there are reports of diversification in the next generation, through training some children in a skill such as driving, educating others, and bringing some into trade (Galal-el-Din 1977; Duffield 1981). Duffield points out that "amongst the petty-bourgeoisie the family represents a real means of attaining wealth" (Duffield 1981:96). In the villages of Dar Masalit the new elite classes are rather young and it is too early to know what may occur in the next generation; however, there are a number of possibilities. Currently government service jobs are largely in the hands of non-Masalit; there are few Masalit in teaching, health, or other salaried jobs. The new elite may have the resources to educate some of their children to the point where these jobs are accessible. For a more rapid return, merchants may be able to underwrite an attempt by a son to get lucrative work abroad. A son might be trained as a tailor, or one might become a full-time herder if the family livestock holdings are large enough. Assuming that trade and other merchant activities continue to provide a source of wealth in Dar Masalit, there are numerous opportunities for the advancement of the children of the rich. The general population is denied opportunity by the lack of cash resources, but with a little cash a great deal is possible.

Summary

In chapter 4, changes in the most important economic activities carried out by the rural people of Dar Masalit have been discussed in detail. Such an analysis was essential to understanding overall change, however it was incomplete. The activities discussed required access to varying amounts of productive assets and resources, and these have not remained the same in the context of new activities. Land and forest resources have become scarce due to increased demand; labor has become more difficult to obtain through non-capitalist relations of reciprocity within the family and the village, while wage labor has become a source of profit; and money can now be used as investment capital in trade, agriculture, herding, and other activities. These changes in the position of the various productive assets affect everyone, whether or not they take part in the activities which generate the changes.

In addition, due to changes in the relative importance of assets and the potential for new levels of consumption, the basis and meaning of wealth and power have changed. From a situation where the political elite was wealthy by virtue of its control of people, there a situation has emerged where wealth and power come from the control of capital. While not fully developed, there are incipient classes within the villages of Dar Masalit that may promote their own interests in the future, probably at the expense of other villagers. However, a number of factors inhibit the development of open conflict and class consciousness, among which is the perception that conflicts of interest between the villagers and the urban elite are more important than those among villagers. This perception does not, in fact, seem far wrong.

6. The Transformation of Masalit Economy and Society

In the preceding chapters, I have presented the most important changes to occur in the environment and economy of Dar Masalit during the colonial and postcolonial period. These include the development or decline of a number of economic activities, changes in the relative importance of the various productive assets, and shifts in the power structure of Dar Masalit. At this point I attempt to gather some of the main themes that have run throughout this analysis, and reassemble the presentation of recent Masalit economic history.

There are three major trends underlying the other changes in the Masalit situation. The simplest to understand is the decline in rainfall, which affects almost all agricultural or forest-related activities. Second is the increasing population density. As argued in chapter 3, the increase has in large part resulted from colonial economic policies, warfare, Dar Masalit's border location, and a lack of appreciation by administrators of problems associated with population growth in a limited area. The population and rainfall trends have played important roles in the transformation of the Masalit economy, but they have mostly been factors that supplemented or compounded the effects of the third major trend—that towards greater incorporation of Dar Masalit in the global economy. A brief summary of that process follows.

Under the Ancien Regime and during Masalit independence, there was a certain degree of contact with European markets through the trans-Saharan trade. Direct participation was limited to the elite, and while commoners paid tribute that was used in trade, the production and consumption of trade goods were almost entirely out of their hands. Kapteijns (1985:6–8; 1983) vigorously rejects the argument that this trade was an important basis for local political power; on the contrary it appears that the control of trade was one of the benefits of political power. After the advent of the colonial period, there was an increase in direct market contact by commoners. From British occupation to the late 1940s, this was limited due to the depression and the Second World War, but some money began to pass through local people's hands, and some Masalit began to migrate to get money. Since the war, Dar Masalit rapidly moved from a situation of local autonomy to one of significant dependence on the market.

The number of ways in which people participate is large, and each has secondary effects. In fact the nexus of market integration is so complex that it is impossible to distinguish causes from effects in many cases. I find it useful, however, to focus on five striking changes, and the ways in which they feed back upon each other or induce other effects. These are the following:

PRODUCTION OF CROPS FOR SALE, ESPECIALLY GROUNDNUTS FOR EXPORT. This is the most obvious way in which local resources are being used in response to world market demands. Groundnut cultivation increases the pressure on limited land, and quite possibly has a long-term degrading effect on farmland. The groundnut market creates new opportunities for profit through investment in growing, transporting, and accumulating them for export. The export orientation of the economy stimulates a hierarchical organization of markets and roads leading to Geneina, and thus contributes to urbanization. Export of groundnuts leads to more money coming into Dar Masalit, which can be used for consumption or reinvestment.

URBANIZATION. Geneina and the smaller towns of Dar Masalit, while acting as market centers for import and export, are also centers of concentrated population. As such, they require food, fuel and shelter, which creates an opportunity for rural people to sell millet, livestock, firewood, and building materials. Concerning the latter two, the demand of the towns has resulted in denudation of former forests in ever-larger circles. This has made it increasingly difficult for most villagers to provide their own fuel and shelter requirements. The owners of camels control the remaining forest resources because they alone are able to transport heavy loads over a distance. This situation produces a source of income for them, but a cash requirement for the other villagers. Furthermore, the forest has been eliminated as an imporant source of food for rural people, thereby increasing the amount of cultivated land needed for subsistence.

LABOR MIGRATION. By working as laborers on enterprises that supply the demands of foreign or Sudanese urban consumers, Masalit are directly engaged in production for the world market. The selective removal of young and middle-aged men from the local setting has had a number of effects: a reduction in the labor force available for familial or cooperative projects; a decrease in the number of craftsmen, and therefore, increased dependence by residents on purchases of import substitutes; and an increasing female specialization in agriculture. Returning temporary migrants have raised local standards of consumption, and also have included a significant number of individuals with enough capital for investment in a camel, sewing machine, or trade.

PURCHASES OF IMPORTED GOODS. Production for sale on the market has been matched by increasing consumption of imports. This has contributed to a reduction in the importance of local crafts, such as weaving and bowl carving, in favor of imported woven cloth and utensils. It has also made possible inequalities in consumption within the village that exceed by far the level of local inequality during the Ancien Regime. Increasing purchases at all levels have required more production of millet, groundnuts and livestock for sale in the market, with their associated pressures on the land. Rising average levels of consumption encourage the young to migrate in search of cash, and encourage those who stay to produce more goods or services at the highest prices possible. Most of these must now be export goods, such as crops or hides, or services associated with export and import, such as transport or trade.

DEVELOPMENT OF ELITES WITH CONTROL OF CAPITAL. Market integration has made possible both the accumulation of money, and the investment of it in profitable enterprises, such as the production of groundnuts for export, trade, sewing and transport. Investment capital is distributed unequally, and the high returns to capital are increasing that inequality. Those with accumulated capital use their resources to produce and encourage the production of more export products and to increase the market for imported goods. They support increasing market dependence by providing credit, employment, and a market for purchase and sale of imports and exports, all of which are profitable enterprises.

The reader will appreciate that the circularity of the various cause and effect relations mentioned above is intentional. The point is that these trends support each other, and all of them are closely linked to national and international market forces. If the integration of this area into the world market simply involved people planting groundnuts and buying tea, it would remain peripheral to their lives. In Dar Masalit, as elsewhere in the world, market contact has not been contained at that level; production and consumption have gone beyond superficial contact, such that now market forces permeate rural life and participation is not optional.

This book has largely been concerned with demonstrating the deep penetration of market forces into every aspect of Masalit life, including those aspects that are most directly connected to subsistence. It is the multifaceted nature of the market, with its variety of goods and requirements, that seems to seek out every nook of supply and cranny of demand which might conceivably exist. The 'hidden hand' of the market is more far-reaching and detailed than any administrative policy could be. The colonial officers who applied the simple faith that buying and selling (of anything) is a higher form of human existence than producing one's needs, did not need to understand the local economy very well in order to start the process of transformation. In finding a few things to buy and a few things to sell, they began a trend towards circulation of money, intensification of production, and increased consumption. Rather than simply 'venting surplus', this quickly produced local elites to further the process and find new ways to expand their role. All they have required of government was protection of trade and maintenance of communications.

The transformation of the economy has required general participation to be successful. This relates one of the questions often asked by anthropology students, who have been assigned one of the many functionalist ethnographies concluded by a chapter on 'modernization' or 'social change' that is, why do people give up their culture? Is life without the market so bad that people cannot wait to drop their former mode of life in favor of a new one? Are tea and sugar so attractive that they are worth renouncing a whole way of life?

These are not easy questions, but to a great extent they are based on two spurious notions: first, that such a choice is presented, and second, that the decision is made by the entire population. The market does not work this way.

The Masalit were not polled on whether they were willing to become dependent on the market in order to consume sugar, any more than sixteenth century Europeans were polled on whether it was worth destroying or enslaving entire peoples in the New World in order to consume sugar. The power of the market comes from its fragmented character. A people does not decide to enter the market as a whole. Rather, individuals decide to sell a goat and buy some cloth, grow some groundnuts and drink tea, or go east for awhile to earn bridewealth. Some look for ways in which profits can be made, and try to raise money to carry out their schemes.

All of these individuals bring market forces closer to their families and neighbors. None can be said to be acting on behalf of their neighbors, nor to possess full information about the effects of their actions, but the overall direction of change seems always to be towards a greater market participation by a larger number of people. The changes reinforce and accelerate one another, as pointed out above. In a fairly short period of time, the accumulation of small, individual decisions results in a transformation of the economy, as well as the social organization, which effects everyone.

The rural Masalit population is thus brought into the market, but in a disadvantageous position. They have few options; most Masalit are obliged to remain in unremunerative forms of agricultural employment, whether in Dar Masalit, the Nile Valley or both in rotation. Agricultural income in Dar Masalit is limited by land, climate and technique, as well as prices. The possibility of increasing one's income locally through nonagricultural investment is limited by the fact that almost all income ultimately derives from agriculture. There is little 'round-aboutness' in the rural economy; the growing occupations are those that facilitate the import and export of world-market goods, produced and consumed in Europe, America and Asia, as well as Sudan's urban centers. As J. H. Boeke found in Indonesia, the large flows of money are between the village and the local extremities of the world market, and the money spends little time in the rural areas (1953:68–69).

Nevertheless, the village, the family, and the local economy continue to be of great importance in Masalit life. The primary consideration of every farmer is the production of food for household consumption; even if the market value of subsistence production is a minority of total output, it is of first importance from the producer's point of view. While money transactions among villagers in day-to-day life are small compared to the money involved in export and import, there is still a large grants economy among neighbors and kin; far more labor is given than is hired, and more millet is pooled than is purchased. In spite of the strains created by market integration, which have been discussed above, and in spite of the transformation of interpersonal relations that has resulted from the deep penetration of market forces, village and family are elements of continuity and stability in rural life.

The village is still home, a source of security and identity, and a place where one can be proud to be Masalit.

The persistence of a degree of local orientation is partially a result of the fact that the majority of the population is somewhat insulated from the market. I have argued elsewhere (Tully 1981b) that *direct* contact with the market—as an employee, export producer, merchant, or purchaser of consumer goods—is carried out to a great extent by young and middle-aged males. They grow most of the groundnuts, tan all of the hides, do all of the transport work, and make up the migrant labor pool for the eastern plantations. The definition of male and female responsibilities within the family, adjusted to reflect current conditions, leaves the primary responsibility for acquiring market goods—clothing, tea, meat, and others—on the husbands and fathers.

While it is clear that women's food crop production makes the male export-oriented activities possible, this division of labor makes it less likely that women and children can enter the market directly, learn Arabic, or attend to national politics affecting crop prices or migration. Women and children are able to maintain a local orientation to a greater extent than adolescent and adult males. Reciprocity in the village and concentration on food crop production are themes of Masalit culture that continue to be particularly meaningful in their lives. In this they are joined by the elderly of both sexes who also produce little for export, and many of whom have never emigrated. Together, the stable residents of the villages; that is, excluding males of migrating age—form a majority of the population, sharing a local orientation, close social relationships, and a basic concern with each other's survival. This has broken down to a certain extent because of the many families without adult males to assume responsibility for cash needs; however, in these cases the consumption of imported goods is usually reduced and market production is still low.

Goran Hyden has referred to "an economy in which the affective ties based on common descent, common residence, etc., prevail . . . as an 'economy of affection' . . . [which is] primarily concerned with the problems for reproduction rather than production" (1980:18). He suggests that individuals are willing to invest considerably in social relationships which increase individual ability to survive and bear risks; furthermore, "this economy of affection is being maintained and defended against the intrusion of the market economy . . . the market economy does not unilaterally cause the destruction of the economy of affection. The latter has the ability to survive and also to affect the mode of operation of the market economy" (1980:19).

In the Masalit case the economy of affection is found in the nexus of village ties; the common purpose of the village is survival. The existence of the village allows men to migrate, because if they are injured or impoverished they can always return. Unless social relations reach a very sorry state in the rural area, no one will starve unless everyone starves.

This security is, as Heyden points out, valued and defended. However, he does not go far enough in his argument. The village preserves economic security, certainly, but this security is associated with a system of meaning and a way of life. In the perspective of the world economy, the villagers of Dar Masalit are anonymous, and as individuals each is dispensable. The Masalit are aware of the fickleness of the market and the lack of control they have over it, how prices change and demand shifts, and they know that to the extent they enter into a relationship with the world market they lose control; their position is on the bottom rung of a very large ladder. It is also important to note that this position is paralleled in the social and cultural spheres. In contact with Sudanese of the urban elite, Masalit face discrimination and racism, and are made painfully aware that their personal habits, religious practices, and linguistic abilities are considered inferior from a Nile Valley perspective. The village is not only a refuge of economic security, where people can produce for themselves; it is also a place where they can act as they are raised to, solve their own problems, and enjoy positions of respect and meaning in their own social world.

Thus, we see in action the paradox of dualism. The rural areas of Dar Masalit are certainly not separated or independent from the urban industrial areas or from the export economy of Sudan. They play vital roles in the production of groundnuts and hides, and as laborers in the plantations that feed the urban sector. Money and market forces have penetrated deeply into village life. And yet a level of autonomy and local orientation is preserved in the village. It may be false consciousness and it may be only an illusion of autonomy, but it is one that makes survival possible in the unfavorable position in which most Masalit find themselves.

The penetration of market forces at the village level does not represent a breakdown of dualism as predicted by modernization theorists. There has been little transfer of capital from the urban sector, and such capital as exists has not been invested in increasing the productivity of local agriculture. On the contrary, the surplus value produced in the rural areas has been exported in exchange for consumer goods. A portion of the surplus value is captured locally and some of it is invested in agriculture, but even this is not invested in any way that can increase productivity; rather it is used to expand the application of labor-intensive techniques. The benefits are concentrated in the hands of a few, while the majority of the population finds it harder and harder to get by. This is dualism almost exactly as formulated by the oft-misrepresented J. H. Boeke (1953, 1954). It is not founded on the failure of urban capitalism to interact with the rural areas, but rather on the development of the urban areas at the expense of the countryside. In this sense dualism can be seen as a relationship, not a typology. It is the final link in an international structure of dependency which connects the metropole to the most diverse and distant hinterlands of the world.

Hyden has argued that where the economy of affection operates, it reduces the likelihood of the emergence of class consciousness (1980:192). This agrees with my description of Masalit village relationships; as long as merchants fulfill their obligations as wealthy villagers by redistributing some amount of their wealth, village solidarity is maintained and conflict is minimized. However, if the main conflict in Dar Masalit is, as I have suggested and as argued generally by Michael Lipton (1977), between the villages and the urban-based elite of Sudan, it is also important to inquire how this division of interests is conceived. Is there a consciousness of this relationship that might be construed as emerging class consciousness? While this was not specifically a focus of field research, there are some comments and events recorded which suggest that this may be the case.

In general, migrants are aware of the fact that Masalit levels of consumption are low compared to the eastern Sudan, and they often experience poor treatment there. Western Sudanese generally find it more difficult to be accepted as citizens, both socially and officially, which restricts their work opportunities and leaves them vulnerable to abuse. Upon returning, migrants are reminded of the lack of local services and investments in development made by the government compared to the eastern Sudan, and the irrelevance of many government policies to their needs. Feelings of being left out of the Sudan are commonly expressed in Dar Masalit as well as other areas of the west, and undoubtedly contributed to western support for the recent Sudanese regionalization program, which gave Darfur greater autonomy in administration and policy.

Yet those who are most aware of Dar Masalit's (and Darfur's) low position in Sudan and are most active in trying to use political means to change it, also tend to be those who are already directed to external affairs, be they economic, social or political, for example, town elite, merchants, or local representatives to the national political system. An alternative reaction to the Masalit situation, by individuals with less to gain from integration, is the more visceral one; anger over the injustice, cynicism about the ideals expressed by national government, distrust of those who are involved in it, and pessimism about the possibility of changing anything. Sentiments like these are also widespread, but they are not a strong basis for organization; they are diffuse and passive, and cannot promote progressive action. They can, however, be the basis for resistance.

It has been suggested in the last chapter that local class relations define groups which are also defined by their relationship to the world market; the new elites have an interest in promoting national integration, while others may resent it. What I am suggesting here is that those who resist integration, who can easily be construed as hide-bound traditionalists clinging to their old ways, may be just as aware of the national arena and experienced in it as those who are promoting integration. Resistance can reduce the efficiency of government institutions, which preserves local autonomy, and it can also be a way of blocking the ambitions of local people who enter Sudanese politics with intentions of forming close ties with urban elites. It can be carried out through many indirect actions; gossip or personal accusations of corruption, nonparticipation in projects, or even attainment of a major position in a project and then failure to carry it out. If local politics are considered in terms of the forces of integration and the forces of local autonomy, we may find that most confrontations are of this covert, indirect sort.

The question of where one's loyalty lies—with village or nation—was graphically illustrated in an entirely non-economic manner on the Little Id (*ᶜi:d al-faTur*) in 1979. This is the day of fastbreaking, the first day following the Muslim month of Ramadan, during which no food or water is taken until sundown each day. In 1979, Ramadan fell in the weeding season, which added to the usual hardship because of the thirst and hunger created by physical labor. It is considered important that the community of Islam pray together and break the fast together on this day, in the form of local communities. The end of the fast is indicated by the appearance of the crescent moon (*Hila:l*) that defines the beginning of a new month, and so one does not know exactly which day is to be the Id until the night before it. Towards the end of Ramadan, then, people in the village were gathering in the evenings at the homes of the merchants (and the anthropologist) who had radios, listening to Radio Omdurman (the Sudanese national station) for news of the hilal. At last, Omdurman announced the moon had been seen, and word was spread through the village that the Id would take place the next day. Preparations went late into the night.

By the next morning, however, word had come from Buga that a certain feki refused to celebrate the Id, because no one in Buga reported seeing the hilal. Now this man was a known opponent of the fursha; the fursha was a merchant, and active in politics and the promotion of government projects, while the feki involved was generally considered a spoiler—with a large constituency for exactly that reason. The fursha and the imam of Buga (also a government appointee) took the position that Sudan was praying and they were going to pray with them; if anyone wanted to pray on a different day, they must do it outside town limits. And so they did; the fursha and most of the town prayed in the mosque on the day observed by the nation, while this feki led prayer outside of town the next day.

Meanwhile, the village was abuzz. Instead of greeting each other with the traditional Id greetings, the word on everyone's lips was "*ayyadta?*" "Are you observing the Id?" The rumor arose that the village imam would not lead prayer that day (although he did), and many village men, anxious to pray with the rest of the country, went to Buga to join the townspeople in prayer. These included many of the pious group in high-capital occupations that have been discussed above. In their wish to do the right thing, they made a statement that their identification with the larger community of Islam is stronger than their identification with the village community.

Later I visited the male teachers in Buga, of whom only one was Masalit. I asked them what they thought of the events; I also wanted to know whom, of Buga political figures, they had seen at the mosque on the day of the Id announced on Radio Omdurman. Much to my surprise, they said they had not prayed on that day, but the previous one. They had heard on Radio Monte Carlo that the crescent moon had been sighted in Saudi Arabia, and they prayed and broke the fast one day before the official Sudanese day, joined by the police and the health practitioner. While the town elite was trying to pray with the nation, these representatives of the nation were praying with the international community of Islam.

We should not go too far in applying significance to this event, but it does echo one of the important themes in Masalit life today—the conflict and ambivalence over how large a world one is attached to. In this book I have attempted to demonstrate the deep penetration of global forces at the village level. Capitalism is evolving at a global level and the processes are largely beyond the control of small farmers in rural villages. Nevertheless to understand the meaning of market integration in people's lives, the processes by which its penetration is brought about, and the effect of local efforts in shaping the process, it is necessary to take an intimate look at a small piece of the world system. It is easy to forget that this system is composed of individuals who are attempting to understand it as a matter of survival, finding ways to profit, ways to cope, or ways to preserve autonomy. Therefore in the Masalit case we have turned our attention to the smallest levels—the community, the family, the individual—and considered what market integration means to them.

Notes

Chapter 1. World Systems and Local Processes

1. Pierre-Philippe Rey and colleagues build upon Louis Althusser and Etienne Balibar's influential approach to Marx (1970). Valuable summaries and critiques of Rey's position are found in Barbara Bradby (1975) and Aidan Foster-Carter (1978).

2. In more recent work, Frank has continued to give priority to "the historical process of capital accumulation in a world scale" (1979:43). However, although he references none of the articulation literature, he also considers "how it was mediated through differing modes of production" (ibid). His emphasis is still on very large regions, and in a later chapter, continents; subsequent work (1980) focuses squarely on processes at the global level.

3. Wallerstein also stresses that the effect of capitalist forces are variable over time: "Neither the 'development' or the 'underdevelopment' of any specific territorial unit can be analyzed or interpreted without fitting it into the cyclical rhythms and secular trends of the world-economy as a whole" (1979:73). D. R. Tully (1985) discusses variation as a result of changing policies.

4. And studies by nonanthropologists as well; see L. Berry 1975; John Illiffe (1983:31–34).

5. It might be the case that an increase in environmental resources per person would have the same effect; given a new linkage to the market, any disturbance of a stable ecological adaptation could create a response that tightens that linkage. This hypothesis needs to be considered in terms of data from a wide variety of cases, but given that environmental conditions are rarely stable, it could be a significant part of an explanation of the unidirectional expansion of the world market.

6. But only just. Jacques Chevalier (1982) has drawn attention to recently published material from an early draft of *Capital* (appendix, Marx 1977) in which it is explicitly stated that usurers and merchants exploit simple commodity producers. Still, given the continued importance of such production, such brief mention is rather unsatisfying.

7. The reader will note in subsequent chapters that the word class is used cautiously, because I consider that the existence of class in a particular instance must be demonstrated rather than assumed. Where I use words such as 'inequality' or 'elite,' it is because I have not demonstrated the existence of class relations in these instances, but this does not mean that a class analysis is impossible. This issue will be taken up in chapter 5.

8. Another set of questions deals with the analysis of migration. Where adult males migrate to work directly for urban capitalist classes, their exploitation is direct; however, the low wages they receive are made possible by the increased labor of women and children in the rural areas, who bear the costs of reproducing the labor force while also producing commodities (Meillassoux 1972). Are the women being exploited by the urban capitalist class in subsidizing wage labor, or by their husbands? Simultaneously, are they being exploited by the rural capitalist class in producing commodities that ultimtely satisfy urban demand? Such complicated cases are the norm rather than the exception.

Chapter 2. Masalit History, Society and Culture

1. 1973 census figures; see chapter 3.

2. Gimr were also allotted an area directly east of Geneina at the eastern border of Dar Masalit. In 1979, this area was removed and incorporated into a newly created district of Northern Darfur. The Erenga appear to be a creation of the last one hundred years, initially as a political amalgamation of smaller groups of people speaking related languages (Kapteijns 1985:16–17).

3. It appears that three of the sheikhs mentioned by Kapteijns (1985:265) are actually comparable to maliks, as the word is used here.

4. I am grateful to Lidwien Kapteijns (personal communication) for correcting my previously published opinion concerning the significance of the fursha in nineteenth-century political organization, which was based on observation of the current adminstrative structure (Tully 1981a:130).

5. It was a general policy in Sudan to establish high salaries where expedient. A 1927 minute from the Governor-General reads: "Be prepared to grant a worthy scale of remuneration to the Chiefships we foster, great and small, in order to give them dignity and status, in the confident hope that we shall thereby be saved in the long run from costly elaborations of our own administrative machinery" (quoted in Cooke 1935:195).

6. I was unable to fully define the role of the sheikha, but it appeared that she was most closely associated with unmarried females. Thus, this position may be related to that of the *umm al-bana:t*, a female counterpart of the wornung, discussed by Kapteijns (MS).

7. In Dar Masalit, men with horses were said to cultivate one field specifically to feed the horse. I encountered only one man who did so in 1979; frequently, men with horses buy grain for them.

8. Kapteijns (MS) states that in Wadai a man had to provide his wife with twelve bushels of grain if she were his sole wife, but only six if he had two or more.

NOTES

Chapter 3. Dar Masalit in Context: Environment, Ecology and Demography

1. The comparative description is based on my own observations as well as interviews with agricultural, medical, veterinary, and political officers of Dar Masalit, furshas of the varying regions, and the study of Landsat images and maps. See figure 3.1 for a list of the main sources.

2. Kapteijns comments on this: "I think that Dar Gimr was 'marginalized' even before the beginning of the colonial period, as a result of drought, excessive exploitation by the sultan and particularly the abbonga [sultanic elite] who 'ate' the dar, partly because the royal family was internally divided and competing for resources" (personal communication). There are several reports of famine in the colonial record concerning Dar Gimr, and the north had the highest rate of emigration in the 1955–56 census (see below).

3. For example, West African matches, made with high phosphorous for humid conditions, are in high demand in the rains, when Sudanese matches will not light, but in the dry season they are somewhat unsafe and Sudanese matches are favored.

4. One fursha complained that trees have been cut to bring down the nests of the *sagr jidya:n*, the eagle that is the national symbol of the Sudan. Possessing such a captive eagle is a source of prestige, apparently, in some circles.

5. Kapteijns (1985:256) cites another 1923 estimate of ninety thousand, and a 1934 estimate of one hundred twenty thousand. A 1928 report estimates the adult male population at twenty thousand, which suggests a total population of approximately one hundred thousand (Darfur 1/37/188).

6. The child-women ratio is defined as the number of children under five per one thousand women of childbearing age. Average complete family size is the number of children born to women now past childbearing age, divided by the number of such women.

7. The omdas of the 1955–56 census are categorized as follows: North: Osman Hashim (Gimr) and Ahmed Mahdi (Jabal); Goz: Bashir Abdullahi, Bashir Ahmed, Mohd Ulma, Ibrahim Idris, A. Banat Mohd, Dafanja Mohd (Erenga and Awra); Abdullahi Ali Mekki, Suleiman Harun, Mohd Abedalla, Osman Abdalla (Arab), Yusif Abdullahi Kaskus (Marasi); Ali Hano, Shalabi Mohd, Abakr Zobeir, Mohd Musa, Zakarriya Abakr, Harun Hassan, Ya'goub Rizik, Idris Mohammed, Ismail Tuga (Masalit); South: A Rahman Nurein, Ya'coub Arbab, Eisa Ed Dom, Nitiko Adam, Nitik Adam, Yacoub Adingi, Yacoub Ishaac, Yusif A. Gadir, Belal Bara, Adam Idris Dabba, Harun To (Masalit); Ishak Naheed (Senyar) Unknown: Daris El Doma, Abdel Rahman Ahmed Berda, El Ghali El Kidheir, Mustafa Sayara, and two special categories; Nomads: Rest.

The Marasi territory near Saraf Umra, as well as a recently created Gimr territory on the eastern border, were placed in a newly established subprovince of Northern Darfur in 1979, and were thus removed from Dar Masalit.

Chapter 4. Production and Exchange

1. The value in sampling of such a variable, which draws on local definitions of wealth and poverty, was suggested by Polly Hill (1972:5).

2. The prevalence of import over export is indicated by the pricing structure: the price of oil is lower in larger quantities, as with sugar and cloth. This is the opposite of the prices of millet and groundnuts, which increase with quantity, due to the strong export market. Clarified butter (*semn*) may be substituted for oil, and, thus, women with livestock make less oil. Butter production is discussed in the section on livestock.

3. This is comparable to the 4.0 hours per day that Robert B. Tripp (1982:394) found for women in a Ghanaian farming settlement, based on the period 6:00 A.M. to 7:00 P.M. only. (Substantial domestic labor is carried out outside of this time period in the villages I studied). Tripp finds that women reduce (or reschedule) their daily domestic labor time from an average of 4.6 hours in the dry season to 3.4 hours in the wet season. Compare Galal-el-Din 1978:58–59.

4. Among the Arabs who pass through this area, women are responsible for setting up and packing the family housing.

5. In Masterei, a mahammas is conceived as a rectangle of 20 x 30 *habl* (rope). A habl is 6 *dira*^{c} long, and a dira (the distance from elbow to fingertip) is 51–52 cm. Elsewhere in Darfur, the mahammas is also based on the habl and dira, but their size and the numbers of each used in calculating the mahammas vary from one site to another. (Hunting Technical Services 1977). There may be some variation within Dar Masalit, as there is for other common measures, such as the mid and kora.

6. Lennart Olsson and Mikael Stern (1981:22) note that yellowing of leaves frequently indicates nitrogen deficiency in millet, which is consistent with this explanation.

7. In similar conditions in Northern Nigeria, K. Klinkenberg found that: "The main feature is the accumulation of clay between a depth of 36 and 119 cm (14 and 47 in)" (1970:55). These depths would normally be reached by millet and groundnut roots.

8. E. Walter Russell (1968) has noted that nitrogen fertilizers must be used carefully in arid zones, since they may encourage rapid early growth and depletion of soil water supplies if there is a break in the rains. Masalit

farmers have stated that dayar is risky for the same reason; that is, the millet could "burn" easily if there was a break in the rains.

9. Jan S. Hogendorn (1978:41) believes that nuts fix nitrogen when intercropped, but also states that each ton of nuts removes 125 lbs. of phosphate, or over 20 kg of phosphorous per 1000 kg, which seems high.

10. The cultivation of groundnuts may also cause higher losses of nutrients through leaching. Unlike millet, which is planted with the first rains, groundnut soil is weeded completely clean after the first growth of weeds; *then* it is planted. This means that the 'first flush' of nutrients—mineralized in the hot season, and released with the first rains—is leached into deeper soils, and may not be recovered.

11. J. M. Cocheme and P. Franquin (1967:95), analyzing millet yields in eleven years of varying rainfall, found 800 mm to be the optimum amount of rainfall for millet, with decreasing yields above and below this figure. Nevertheless, with 460 mm in one year, a yield of 960 kg/ha was produced—approximately 75 percent of the best yields recorded. While it is possible that this crop used stored moisture from the previous year (rainfall 820 mm), this illustrated the ability of millet to resist drought. Since the soil type was not reported, it is not certain that the optimal rainfall in Dar Masalit would be the same. Lennart Olsson (1983), analyzing Kordofan yields of millet for the period 1952–1974, found that the number of days with rainfall in combination with July-September total rainfall explained yield variation much better than total annual rainfall.

12. I was unable to determine if moloxiyya was identical to the plant of this name used widely in the Middle East, but it is a popular stew ingredient and was grown in most gardens.

13. Animal theft was a recurring problem, and it was little hindered by the minimal supervision given to animals. Villagers frequently blamed nomads for theft, but in 1979 a series of losses of small stock was traced to a group of young male villagers, who were roasting and eating them. Another villager was convicted of stealing a camel, which he took to Geneina and sold. These cases pointed out the difficulty of being a successful thief in an area where people and animals were fairly well-known; it was nearly impossible for a villager to go to any nearby market, especially with animals, and not be noticed.

14. Based on seventeen fields in which manuring was completed within the last ten years, and counting six goats as the equivalent of a cow, it was determined that on the average one hundred twelve cows manure 1 hectare per year. Usually this is carried out intensively with large herds, but one family has continuously manured its 2 hectare field for nine years with approximately ten cows and fifteen goats; it was one of the most pro-

ductive fields in the village. In outlying villages where people have more animals, this appears to be a common pattern.

15. Lidwien Kapteijns (1985:26) states that the village herd was tended communally in the nineteenth century. Since villages were smaller, it was quite possible that a village's animals were kept in one herd, and the current practice by owners of helping out in herding would be consistent with the communal practice. However, soil was being manured at least as early as the 1920s, and it seems likely that field owners took greater responsibility for herding then as they do now.

16. Manured fields also produce longer and better millet stalks which are useful in fencing and housing, and can be sold. Crops on manured fields clearly exceed other fields in height, even after several years of cultivation.

17. In one case, which other men said they would emulate, a merchant invited a group of nomadic camel herders to stay on his field in the dry season of 1979. They spent four months with approximately eighty camels and two hundred sheep; the merchant gave them millet for their horses, sugar and tea worth approximately LS 10. This year, he reported: "You cannot walk through the field," (that is, because the millet stand is so thick). Since camels do not compete with Masalit livestock for grazing, this may be a way of improving more fields in the future.

18. Camels were first owned in numbers by Masalit of this area in the 1960s, when the transport of import and export goods flourished. See below, "High Capital Activities."

19. These five new camels were not yet being worked and were therefore not included. Two of the five recent buyers owned and worked adult camels, one worked his father's camel, and one recently had his camel stolen.

20. It would appear that in a barter economy with fixed rates of exchange, there is theoretically no difference between money and a commodity. This would only be likely to occur in full form when the number of commodities is low. In the Masalit case, because several goods dominated the exchange economy, it was feasible to fix exchange rates among them; for minor goods, if the rate of exchange with one major commodity was known, the rate with any other could be calculated in one step.

21. Dar Masalit's situation was not unique. Nineteen years after the conquest of Darfur, Reginald Davies wrote, "most of Darfur, for example, is, economically, hardly part of the Sudan at all, except in respect of animals, which transport themselves, on the hoof or pad, at small cost to the exporter. An abundance of grain in Darfur would do little or nothing to relieve a famine in the central Sudan" (1935:305).

22. In Murne (eastern Dar Masalit) and neighboring Fur areas K. M. Barbour observed in 1948 and 1949 that women were wearing *zarag* from Egypt and cottons from India. However, men still wore local cloth, and sugar and tea were not used much. Barter was the prevailing means of exchange; local monetization was limited: "Money itself was regarded as merely a commodity, varying in demand and in price at different seasons. . . . The most striking features of the Fur economy are its self-sufficiency and its isolation" (1950:127; compare Tothill 1948:868–69).

23. Hunting Technical Services (1977) reports that in Jabal Marra, the use of shail is also limited and essentially acts as consumer credit. However, in that case the borrower receives only about one-sixth of the value of his crop. Tony Barnett (1977) found that even though shail is quite profitable in the Gezira, borrowers consider that the lender is doing them a favor.

24. Emigrants to urban areas, but not to other villages, were included. See below, "Dar Masalit Internal Migration."

25. The measure of land per capita does not make distinctions by age or sex. Adjustment may be made for these factors through the use of fractional consumption and production coefficients. Using some common estimates, the T-value of this comparison was further increased.

Chapter 5. Assets and Resources

1. These terms are used with very different meanings in other parts of Darfur. The words were probably introduced as part of the system of estates granted by the Fur sultanate, as described by G. Michael La Rue (1984), but in Dar Masalit the names were simply applied to traditional patterns. Thus, while La Rue suggests that hakura and fas rights conflicted with traditional ethnic and lineage rights (1984:12), in most of Dar Masalit, they were the same things.

2. It may be the case that a sid who became powerful enough could become a malik, especially if he were of a different clan than the original malik; he might secede from the clan territory or even overthrow a weak malik. The clan territories were not engraved in stone or protected by a supernatural charter.

3. The principle of acquiring land rights through use, including use that is not authorized, is also found in Washington State law; see "An 'adverse possession' is hard to fight", Seattle Post-Intelligencer, 10 February 1983, p. D2.

4. Male and female tasks may be the same or different, depending on the number of each sex present. For example, if there are only a few women at a harvesting nafir, they collect and transport the ears of millet to a cen-

tral point, whereas if the women are numerous they also cut the ears from the stalks. Still, women tend to do all of the collecting at harvest nafirs, and also all of the *guhu:r*, or close weeding at a hoeing nafir, even though both men and women carry out these tasks on their own fields.

5. Kapteijns (1983) states that advances of grain from public granaries by the sultan's governors, to be repaid at harvest, were used to create personal relationships of patronage. This opportunity would not have been available to the 'unofficial' elite of the villages, but the existence of this practice supports the hypothesis that generosity with grain was a means of political advancement. For parallel cases of the undermining of local redistributive patterns by market integration, see Raymond Firth 1939:363–65; S. F. Nadel 1947:56–84; James B. Watson 1952:108; Bob Shenton and Mike Watts 1979.

6. Taxes were (and are) assessed every three years. In the year of assessment, a double tax was collected, and no tax was collected in the second year. In the third year, a single tax was collected, and in the following year a new assessment was made.

7. According to Kapteijns, commoners also had slaves; it would seem most likely that, since their purchase would be rather difficult for most commoners, any slaves they had would be from the ranks of the refugees or the unfortunate who sold or volunteered themselves in order to survive. Local big-men or village founders may have acquired slaves in this way.

8. Total animal value was approximated in cow equivalents by the following formula, which reflects relative livestock prices in the 1978–79 period: value = cows + goats/6 + donkeys/2 + horses + camels x 2. Based on a 1978 survey, tailors and jammala owned an average of 6.8 cow equivalents per family compared with 4.7 for other non-merchants. Excluding camels the values were 5.7 and 4.5. Most merchants refused to participate or gave answers considered by my assistants to be low. In 1979 three merchants admitted to having herds of thirty or more cow equivalents, while several others were estimated by third parties to have holdings at least at this level. The determination of livestock holdings is notoriously difficult in western Sudan due to the fact that livestock taxes are the main form of personal taxation (Wilson 1977, 1979).

References

Abdalla, Ismail H. 1983. The Killer Ax: Farming and Deforestation in a Fragile Ecological System in Kordofan. Paper presented at the Twenty-Sixth Annual Meeting of the African Studies Association, Boston December 7–10.

———. 1985. Ecological, Economic and Cultural Change in an Agrarian Setting in Western Sudan: The Case of Awana Village. In Mahjoub El-Bedawi and David Sconyers (eds.), *Sudan Studies Association Selected Conference Papers 1982–1984*, 129–146. Baltimore: Sudan Studies Association.

Abrahams, R.G. 1965. Neighborhood Organization: A Major Sub-System among the Northern Nyamwezi. *Africa* 35:168–186.

Adam, Farah Hasan, and **William Andrea Apaya.** 1973. Agricultural Credit in the Gezira. *Sudan Notes and Records* 54:104–115.

Ahmed, Abdel Ghaffar M., and **Mustafa Abdel Rahman.** 1979. Small Urban Centers: Vanguards of Exploitation. *Africa* 49:258–271.

Althusser, Louis, and **Etienne Balibar.** 1979. *Reading Capital.* London: New Left Books.

Amin, Samir. 1972. Underdevelopment and Dependence in Black Africa: Origins and Contemporary Forms. *Journal of Modern African Studies* 4:503–24.

———. 1974a. *Accumulation on a World Scale.* New York: Monthly Review Press.

———. 1974b. (ed.) *Modern Migrations in West Africa.* London: Oxford University Press.

———. 1976. *Unequal Development: An Essay on the Social Formations of Peripheral Capitalism.* New York: Monthly Review Press.

Anderson, G.D. 1970. Fertility Studies on a Sandy Loam in Semi-Arid Tanzania II: Effects of Phosphorous, Potassium, and Lime on Yields of Groundnuts. *Experimental Agriculture* 6:213–222.

Andrews, F.W. 1948. Weeds in the Sudan. In J.D. Tothill (ed.), *Agriculture in the Sudan.* London: Oxford University Press.

Arizpe, Lourdes. 1982. Relay Migration and the Survival of the Peasant Household. In Helen I. Safa (ed.), *Towards a Political Economy of Urbanization in the Third World Countries*, 19–46. London: Oxford University Press.

Arrighi, G. 1973. Labor in Historical Perspective: A Study of the Proletarianization of the African Peasantry in Rhodesia. In G. Arrighi and J.S. Saul (eds.), *Essays on the Political Economy of Africa*, 180–234. New York: Monthly Review Press.

Baier, Stephen. 1976. Economic History and Development: Drought and the Sahelian Economies of Niger. *African Economic History* 1:1–16.

Bakhit, A/Hamid M.A. 1983. Desertification, Rehabilitation and Conservation: The Case of Western Sudan. *At-tasahhur* 1:5–9.

Balamoan, G. Ayoub. 1976. *Migration Policies in the Anglo-Egyptian Sudan 1884–1956.* Cambridge, MA: Harvard University Center for Population Studies.

Barbour, K.M. 1950. The Wadi Azum from Zalingei to Murnei. *Sudan Notes and Records* 31:105–28.

———. 1961. *The Republic of Sudan: A Regional Geography.* London: University of London Press.

Barlett, Peggy F. 1980. Adaptive Strategies in Peasant Agricultural Production. *Annual Review of Anthropology* 9:545–73.

———. 1982. *Agricultural Choice and Change: Decision Making in a Costa Rican Community.* New Brunswick, NJ: Rutgers University Press.

Barnett, Tony. 1975. The Gezira Scheme: Production of Cotton and the Reproduction of Underdevelopment. In Ivar Oxall, Tony Barnett, and David Booth (eds.), *Beyond the Sociology of Development: Economy and Society in Latin America and Africa.* London: Routledge and Kegan Paul.

———. *The Gezira Scheme.* London: Cass.

Barth, Fredrik. 1967a. *Human Resources.* Occasional paper No. 1, Sosialantropologisk Institutt, Universitet I Bergen.

———. 1967b. Economic Spheres in Darfur. In R. Firth (ed.), *Themes in Economic Anthropology*, 149–174. London: Tavistock Publication.

Bayoumi, Abdel Aziz. 1983. Sudan Government Efforts in Controlling Desertification. Presented at the workshop on Monitoring and Controlling Desertification in Sudan; Institute of Environmental Studies, University of Khartoum, February 20–24.

Bebawi, Faiz F. 1984. A Review of Cultural Control of *Striga hermonthica* in Sudan. In C. Parker, L.J. Musselman, R.M. Polhill, and A.K. Wilson (eds.), *Proceedings of the Third International Symposium on Parasitic Weeds*, ICARDA/International Parasitic Seed Plant Research Group, 7–9 May 1984, Aleppo, Syria, 148–155. Aleppo: ICARDA.

Bernstein, Henry 1977. Notes on Capital and Peasantry. *Review of African Political Economy* 10:60–73.

Berry, L. 1975. The Sahel: Climate and Soils. In *The Sahel: Ecological Approaches to Land Use*, 9–17. MAB Technical Note. Paris: UNESCO Press.

Berry, Sara S. 1975. *Cocoa, Custom and Socio-Economic Change in Rural Western Nigeria.* Oxford: Clarendon Press.

Boeke, J.H. 1953. *Economics and Economic Policy of Dual Societies.* New York: Institute of Pacific Relations.

———. 1954. Three Forms of Disintegration in Dual Societies. *Indonesie* 7:278–295.

Bohannan, Paul. 1959. The Impact of Money on an African Subsistence Economy. *Journal of Economic History* 19:491–503.

Bohannan, Paul, and **George Dalton**. 1962. Introduction. In Bohannan and Dalton (eds.), *Markets in Africa.* Evanston: Northwestern University Press.

Boulding, K.E. 1973. *The Economy of Love and Fear.* Belmont: Wadworth.

Boyd, David J. 1985. "We Must Follow the Fore": Pig Husbandry Intensification and Ritual Diffusion Among the Irakia Awa, Papua New Guinea. *American Ethnologist* 12:119–136.

Bradby, Barbara. 1975. The Destruction of Natural Economy. *Economy and Society* 4:127–161.

Brady, Nyle C. 1974. *The Nature and Properties of Soils.* New York: Macmillan.

Bryson, R.A. 1974. A Perspective on Climate Change. *Science* 184:753–60.

Byerlee, Derek, Carl K. Eicher, Carl Liedhom,, and **Dunstan S.C. Spencer.** 1977. *Rural Employment in Tropical Africa: Summary of Findings.* African Rural Economy Program, Working Paper No. 20. East Lansing: Michigan State University.

Caldwell, John C. 1975. *The Sahelian Drought and its Demographic Implications.* Overseas Liaison Committee, Paper No. 8. Washington: American Council on Education.

Charney, J.G. 1975. Dynamics of Deserts and Drought in the Sahel. *Quarterly Journal of the Royal Meteorological Society* 101:193–202.

Chase-Dunn, Christopher. 1985. The Kernel of the Capitalist World-Economy: Three Approaches. In William R. Thompson (ed.), *Contending Approaches to World-System Analysis*, 55–78. Beverly Hills: Sage.

Chevalier, Jacques M. 1982. There is Nothing Simple about Simple Commodity Production. *Journal of Peasant Studies* 10:153–186.

Chibnik, Michael. 1980. The Statistical Behavior Approach: The Choice Between Wage Labor and Cash Cropping in Rural Belize. In Peggy F. Barlett (ed.), *Agricultural Decision Making*, 87–113. New York: Academic Press.

Clarence-Smith, Gervase, and **Richard Moorsom.** 1977. Underdevelopment and Class formation in Ovamboland, 1844–1917. In Richard Palmer and Neil Parsons (eds.), *The Roots of Rural Poverty in Central and Southern Africa*, 96–112. Berkeley: University of California Press.

Cliffe, Lionel. 1977. Rural Class Formation in East Africa. *Journal of Peasant Studies* 4:195–224.

Cliffe, Lionel, and **Richard Moorsom.** 1979. Rural Class Formation and Ecological Collapse in Botswana. *Review of African Political Economy* 15–16:35–52.

Cloudsley-Thompson, J.L. 1978. Human Activities and Desert Expansion. *The Geographical Journal* 144:416–423.

Cocheme, J., and **P. Franquin.** 1967. *An Agroclimatology Survey of a Semiarid Area in Africa South of the Sahara.* Technical Note No. 86, World Meteorological Organization.

Collier, George A. 1975. *Fields of the Tzotzil: The Ecological Bases of Tradition in Highland Chiapas.* Austin, TX: University of Texas Press.

Collins, Jane. 1984. The Maintenance of Peasant Coffee Production in a Peruvian Valley. *American Ethnologist* 11:413–438.

Comaroff, John L. 1984. The Closed Society and its Critics: Historical Transformations in African Ethnography. *American Ethnologist* 11:571–583.

Cooke, B.K. 1935. Native Administration in Practice: Historical Outline. In J.A. deC. Hamilton (ed.), *The Anglo-Egyptian Sudan from Within*, 191–204. London: Faber & Faber.

Cooper, Frederick. 1981. Africa and the World Economy. *African Studies Review* 24(2/3):1–86.

Cordell, D. 1977. Eastern Libya, Wadai and the Sanusiya: A Tariga and a Trade Route. *Journal of African History* 18:21–36.

Daly, M.W. 1980. *British Administration and the Northern Sudan 1917–1924: The Governor-Generalship of Sir Lee Stack in the Sudan.* Istanbul: Witgoven.

Davies, Reginald. 1926. The Masalit Sultanate. *Sudan Notes and Records* 9:49–62.

———· 1935. Economics and Trade. In J.A. deC. Hamilton, *The Anglo-Egyptian Sudan from Within*, 294–309. London: Faber & Faber.

———. 1957. *The Camel's Back: Service in the Rural Sudan.* London: J. Murray.

Ddirar, Hamid Ahmed. 1978. The Art and Science of Merissa Fermentation. *Sudan Notes and Records* 57:115–129.

DeJanvry, Alain, and **Carlos Garramon.** 1977. The Dynamics of Rural Poverty in Latin America. *Journal of Peasant Studies* 4:206–216.

Delbosc, G. 1968. Etudes sur la Regeneration de la Fertilite du Sol dans la Zone Arachidiere du Senegal. *Oleagineux* 23:27–33.

DeSchlippe, Pierre. 1956. *Shifting Cultivation in Africa: The Zande System of Agriculture.* London: Routledge and Kegan Paul.

DeVroey, Michel. 1982. On the Obsolescence of the Marxian Theory of Value: A Critical Review. *Capital and Class* 17:34–59.

DeWalt, Billie. 1982. The Big Macro Connection: Population, Grain and Cattle in Southern Honduras. *Culture and Agriculture* 14:1–12.

DeWilde, John C. 1967a. *Experiences with Agricultural Development in Tropical Africa. Vol. I: The Synthesis.* Baltimore: Johns Hopkins Press.

———. 1967b. *Experiences with Agricultural Development in Tropical Africa. Vol. II: The Case Studies.* Baltimore: Johns Hopkins Press.

Dickey, Christopher. 1985. Age-Old Skills Helped Villagers Survive Sudanese Famine. *The Guardian Weekly*, Manchester, October 17:17.

Doornbos, Paul. 1982. A Sinyar Tale of Friendship. *Sudan Texts Bulletin* 5:36–46.

———. 1984a. Haddad. In Richard V. Weekes (ed.), *Muslim Peoples: A World Ethnographic Survey* (2nd edition), 309–313. Westport, Connecticut: Greenwood Press.

———. 1984b. Sinyar. In Richard V. Weekes (ed.), *Muslim Peoples: A World Ethnographic Survey* (2nd edition), 690–695. Westport, Connecticut: Greenwood Press.

Doornbos, Paul, and **Lidwien Kapteijns.** 1984. Tama-Speaking Peoples. In Richard V. Weekes (ed.) *Muslim Peoples: A World Ethnographic Survey* (2nd edition), 745–754. Westport, Connecticut: Greenwood Press.

Duffield, Mark R. 1978. *Peripheral Capitalism and the Social Relations of Agricultural Production in the Village of Maiurno near Sennar.* Bulletin No. 66, Economic and Social Research Council, Khartoum, Sudan.

———. 1979. Observations Concerning the Demographics and Settlements of Nigerians in Northern Sudan (mula:Hiza:t Hawl di:maGrafiyya wa mustawtana:t al ni:ji:riyi:n fi: ʃama:l as su:da:n). In Mohammed El Awad Galal-el-Din and Mohammed Yusif Ahmed El Mustafa (eds.), *Immigration and Inter-*

nal Migration in Sudan (al hijra al wa:fida ila: wa al hijra ad da:xiliyya fi: as su:da:n). Khartoum: Economic and Social Research Council, National Council for Research.

———. 1981. *Maiurno: Capitalism and Rural Life in Sudan*. London: Ithaca Press.

Dupre, George, and **Pierre-Philippe Rey.** 1973. Reflections on the Pertinence of a Theory of the History of Exchange. *Economy and Society* 2:131–163.

Emmanuel, Arghiri. 1972. *Unequal Exchange: A Study of the Imperialism of Trade*. New York: Monthly Review Press.

Erasmus, Charles J. 1965. The Occurrence and Disappearance of Reciprocal Farm Labor in Latin America. In D.B. Heath and R.N. Adams (eds.), *Contemporary Cultures and Societies of Latin America*. New York: Random House.

Evans-Pritchard, E.E. 1940. *The Nuer: A Description of the Modes of Livelihood and Political Institutions of a Nilotic People*. Oxford: Oxford University Press.

FAO. 1968. *Land and Water Resources Survey in the Jebel Marra Area: The Sudan. Final Report*. FAO/SF: 48:SUD–17.

Faulkingham, Ralph H. 1977. Ecological Constraints and Subsistence Strategies: The Impact of Drought in a Hausa Village, A Case Study from Niger. In David Dalby, R.J. Harrison Church, and Fatima Bezzaz (eds.), *Drought in Africa 2*. London: International African Institute.

Feierman, Steven. 1985. Struggles for Control: The Social Roots of Health and Healing in Modern Africa. *African Studies Review* 28(2/3):73–147.

Feldman, Rayah. 1975. Rural Social Differentiation and Political Goals in Tanzania. In Ivar Oxaal, Tony Barnett, and David Booth (eds.), *Beyond the Sociology of Development: Economy and Society in Latin America and Africa*. London: Routledge and Kegan Paul.

Firth, Raymond. 1939. *Primitive Polynesian Economy*. London: Routledge & Sons.

Foster-Carter, Aidan. 1978. The Modes of Production Controversy. *New Left Review* 107:47–78.

Frank, Andre Gunder. 1967. *Capitalism and Underdevelopment in Latin America: Historical Studies of Chile and Brazil*. New York: Monthly Review Press.

———. 1969. *Latin America: Underdevelopment or Revolution*. New York: Monthly Review Press.

———. 1972. *Lumpenbourgeosie: Lumpendevelopment: Dependence, Class and Politics in Latin America.* New York: Monthly Review Press.

———. 1979. *Dependent Accumulation and Underdevelopment.* New York: Monthly Review Press.

———. 1980. *Crisis: In the World Economy.* New York: Holmes and Meier.

Franke, Richard W. 1982. Class Formation and Environmental Maintenance in the West African Sahel. Paper presented at the 81st Annual Meeting of the American Anthropological Association, Washington, D.C., December 1982.

Franke, Richard W., and **Barbara H. Chasin.** 1980. *Seeds of Famine: Ecological Destruction and the Development Dilemma in the West African Sahel.* Montclair, NJ: Allanheld, Osmin & Co.

Frankenberger, Tim. 1983. Understanding the Process of Desertification through Farming Systems Research: A Case Study from the Sudan. *Practicing Anthropology* 5 (3).

Galal-el-Din, Mohamed El Awad. 1977. The Rationality of High Fertility in Urban Sudan. In J.C. Caldwell (ed.), *The Persistence of High Fertility*, 633–658. Canberra: Australian National University.

———. 1978. Population Dynamics and Socioeconomic Development in Rural Sudan (mimeo). Development Studies and Research Center, University of Khartoum.

Galal-el-Din, Mohammed El Awad, and **Mohamed Yusif Ahmed El Mustafa.** 1979. *Immigration and Internal Migration in Sudan (al hijra al wa:fida ila: wa al hijra ad da:xiliyya fi: as su:da:n).* Khartoum: Economic and Social Research Council, National Council for Research.

Gartrell, Beverly. 1983. British Administrators, Colonial Chiefs, and the Comfort of Tradition: An Example from Uganda. *African Studies Review* 36(1):1–24.

Ghabbour, Samir J. 1972. Some Aspects of Conservation in the Sudan. *Biological Conservation* 4:228–229.

Gladwin, Christina H., and **John Butler.** 1984. Is Gardening an Adaptive Strategy for Florida Family Farmers? *Human Organization* 43:208–216.

Glickman, Maurice. 1972. The Nuer and the Dinka: A Further Note. *Man* (n.s.) 7:586–594.

Gluckman, M. 1941. *Economy of the Central Barotse Plain.* Rhodes-Livingstone Papers, No. 7. Livingstone: The Rhodes-Livingstone Institute.

Goddard, A.D. 1973. Changing Family Structures among the Rural Hausa. *Africa* 43:207–218.

Goodman, David, and **Michael Redclift.** 1981. *From Peasant to Proletarian: Capitalist Development and Agrarian Transitions.* Oxford: Basil Blackwell.

Goody, Jack. 1971. *Technology, Tradition and the State in Africa.* London: Oxford University Press.

Greenberg, Joseph H. 1966. *The Languages of Africa.* Bloomington: Indiana University.

———. 1971. Nilo Saharan and Meroitic. *Current Trends in Linguistics* 7:421–442.

Grossman, Lawrence, S. 1983. Cattle, Rural Economic Differentiation, and Articulation in the Highlands of Papua New Guinea. *American Ethnologist* 10:59–76.

Grove, A.T. 1977. Desertification in the African Environment. In David Dalby, R.J. Harrison Church, and Fatima Bezzaz (eds.), *Drought in Africa 2.* London: International African Institute.

———. 1978. Geographical Introduction to the Sahel. *Geographical Journal* 144 (part 3):407–415.

———. 1981. The Climate of the Sahara in the Period of Meteorological Records. In J.A. Allen (ed.), *The Sahara: Ecological Change and Early Economic History.* Cambridgeshire, England: Menas Press.

Guillet, David. 1980. Reciprocal Labor and Peripheral Capitalism in the Central Andes. *Ethnology* 19:151–167.

Gulliver, P.H. 1971. *Neighbors and Networks: The Idiom of Kinship in Social Action among the Ndendeuli of Tanzania.* Berkeley: University of California Press.

Guyer, Jane I. 1980. Food, Cocoa and the Division of Labour by Sex in Two West African Societies. *Comparative Studies in Society and History* 22:355–373.

———. 1981. Household and Community in African Studies. *African Studies Review* 24:87–137.

Haaland, Gunnar. 1980. Ethnic Groups and Language Use in Darfur. In Robin Thelwall (ed.), *Aspects of Language in the Sudan.* Coleraine: New University of Ulster.

———. 1984. Fur. In Richard V. Weekes (ed.), *Muslim Peoples: A World Ethnographic Survey* (2nd edition), 264–269. Westport, Connecticut: Greenwood Press.

Hansen, William, and **Brigitte Schulz.** 1981. Imperialism, Dependency and Social Class. *Africa Today* 28(3):5–36.

Hardin, Garret. 1977. The Tragedy of the Commons. In Garret Hardin and John Baden (eds.), *Managing the Commons*, 16–30. San Francisco: W.H. Freeman.

Hare, F. Kenneth. 1977. Climate and Desertification. In *Desertification: Its Causes and Consequences.* Proceedings of the United Nations Conference on Desertification, Nairobi 29–August to 9–September 1977. Oxford: Pergamon Press.

Hart, Keith. 1982. *The Political Economy of West African Agriculture.* Cambridge: Cambridge University Press.

Hedlund, Hans, and **Mats Lundahl.** 1984. The Economic Role of Beer in Rural Zambia. *Human Organization* 43:61–65.

Hill, Polly. 1972. *Rural Hausa: A Village and a Setting.* Cambridge: Cambridge University Press.

Hogendorn, Jan S. 1978. *Nigerian Groundnut Exports: Origins and Early Development.* Zaria: Ahmedu Bello University Press.

Holy, Ladislav. 1974. *Neighbors and Kinsmen: A Study of the Berti People of Darfur.* London: C. Hurst.

Hulse, Joseph H., Evangeline M. Laing, and **Odette E. Pearson.** 1980. *Sorghum and the Millets: Their Composition and Nutritive Value.* New York: Academic Press.

Hunting Technical Services. 1977. *Agricultural Development in the Jebel Marra Area, Annex V, Social Organization and Structure.* Borehamwood, England: Hunting Technical Services.

Hyden, Goran. 1980. *Beyond Ujamaa in Tanzania.* Berkeley: University of California Press.

Ibrahim, Fouad N. 1978. *The Problem of Desertification in the Republic of the Sudan with Special Reference to Northern Darfur Province.* Monograph No. 8, Development Studies and Research Center, University of Khartoum.

Iliffe, John. 1983. *The Emergence of African Capitalism.* London: Macmillan Press.

James, Wendy R. 1972. Beer, Morality and Social Relations among the Uduk. *Sudan Society* 5:17–27.

Jernudd, Bjorn. 1968. Linguistic Integration and National Development: A Case Study of the Jebel Marra Area, Sudan. In J.A. Fishman, C.A. Ferguson, and

J. Das Gupta (eds.). *Language Problems of Developing Nations.* New York: John Wiley and Sons.

Jones, Brynmor. 1938. Desiccation and the West African Colonies. *Geographical Journal* 41:401–23.

Jones, Christine. 1983. The Mobilization of Women's Labor for Cash Crop Production: A Game Theoretical Approach. *American Journal of Agricultural Economics* 65:1049–1054.

Jones, M.J., and **A. Wild.** 1975. *Soils of the West African Savanna.* Technical Communication No. 55, Commonwealth Bureau of Soils. Farnham Royal: Commonwealth Agricultural Bureau.

Kapteijns, Lidwien. 1983. The Emergence of a Sudanic State: Dar Masalit, 1874–1905. *International Journal of African Historical Studies* 16:(4).

———. 1985. *Mahdist Faith and Sudanic Tradition: The History of the Masalit Sultanate, 1870–1930.* London: KPI.

———. MS. Islamic Rationales for the Changing Social Roles of Women in the Western Sudan.

Kapteijns, Lidwien, and **I.Y. Abdel Rahman.** 1979. In Search of the Past. *Sudanow*, May 1979:36–43.

Kapteijns, Lidwien, and **Jay Spaulding.** 1982. Precolonial Trade Between States in the Eastern Sudan, ca. 1700–1900. *African Economic History* 11:29–62.

Karrar, Siddiq. 1966. The Markets for Sudan's Agricultural Products (With Reference to Diversification of Agricultural Production). In D.J. Shaw (ed.), *Agricultural Development in the Sudan*, Vol. 2, 255–269. Khartoum: Philosophical Society of the Sudan with the Sudan Agricultural Society.

Kassas, M. 1970. Desertification versus Potential for Recovery in Circum-Saharan Territories. In Harold E. Dregne (ed.), *Arid Lands in Transition.* Washington, D.C.: AAAS.

Klinkenberg, K. 1970. Soils. In M.J. Mortimore (ed.), *Zaria and its Region*, 55–60. Occasional paper No. 4, Department of Geography, Ahmedu Bello University, Zaria.

Lamb, Peter J. 1982. Persistence of Subsaharan Drought. *Nature* 299:46–47.

Landsberg, H.E. 1975. Sahel Drought: Change of Climate or Part of Climate? *Archiv der Meteorologie, Geophysik und Bioclimatologie, B*, 23:193–200.

Larson, Barbara. 1983. Tunisian Kin Ties Reconsidered. *American Ethnologist* 10:551–570.

LaRue, G. Michael. 1984. *Land and Social Stratification in Dar Fur, 1785–1875: The Hakura System.* African Studies Center, Working Paper No. 96. Boston: Boston University.

Lebeuf, Annie M.D. 1959. *Les Populations du Tchad.* Paris: Presses Universitaires de France.

LeHouerou, H.N. 1968. La Desertisation du Sahara Septentrional et des Steppes Limitrophes. In *Proceedings of the IBP Hammamet Technical Meeting on the Conservation of Nature*; Hammamet, Tunisia. Cited in Kassas 1970:123–124.

Lenin, V.I. 1964. *The Development of Capitalism in Russia.* Moscow: Progress Publishers.

LeRouvreur, A. 1962. *Sahariens et Saheliens du Tchad.* Paris: Berger-Levrault.

Lewis, Herbert S. 1974. Neighbors, Friends, and Kinsmen: Principles of Social Organization among the Cushitic-Speaking Peoples of Ethiopia. *Ethnology* 13:145–157.

Lewis, W.A. 1954. Economic Development with Unlimited Supplies of Labour. *Manchester School of Economic and Social Studies* 22:139–191.

Lippi, Marco. 1980. *Value and Naturalism in Marx.* London: New Left Books.

Lipton, Michael. 1977. *Why Poor People Stay Poor: Urban Bias in World Development.* Cambridge, MA: Harvard University Press.

———. 1982. Migration from Rural Areas of Poor Countries: The Impact on Rural Productivity and Income Distribution. In Richard H. Sabot (ed.), *Migration and the Labor Market in Developing Countries*, 191–228. Boulder, Colo: Westview Press.

Lovejoy, P.E., and **S. Baier.** 1976. The Desert-side Economy of the Central Sudan. In Micahel H. Glantz (ed.), *The Politics of Natural Disaster: The Case of the Sahel Drought*, 145–175. New York: Praeger.

Lugard, (Lord). 1965. *The Dual Mandate in British Tropical Africa*, (5th edition). London: Frank Cass.

MacLeod, N.H. 1976. Dust in the Sahel: Cause of Drought? In M.H. Glantz (ed.), *The Politics of Natural Disaster: The Case of the Sahel Drought*, 214–31. New York: Praeger.

MacMichael, Sir Harold. 1934. *The Anglo-Egyptian Sudan.* London: Faber and Faber.

Mahmoud, Fatima Babiker. 1984. *The Sudanese Bourgeoisie: Vanguard of Development?* London: Zed.

Marx, Karl. 1972. The Eighteenth Brumaire of Louis Bonaparte. In Robert C. Tucker (ed.), *The Marx-Engels Reader*, 436–525. New York: W.W. Norton.

———. 1977. *Capital, Vol. I.* trans. Ben Fowkes. New York: Vintage Books.

Mather, D.B. 1956. Migration in the Sudan. In R.W. Steel and C.A. Fisher (eds.), *Geographical Essays on British Tropical Lands.* London: George Philip and Son.

Mbithi, Philip M., and **Fred E. Chege.** 1973. Linkages Between Agriculture and Rural Small-Scale Enterprises. In Frank C. Child and Mary E. Kempe (eds.), *Small Scale Enterprise*, 33–50. Occasional Paper 6, Institute for Development Studies, University of Nairobi.

Meillassoux, C. 1972. From Reproduction to Production: A Marxist Approach to Economic Anthropology. *Economy and Society* 1:93–105.

Moore, M.P. 1975. Cooperative Labour in Peasant Agriculture. *Journal of Peasant Studies.* 2:270–291.

Mosely, K.P., and **I.M. Wallerstein.** 1978. Precapitalist Social Structures. *Annual Review of Sociology* 4:259–290.

Mureithi, Leopold P. 1973. Nonfarm Economic Activities in Rural Areas. In Frank C. Child and Mary E. Kempe (eds.), *Small Scale Enterprise*, 128–138. Occasional Paper 6, Institute for Development Studies, University of Nairobi.

Murray, Colin. 1981. *Families Divided: The Impact of Migrant Labour in Lesotho.* Cambridge: Cambridge University Press.

Nachtigal, Gustav. 1971. *Sahara and Sudan; Vol. 4, Wadai and Darfur.* trans. A.G.B., and H.J. Fisher. Berkeley: University of California Press.

Nadel, S.F. 1947. *The Nuba: An Anthropological Study of the Hill Tribes in Kordofan.* London: Oxford University Press.

Nash, June. 1981. Ethnographic Aspects of the World Capitalist System. *Annual Review of Anthropology* 10:393–423.

Netting, Robert McC. 1964. Beer as a Locus of Value among the West African Kofyar. *American Anthropologist* 66:375–384.

Newcomer, Peter J. 1972. The Nuer are Dinka: An Essay on Origins and Environmental Determinism. *Man* (n.s.) 7:5–11.

Nicholson, Sharon E. 1980. Saharan Climates in Historic Times. In Martin A.J. Williams and Hugues Faure (eds.), *The Sahara and the Nile.* Rotterdam: A.A. Balkema.

Nye, P.H., and **D.J. Greenland.** 1960. *The Soil under Shifting Cultivation.* Technical Comm. No. 51, Commonwealth Bureau of Soils, Harpendon.

O'Brien, John James III. 1980. *Agricultural Labor and Development in Sudan.* Doctoral Dissertation, University of Connecticut.

O'Fahey, R.S. 1979. Islam, State and Society in Dar Fur. In N. Levtzion (ed.), *Conversion to Islam*, 189–206. New York: Holmes and Meier.

———.1980. *State and Society in Dar Fur.* London: C. Hurst & Co.

O'Fahey, R.S., and **J.L. Spaulding.** 1974. *Kingdoms of the Sudan.* London: Methuen and Co.

Oboler, Regina Smith. 1982. *Women, Men, Property and Change in Nandi District, Kenya.* Doctoral Dissertation, Temple University.

Olsson, Lennart. 1983. *Desertification or Climate? Investigation Regarding the Relationship between Land Degradation and Climate in the Central Sudan.* Lund Studies in Geography, Series A Physical Geography, No. 60. University of Lund, Sweden.

Olsson, Lennart, and **Mikael Stern.** 1981. *Large Area Data Sampling for Remote Sensing Applications and Statistical Analysis of Environment, Exemplified by an Investigation in the Sudan.* Lunds Universitets Naturgeografiska Institution, Rapporter Och Notiser 49. Lund, Sweden.

Orlove, Benjamin S. 1980. Ecological Anthropology. *Annual Review of Anthropology* 9:235–273.

Parker, C. 1984. The Influence of Striga Species on Sorghum under Varying Nitrogen Fertilization. In C. Parker, L.J. Musselman, R.M. Polhill, and A.K. Wilson (eds.), *Proceedings of the Third International Symposium on Parasitic Weeds*, ICARDA/International Parasitic Seed Plant Research Group, 7–9 May 1984, Aleppo, Syria, 90–98. Aleppo: ICARDA.

Pedlar, F.J. 1955. *Economic Geography of West Africa.* London: Longmans, Green & Co.

Peoples, James G. 1978. Dependence in a Micronesian Economy. *American Ethnologist* 5:535–552.

Pilling, Geoffrey. 1973. Imperialism, Trade and 'Unequal Exchange': The Work of Arghiri Emmanuel. *Economy and Society* 2:164–185.

Platt, B.S. 1955. Some Traditional Alcoholic Beverages and their Importance in Indigenous African Communities. *Proceedings of the Nutrition Society* 14:115–124.

Polanyi, Karl. 1957. The Economy as Instituted Process. In Karl Polanyi, Conrad M. Arensberg, and Harry W. Pearson (eds.), *Trade and Market in the Early Empires*. New York: The Free Press.

Portes, Alejandro, and **John Walton.** 1981. *Labor, Class and the International System.* New York: Academic Press.

Redfield, Robert. 1960. *Peasant Society and Culture.* Chicago: University of Chicago Press.

Reeves, Edward B. 1983. Farm Systems Research and Village Shopkeepers in North Kordofan, Sudan. *Practicing Anthropology* 5(3):8–9.

Republic of Sudan, Department of Statistics. 1960. *First Population Census of the Sudan, 1955–56.* Khartoum: Government Printing Press.

Rey, Pierre-Philippe. 1973. *Les Alliances de Classes.* Paris: Maspero.

———. 1975. The Lineage Mode of Production. *Critique of Anthropology* 3:27–29.

Reyna, S.P. 1975. Age-Differential, Marital Instability, and Venereal Disease. In Moni Nag (ed.), *Population and Social Organization.* Chicago: Aldine.

———. 1979. The Rationality of Divorce: Marital Instability among the Barma of Chad. In George Kurian (ed.), *Cross-Cultural Perspectives of Mate-Selection and Marriage.* Westport, Connecticut: Greenwood Press.

———. 1984. Arabs, Chadian. In Richard V. Weekes (ed.), *Muslim Peoples: A World Ethnographic Survey* (2nd edition), 45–49. Westport, Connecticut: Greenwood Press.

Reynolds, Dorene R. 1982. The Household Divided: Competition for Cash Between Husbands and Wives in West Pokot District, Kenya. Paper presented at the 81st Annual Meeting of the American Anthropological Association, Washington D.C., December 3–7.

Richards, Paul. 1983. Ecological Change and the Politics of African Land Use. *African Studies Review* 26(2):1–72.

Roberts, Ron E., and **Douglas E. Brintnall.** 1983. *Reinventing Inequality: An Inquiry into Society and Stratification.* Cambridge, MA: Schenkman.

Roemer, John E. 1982. New Directions in the Marxian Theory of Exploitation and Class. *Politics and Society* 11:253:287.

Ross, Clark G. 1982. A Village Level Study of Producer Grain Transactions in Rural Senegal. *African Studies Review* 25:65–84.

Roth-Laly, Arlette. 1969–1972. *Lexique des parlers Arabes Tchado-Soudanais* (four volumes). Paris: Centre National de la Recherche Scientifique.

Russell, E. Walter. 1968. Some Agricultural Problems of Semi-Arid Areas. In R.P. Moss (ed.) *The Soil Resources of Tropical Africa*, 121–135. Cambridge: Cambridge University Press.

Sacks, Karen. 1979. Causality and Chance on the Upper Nile. *American Ethnologist* 6:437–448.

Sahlins, Marshall D. 1961. The Segmentary Lineage: An Organization of Predatory Expansion. *American Anthropologist* 63:322–45.

———. 1963. Poor Man, Rich Man, Big-Man, Chief: Political Types in Melanesia and Polynesia. *Comparative Studies in Society and History* 5:285–303.

———. 1972. *Stone Age Economics.* Chicago: Aldine.

Samoff, Joel, and **Rachel Samoff.** 1976. The Local Politics of Underdevelopment. *African Review* 6(1):69–97.

Saul, Mahir. 1981. Beer, Sorghum and Women: Production for the Market in Rural Upper Volta. *Africa* 51:746–764.

———. 1983. Work Parties, Wages and Accumulation in a Voltaic Village. *American Ethnologist* 10:77–96.

Schone, D.J. 1977. African Droughts and the Spectrum of Time. In David Dalby, R.J. Harrison Church and Fatima Bezzaz (eds.), *Drought in Africa 2.* London: International African Institute.

Scott, C.D. 1976. Peasants, Proletarianization and the Articulation of Modes of Production: The Case of Sugar Cane Cutters in Northern Peru, 1940–69. *Journal of Peasant Studies* 3:321–341.

Shaw, D.J. 1966. The Effects of Moneylending (Sheil) on Agricultural Development in the Sudan. In D.J. Shaw (ed.), *Agricultural Development in the Sudan.* Vol. 2, D56–D59. Khartoum: Philosophical Society of the Sudan with the Sudan Agricultural Society.

Shenton, Bob, and **Mike Watts.** 1979. Capitalism and Hunger in Northern Nigeria. *Review of African Political Economy* 15–16:53–62.

Smith, Carol. 1978. Beyond Dependency Theory: National and Regional Patterns of Underdevelopment in Guatemala. *American Ethnologist* 5:574–617.

Smith, Joan, Immanuel Wallerstein, and **Hans-Dieter Evers** (eds.) 1984. *Households and the World Economy.* Beverly Hills: Sage.

Soiffer, Stephen M., and **Gary N. Howe.** 1982. Patrons, Clients and the Articulation of Modes of Production: An Examination of the Penetration of Capitalism into Peripheral Agriculture in Northeastern Brazil. *Journal of Peasant Studies* 9:176–206.

Southall, Aidan. 1976. Nuer and Dinka are People: Ecology, Ethnicity and Logical Possibility. *Man* (n.s.) 11:463–491.

Steedman, Ian. 1978. *Marx after Sraffa.* London: New Left Books.

Sudanow. 1979. Passport to Marriage. February 1979:53–54.

Svandize, I.A. 1968. The African Struggle for Agricultural Productivity. *Journal of Modern African Studies* 6:311–28.

Swift, Jeremy. 1977. Sahelian Pastoralists: Underdevelopment, Desertification and Famine. *Annual Review of Anthropology* 6:457–78.

Talbot, M.R. 1980. Environmental Responses to Climatic Change in the West African Sahel over the Past 20,000 Years. In Martin A.J. Williams and Hugues Faure (eds.), *The Sahara and the Nile.* Rotterdam: A.A. Balkema.

Todaro, Michael P. 1976. *Migration and Economic Development.* Occasional Paper No. 18, Institute for Development Studies, University of Nairobi.

Tornay, Serge. 1981. The Omo Murle Enigma. In M. Lionel Bender (ed.), *Peoples and Cultures of the Ethio-Sudan Borderlands*, 33–60. East Lansing: African Studies Center, Michigan State University.

Tothill, J.D. 1948. *Agriculture in the Sudan.* London: Oxford University Press.

Trimingham, J. Spencer. 1946. *Sudan Colloquial Arabic* (2nd edition). London: Oxford University Press.

Tripp, Robert B. 1982. Time Allocation in Northern Ghana: An Example of the Random Visit Method. *Journal of Developing Areas* 16:391–400.

Tubiana, Marie-Jose, and **Joseph Tubiana.** 1977. *The Zaghawa from an Ecological Perspective.* Rotterdam: A.A. Balkema.

Tucker, A.N., and **M.A. Bryan.** 1956. *The Non-Bantu Languages of North-eastern Africa.* London: Oxford University Press for the International African Institute.

Tully, Dennis. 1981a. Dar Masalit Today: Dynamics of Ecology, Society and Politics. In M.L. Bender (ed.), *Peoples and Cultures of the Ethio-Sudan Borderlands*, 117–136. East Lansing: African Studies Center, Michigan State University.

———. 1981b. Dual Economy or Dual Population: A Western Sudanese Case. Paper presented at the 80th annual Meeting of the American Anthropological Association, Los Angeles, December 2–6.

———. 1984. Masalit. In Richard V. Weekes (ed.), *Muslim Peoples: A World Ethnographic Survey* (2nd edition), 499–504. Westport, Connecticut: Greenwood Press.

———. 1985. Labor Migration in the Economy and Society of Dar Masalit. In Mahjoub El-Bedawi and David Sconyers (eds.), *Sudan Studies Association Selected Conference Papers 1982–1984*, 159–169. Baltimore: Sudan Studies Association.

Tully, Dorene R. 1985. *Human Ecology and Political Process: The Context of Market Incorporation in West Pokot District, Kenya.* Doctoral Dissertation, University of Washington.

Turner, E.L.B., and **V.W. Turner.** 1955. Money Economy among the Mwinilunga Ndembu: A Study of Some Individual Cash Budgets. *Rhodes-Livingstone Journal* 18:19–37.

Turshen, Meredeth. 1984. *The Political Ecology of Disease in Tanzania.* New Brunswick, NJ: Rutgers University Press.

UNCD. 1977. Overview (prepared by the Secretariat, UNCD). In *Desertification: Its Causes and Consequences.* Proceedings of the United Nations Conference on Desertification, Nairobi 29–August to 9–September 1977. Oxford: Pergamon Press.

Van Raay, Hans G.T. 1974. *Fulani Pastoralists and Cattle.* Occasional paper No. 44, Institute of Social Studies, The Hague.

Vincent, Joan. 1971. *African Elite: The Big Men of a Small Town.* New York: Columbia University Press.

———. 1982. *Teso in Transformation: The Political Economy of Peasant and Class in Eastern Africa.* Berkeley: University of California Press.

Vine, H. 1968. Developments in the Study of Soils and Shifting Agriculture in Tropical Africa. In R.P. Moss (ed.), *The Soil Resources of Tropical Africa*, 89–119. Cambridge: Cambridge University Press.

Wallerstein, I.M. 1974a. *The Modern World-System: Capitalist Agriculture and the Origins of the European World-Economy in the Sixteenth Century.* New York: Academic Press.

———. 1974b. The Rise and Future Demise of the World Capitalist System: Concepts for Comparative Analysis. *Comparative Studies in Society and History* 16:387–415.

———. 1978. World-System Analysis: Theoretical and Interpretative Issues. In Barbara Hockey Kaplan (ed.), *Social Change in the Capitalist World Economy.* Beverly Hills: Sage.

———. 1979. Underdevelopment and Phase-B: Effect of the Seventeenth Century Stagnation on Core and Periphery of the European World-Economy. In Walter L. Goldfrank (ed.), *The World System of Capitalism: Past and Present*, 73–83. Beverly Hills: Sage.

Warren, Andrew, and **Judith K. Maizels.** 1977. Ecological Change and Desertification. In *Desertification: Its Causes and Consequences*. Proceedings of the United Nations Conference on Desertification, Nairobi 29–August to 9–September 1977. Oxford: Pergamon Press.

Wasserstrom, Robert. 1978. Population Growth and Economic Development in Chiapas, 1524–1975. *Human Ecology* 6:127–143.

Watson, James B. 1952. *Cayua Culture Change*. Memoir No. 73. Washington D.C.: American Anthropological Association.

———. 1977. Pigs, Fodder, and the Jones Effect in Postpomoean New Guinea. *Ethnology* 16:57–70.

Watson, William. 1958. *Tribal Cohesion in a Money Economy*. Manchester: University Press.

Wiest, Raymond E. (in press). External Dependency and the Perpetuation of Temporary Migration to the United States. In R.C. Jones (ed.), *Spatial Perspectives in Undocumented Migration: Mexico and the United States*. Totowa, N.J.: Littlefield, Adams and Co.

Wilson, Godfrey. 1941–1942. *The Economics of Detribalization in Northern Rhodesia*. Rhodes-Livingstone Papers, Nos. 5 and 6. Livingstone: The Rhodes-Livingstone Institute.

Wilson, R.T. 1977. Temporal Changes in Livestock Numbers and Patterns of Transhumance in Southern Darfur, Sudan. *Journal of Developing Areas* 11:493–508.

———. 1979. The Incidence and Control of Livestock Diseases in Darfur, Anglo-Egyptian Sudan, During the Period of the Condominium, 1916–1956. *International Journal of African Historical Studies* 12:62–82.

———. 1980. Wildlife in Northern Darfur, Sudan: A Review of its Distribution and Status in the Recent Past and at Present. *Biological Conservation* 17(2):85–101.

Winstanley, Derek. 1973. Rainfall Patterns and General Atmospheric Circulation. *Nature* 245:190–194.

Wright, Erik Olin. 1982. The Status of the Political in the Concept of Class Structure. *Politics and Society* 11:321–341.

Index